The HORSES
TOO ARE GONE

The HORSES
TOO ARE GONE

MICHAEL KEENAN

BANTAM BOOKS
Sydney   Auckland   Toronto   New York   London

THE HORSES TOO ARE GONE
A BANTAM BOOK

First published in Australia and New Zealand
in 1998 by Bantam

Reprinted 1998 (five times)

Keenan, Michael, 1943–
    The horses too are gone.

    ISBN 0 7338 0167 6.

    1. Droughts—New South Wales. 2. Cattle—New South Wales
    —Feeding and feeds. 3. Cattle—Queensland—Feeding and
    feeds. 4. Queensland—Social life and customs—1990–
    I. Title.

636.2084

Bantam books are published by

Transworld Publishers (Aust) Pty Limited
15–25 Helles Ave, Moorebank, NSW 2170

Random House (NZ) Ltd
18 Poland Rd, Glenfield, Auckland

Transworld Publishers (UK) Limited
61–63 Uxbridge Road, Ealing, London W5 5SA

Bantam Doubleday Dell Publishing Group Inc
1540 Broadway, New York, New York 10036

Cover design by Liz Seymour
Cover photo by Sarah Keenan
Author photo by Sarah Keenan
Edited by Amanda O'Connell

Typeset by Midland Typesetters, Victoria
Printed by McPherson's Printing Group, Victoria

10 9 8 7 6

From first seeing the original rough copy, Bantam's commissioning editor Jude McGee encouraged me to complete the task. Non-fiction is daunting and hellishly difficult to write. I dedicate The Horses Too Are Gone *to Jude with thanks.*

Author's note: characters in the story

This is a true story. However, the tyranny of distance has made it impossible for me to locate and speak to every character who passes through the following pages so a few fictitious names have been used to avoid embarrassment. Some characters have a distinct role and I felt were more aptly described by a colourful nickname.

Of the Wild Bunch I know very little. I saw groups of people I couldn't identify on two occasions. Names given to the Wild Bunch are fictitious and physical appearances have been altered, so any resemblance to any person is unintentional.

Contents

Acknowledgments   ix

Maps   xi

Introduction   xiii

1. Myall Plains   1

2. Reconnaissance   12

3. The First Lift   20

4. The Forbidden Mare   36

5. The Grass Generals   53

6. The High Plains of Death   79

7. Race Against Time   89

8. The Black Hole   107

9. The Wild Bunch   125

10. Stake-out   141

11. Dwellers of the Rangelands   166

12. Bore Crisis   182

13. Stampede   210

14. An Autumn of Reflection   243

15. Tableland Camp   256

16. The Shadows of Anxiety   280

17. The Dilemma   296

18. Gorge Camp Attack   304

19. The Dingo and the Omen   325

20. Rescue   336

     Epilogue   341

     Glossary   346

Acknowledgments

First and foremost a special thanks goes to Sal, who must have spent hours that could nearly be counted in the hundreds at the computer. It really was a combined effort.

I wish to thank Gil and Eunice Campbell for all their assistance, even to the point of listening to me read out rough copy chapters.

Donna Lamb typed my first rough copy manuscript and she didn't even get a kiss for that, but she may have been very relieved too. Donna also supplied me with valuable historical information.

Scalp, who is so named in the text to fit his formidable reputation as a dingo hunter ($20 bounty paid for each scalp), must be particularly acknowledged for his assistance on geographic locations. He wanted to show me the Kenniffs' principal hideout and I regret that I never found time.

Smokie provided anecdotes of history in the Mitchell district, for example the fatal stampede thought to have occurred in the 1890s.

The Old Boy provided the humour. It was far more than his jokes, it was more his unique style of description. I said to him one day, 'What's this bloke like?' 'Well,' he said, 'if you gutted him there'd be nothing left.'

Noel Hamilton explained in detail a lot of the bushman activities, such as wild bull throwing and pig catching.

Annette Fuller provided the coffee in her air-conditioned coffee lounge, where the first few chapters were written. I also looked upon her as my casual staff recruitment secretary.

Despite his poor health, Bill Anderson opened up his stables and looked after two of my thoroughbred horses. His hearty laugh was still rumbling out of that massive chest only days before he died.

I write quickly and off the cuff, sometimes not analysing too much. The thought arrives and down it goes. It is a free style that makes writing enjoyable, but it requires careful editing and for that I wish to thank Amanda O'Connell and Katie Stackhouse.

Roadtrain route, Myall Plains to Amby Creek

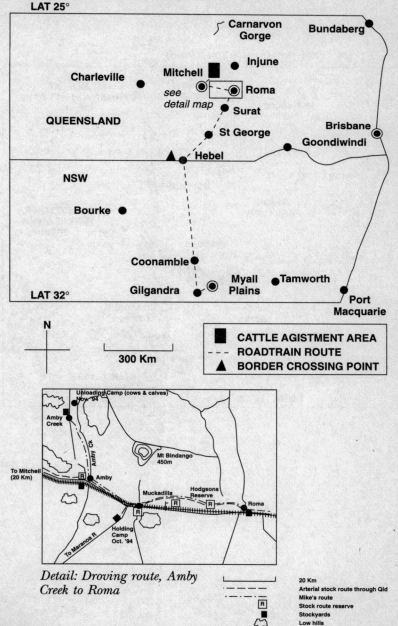

LAT 25°

Carnarvon Gorge

Bundaberg

Injune

Mitchell

see detail map

Roma

Surat

Charleville

QUEENSLAND

St George

Brisbane

Goondiwindi

Hebel

NSW

Bourke

Coonamble

Gilgandra

Myall Plains

Tamworth

Port Macquarie

LAT 32°

N

300 Km

■ CATTLE AGISTMENT AREA
--- ROADTRAIN ROUTE
▲ BORDER CROSSING POINT

Unloading Camp (cows & calves) Nov. '94

Amby Creek

Amby Ck

Mt Bindango 450m

To Mitchell (20 Km)

Amby

Muckadilla

Hodgsons Reserve

Roma

Holding Camp Oct. '94

To Maranoa R.

Detail: Droving route, Amby Creek to Roma

20 Km

Arterial stock route through Qld
Mike's route
Stock route reserve
Stockyards
Low hills

Camps, bores and yards in the rangelands

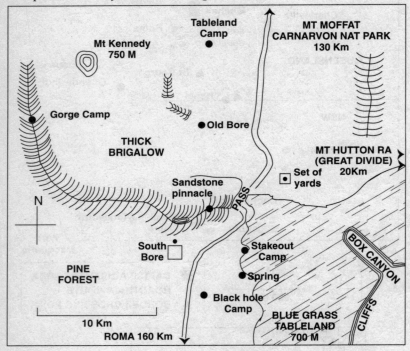

Introduction

A tableland formed by lava flows over some millions of years, gradually tapers away from the Warrumbungle mountains, running towards the Castlereagh river. The property Myall Plains is located on this tableland. In August 1994 the black basalt soils were as bare as a linoleum floor. The dark red poll Hereford cattle looked pathetic and even more pathetic was our attempt to feed so many. Before the calving began we had 1250 head. My wife Sal bagged the grain from the silo, Greg, who was helping us at the time, lifted the bags onto a truck and I lopped kurrajong trees. For a few months it had worked. By August the cows were heavily pregnant and a couple of kilos of wheat, a smell of hay and a few mouthfuls of kurrajong leaves were hopelessly inadequate. The last semi load of hay was down to five hundred bales and no more was available. We only had enough oats for the horses and if we wanted more we had to freight it across the Nullabor from Western Australia. The Wheat Board couldn't keep up with demand and introduced quotas at some silos. Wheat's not very suitable for stockfeed unless hammermilled and blended with roughage. To compound the grim situation, the cattle market in New South Wales had all but collapsed.

There was only one option left remotely open—agistment in

Queensland. Upon enquiry I was told there was feed north of the Roma–Charleville line, a huge journey for cattle already weak.

For most of us life is orderly and reasonably predictable. Heading west or north in search of cattle feed was not something I hadn't done before. The winters are cold on the tableland and it had always been good business to get the young weaner cattle out onto the warmer plains in the spring. The weaners usually went onto the same properties and were well looked after. When I left for Roma on 8 August I didn't expect to be plunged into a desperate struggle for survival, eight hundred kilometres from home.

I feel it is necessary to write a brief background to this drought, because we hear of so many droughts, people might well ask, 'What's new?'.

This drought began in March 1994 and, according to the Coonabarabran Rural Lands Board, officially ended in August 1996. There were falls of rain between those dates, but never that vital follow-up rain. It was so long that in the end none of us were planning to merely come through it, take a few losses and put the cheque book in the drawer. We were fighting to keep our farms—our homes—and not be forced to abandon everything and end up on the unemployment scrap heap. For those of us with Irish genes the prospect of losing our land is particularly abhorrent. We have this distorted view that land is symbolic of freedom; a sentiment that has its roots buried in the dark ages of British rule in Ireland. Old Irish names are common throughout the Australian farming community and it is interesting to note that all the families I grew up with in the bush are still there. They may have sold and moved, but they remain on the land and it is a tribute rarely given to people of Irish descent.

I am fifth generation from Ireland. My great-great-grandfather, James Keenan, arrived in Sydney in 1828 and went to Bathurst to break in horses. In the 1840s he took up his own land along Borenore Creek in the Molong district. He must have thought we would hang onto our land, because he built a vault at Orange and in 1856 was the first one in. My father was the last, in October 1994, one hundred and forty years later.

I have been asked what prompted me to write this book. It is a difficult question for me, because I just started writing when I realised I was mixing with some unique characters, straight out of the brigalow.

An encounter between characters and circumstances is the source of any story, but something has to spark the desire to write a story. In my case I think the spark came from a love of local history. Wherever I find myself I want to know what happened there. Seconds before I crossed the bridge leading into the Queensland town of Mitchell for the first time, I saw the sign, 'The Heart of Kenniff Country'. Immediately it stirred interest. I soon discovered that Mitchell's claim to fame was the escapades of the bushrangers Patrick and James Kenniff between 1891 and 1902. The dramatic horseback shootout in March 1902 against a posse led by Constable George Doyle bears a striking similarity to the final scene of author Rolf Boldrewood's novel *Robbery Under Arms*. Months later I found it a bizarre twist of fate that I should find myself in the same vast rangelands, watching out for unknown horsemen.

In some respects this book is a journey back in time, a story of characters clinging to a way of life that is disappearing in a world committed to progress.

CHAPTER

1 Myall Plains

August 1994

The wind was up again. From the tree top I stared at the high cloud, hoping to see just a hint of moisture. The cloud was white—too white—like splayed cotton wool removed from an old bandage. Up there, maybe four thousand metres, a gale blew. There was no moisture. For six months not even a single scud of fine rain had reached the ground.

My eyes gravitated to the horizon. More like the skeletal remains of a Dreamtime monster than a mountain range, the Warrumbungles stood impervious to all elements of nature. In thirteen million years they had lost only altitude. With a sudden wave of nostalgia I realised they were the only part of my life that remained unaltered.

On the left, all alone, towered the Tonduron. Dangerous and strikingly beautiful, this thousand-metre spire is Australia's Matterhorn. Nestled in the foothills below, the Mountain View Hotel in Tooraweenah is still the source of climbing tales going back a hundred years.

A little to the right the summit of Crater Bluff seemed to be taking a peep through a saddle high in the mountains. With a shiver I remembered my ascent of the south wall in 1960. Further to the right loomed Burrumbuckle—a giant monolith of trachyte rock that resembled a crouched lion.

To look out on those mountains was just an escape, I suppose. It never lasted long. The cows had spotted the vehicle near the tree. They were running and some were calling out. The dust from the bare reddish ground rose from their feet and looking through the rich green branches of the kurrajong tree I wondered what droughts this continent had seen to evolve such an extraordinary tree. If there is a tree anywhere in the world with the characteristics of the kurrajong, I have never heard of it. Cattle and sheep find the leaves as palatable as lucerne hay. The protein content is lower than that of good hay, but given sufficient quantities dry cattle will fatten on kurrajong.

The tree itself has no lateral roots. Moisture is extracted from the soil by a single tap root. In large trees this tap root is thought to descend up to ten metres into the ground, and proof of this hypothesis is that the tree will continue to flourish in a drought when all other plant species are struggling to survive.

I always start lopping branches for fodder at the top of the tree. If you slip and fall the lower branches will cushion you. But sometimes this method creates a tangle of branches before any reach the ground. On this occasion the first branch fell all the way. Within seconds it was torn to oblivion. One of the disadvantages of lopping kurrajong for stock is that the strong are always best fed. The weaker animals must wait until their stronger cousins have had a tummyful. If I am fit I can match it tree to tree with my axe with a powersaw operator. It seems to me that technology has introduced as many problems as it has solved. For the kurrajong tree it has been a disaster. The tree lopper of the 1990s is fast and ruthless. A powersaw in a tree is extremely dangerous and the operator minimises the risk by savagely cutting back the tree. Five to ten percent of the trees fail to recover, and those that do will not provide stock fodder again for more than two decades.

In 1957 my father had an Aborigine and a German immigrant do the drought lopping. They used tomahawks and skilfully pruned the trees. In 1965 the trees were bursting with foliage and were lopped the same way. Today the landscape of the kurrajong belts that cling to the old lava flow soils from the Warrumbungles throws up a sad picture. The lopping in the 1994 drought has left thousands of trees resembling overgrown rose bushes. For anyone who may ponder over the future, it diminishes any confidence in the will of ordinary men to restrain their greed. Yet there are farmers who put aside time, energy and funds to plant trees. For them, the lopping of 1994 must have been a scene of despair.

The dreaming was over. The tally chase had begun. Below me, two hundred cows were streaming in for a mouthful of leaves. None had calved yet, but when I looked down on those bloated stomachs and protruding backbones I knew the first calf would come before the end of the month. There were too many. The mob should have been split in half, but already some of our dams were dry. We were forced to run the herd in just three mobs.

It would take ten trees to feed this mob. The first tree in the morning was the worst. The muscles stiffened overnight and I moved from limb to limb with a slight hesitancy. Then the sweat formed, the jumper came off which I tied around my waist, and I drifted into a world of wind, leaves and the sound of ravenous eating. By the third tree I moved with the ease of a monkey.

By lunchtime this lot were fed. Two kilometres to the north the scene was the same. I had hired an experienced tree man from Tooraweenah. This little man lopped for nearly four hundred cows. He was fearless and lopped trees that we called virgins. They were twenty metres high. One slip would be fatal. Interestingly, there was not a kurrajong the Aboriginal womenfolk had not climbed for the seed long ago. The trunks of the

trees carried scars of stone axeheads. Using stone hand grind-
ers, the women made flour and cooked what we would call
scones.

The best thing about lunch in the bush is the company. After
four hours lopping it's nice to hear someone speak. My wife
Sal is one of those women with a natural gift of elevating the
day above the drab and mundane. She listens to the news. She
keeps in regular contact with friends—not for gossip, but for
the stimulation of what everyone is doing from day to day.
During hard times in the bush the women provide vital
support, for men tend to withdraw into a shell.

Sal plays an additional support role, beyond the reach of
some. She observes stock and watches paddocks. If a cow hasn't
moved for some hours she makes a mental note of it. She will
ask me when I last filled a water tank. Most of us men are on
our own now and we need this sort of help. And most important of all, when we come back from some job it's comforting
to hear the word 'hi'.

This day was a little different. Sal was bright as usual when I
entered the kitchen, but her news was not good. She had taken
a paddock drive through the weaners and the oats would be
eaten into the ground within a fortnight. There were five
hundred and forty of them to feed. Even if rain fell almost
immediately there would be no feed for weeks. At five hundred
and fifty metres above sea level and no protection from the
seasonal south-west wind, our property, Myall Plains, was as
bleak in winter as the Texas Panhandle.

Sal put my sandwiches on the table and sat opposite with a
cup of tea. We waited for the market report on the ABC. I had
already made enquiries in the south and it seemed Victoria was
the place to sell. There, the reliable winter rain had been below
average, but just one good fall would ensure a reasonable
spring.

Fighting a drought is like fighting an invisible enemy. It's there all the time, dug in, and as your resources diminish it tightens its grip. Like a general deploying troops, a cattle grazier makes strategic decisions. Some dig in and feed their stock, besieged but trying to out-wait the enemy. Others move their cattle in an attempt to outflank the drought. Some surrender and sell, taking the prices on offer. Sometimes those who sell are the only winners. Like a fallen city, the fight is over, but when the enemy withdraws you rebuild. The reality, however, is that few are left with sufficient resources to start again.

The radio gave us the bad news: the market at Wodonga in Victoria had dropped. Allowing for time to advertise the Myall Plains weaners and arrange transport, it would be a fortnight before they could be offered for sale. If no rain fell in that time the market would ease further.

'What will you do?' Sal asked. She had that little white-faced look I'd seen so often in the wool crash. Only three years before we had lost our property at Capertee. When wool crashed it was the equivalent of BHP disappearing from the stock exchange board. To have something taken from you that you love leaves a scar for life and, worse still, you live forever in fear that the banks and other vultures of our social system will be back again to perch on the front gate.

'We'll roadtrain to Queensland and drop them on a stock route with a drover. When it rains we'll sell them in Roma.'

'Will your father agree?'

I probably didn't answer. Sal and I know each other so well just a look says it all. Dad had angina and was very ill. Quietly to myself and no one else I put his life expectancy at about six weeks. To watch someone who had such a zest for life slowly die is a harrowing experience. To add to the trauma we no longer liked each other. If you have never liked someone you feel nothing. It's when you have shared a great friendship in the distant past that you look inwardly. What went wrong? Above all else I value the friendship of my boys. To rear children and then have it all fall apart negates life itself, for we can take nothing with us and all we can ever leave is a memory.

I left Sal at the table with a sense of foreboding. Dad and I didn't have many discussions left.

It was only two kilometres to Mum and Dad's home. We called it the cottage. Sal and I had lived there in the early 1970s with our babies. Since then a number of families had passed through. My parents had only been there two years.

I saw them every day. First job in the morning I lit the fire and filled the wood basket. There was never much said. My mother had cancer and although she never once complained I think pain rarely left her alone. I discussed the drought when decisions had to be made.

This time when I pulled up in the little farm truck I felt uncomfortable. To ask a very sick man to contemplate road-trains and Queensland stock routes is a big thing. For a few moments I just sat in the truck, looking out on Dad's withered tomato vines. The frosts would have killed them in the end, but these vines had died in the late autumn through neglect. All his life Dad had grown tomatoes. He loved them. When he no longer had the strength to weed and water his tomato beds I knew the end was near.

I went inside and he was sitting by the fire. Sometimes he read. Mostly he just sat with his memories. Hanging on the wall behind him was a race photograph of Vodka Jack—his last horse. The horse had won a maiden event at Narromine the previous spring. Dad had been on course that day and loved every minute of it. I remember how gaunt and sick he looked, but there was still life in him. Now he was deathly white and almost skeletal.

'The weaners are on top of the oats,' I said at last.

'We better sell them,' he said simply.

'We're too late.'

'I thought your Wodonga plan was a good one.'

'The market dropped twenty dollars this morning. By the time we get there it might be back another forty.'

My assessment of the market was not speculation. I had sold the cast for age cows at Dubbo and received the worst price since the cattle crash of the early 1970s. I had not told Dad. He had forgotten they even existed.

He didn't know what to say. He must have known his days were numbered. To have to concentrate on anything beyond a week would arouse some level of fear.

'I'm thinking about Queensland,' I said. 'Bill says the stock routes are still okay. Water's good. Feed's a bit frosted, but plenty of it.'

Bill was from Roma and had married Dad's niece, Sandra. Dad had a lot of respect for Bill.

'Go on the road yourself!' He stared at me now and I could see a trace of alarm.

'No, we'll find a drover.'

He was silent for a while. I didn't expect him to agree. There was only Sal and me to look after them. He hated hospitals. I knew he wanted to die here if possible.

'We can't feed them?' he queried.

'The kurrajong's nearly finished. We'll have to buy truck loads of grain to feed the cows.' I paused and gave him a moment to think about it. 'The cows are the problem. They're about to drop the calves.'

'The problem too is you're an adventurer.'

I watched him closely for a trace of humour. It may have been there. He was too sick to smile. Maybe he would never smile again. I just sat and waited. Feeding twelve hundred head of cattle was out of the question. We didn't have the equipment. We didn't have the water.

'Keenan Brothers would have gone on the road.'

He wasn't looking at me now. He had gone back to the grand old days. When he spoke of the Keenan brothers I thought of the film *The Sting*. That was how they lived in the 1920s. Poker games on trains where the stakes were measured in thousands of pounds. There were full-time drovers from far western Queensland to Victoria. It was a time when they discussed track form with priests. Dad had seen those days. They were days of great optimism for the small man. The Keenan men had a humble start. Their father died from injuries sustained in a fall from a horse, and their French mother reared them on a farm near Molong. She worked them hard and through her genes she gave them a personality that was later to help them build a land empire, although still small by Australian standards at that time.

'They made money out of droughts and out of crashes,' he went on. 'They trod ground that others drew back from.'

Then he looked at me. 'But they lost it.' He paused for a while, just gazing at me. 'Remember that always. They lost it.'

I waited for a while and then I said simply, 'I'll go up and have a look then.'

'You telephone the agent,' he said firmly. 'Tell him to book you into the hotel at Roma and have him meet you for breakfast each morning.'

I struggled not to smile. In the old days the agents met graziers as the train came in. Dined with them, drank with them; in short, never left their sides. I wondered what reception I would receive if I asked Wesfarmers Dalgety to roll out the carpet like the old AML & F Company did for my grandfather.

Dad had agreed in principle but I felt no relief. Between that moment and when I packed my suitcase that night I asked myself continually if there were no other option. If general rain fell the young cattle would lift a hundred dollars a head almost overnight. We were into August, just weeks from the second-best rain month on the calendar—October. It was gambling on weather—or was it the ghosts of Keenan Brothers that drove me?

In anticipation of being forced to face up to the Queensland option, I'd placed an ad in Roma's *Western Star* for agistment and a drover. In the ad I explained agistment was preferred, but if unavailable a drover would be employed to walk the stock routes.

The paper was delivered to the newsagents each Friday and by coincidence the day I had to make the decision was the cut-off time for ads. If I drove to Roma on Friday, Sal could report any phone calls that came through and I would be on the spot to deal with them. Not resolved was who would do the boggy dam run while I was away.

'If any get bogged why couldn't I pull them out?' Sal asked.

'I'll be away with the Landcruiser.'

'Teach me to drive the tractor.'

'Too dangerous,' I said, still wondering what to do. The tractor was brand new and the only time it had been out of the shed was to pull cows from a bog. In the hands of an inexperienced operator it would be dangerous work. Dams are surrounded by steep banks and provide very unstable ground for wheel tractors.

There had been no solution to the occasional bogging. Those dams we could do without had been fenced off. Others had to be left so the cattle could get a drink. Before they reached the ever receding water they struggled through putrid silt up to their bellies. For old cows it was a death trap.

'Let's do the run early,' Sal said. 'Then you go and if I run into real bother I will phone Peter.'

Poor Peter was our nearest neighbour. Too often he had to come to our rescue. He always came in great spirit and never once made us feel uncomfortable, but he was just as busy as us fighting the drought.

'If only the bugger would ask us to rescue him one day,' I said, knowing damn well we would have to call on him.

One dam was so bad we had a canoe on standby. Sometimes a cow would get stuck, struggle frantically, become exhausted and move out into the water. If they were not soon rescued their bodies would seize up from the cold and after the trauma of being towed out some never regained their feet.

Early on Friday morning we went to this dam first. It was freezing. No frost, but a face-numbing breeze of about five degrees Celsius. There was a cow stuck and she had moved out into the water.

Sal and I had a routine procedure by this stage. We placed the canoe on the silt and Sal pushed me out as far as she could without getting into the bog and then I used the paddle. Upon reaching the water I would paddle slowly across to the cow. The animal was already terrified by this time and the spectacle of a canoe approaching made some panic. I had to be very careful I didn't capsize, as the liquid mud beneath the water was as deadly as quicksand. I carried a chain with me which had a large slip ring at one end and at the other end the chain was attached to a rope. Once I had the slip ring end over the cow's head, Sal took up the slack by pulling the rope. She perceived the whole operation as a potential horror show and always made brave comments to make me laugh.

'Darling, you must feel you're on a holiday in that canoe!'

With the chain attached I came in as quickly as possible and hauled the poor thing out with the tractor. We had a high success rate and when the cow regained her feet we walked her to our hospital paddock which was watered by a trough from the homestead bore.

No matter how well each rescue went the scene was distressing and I asked myself many times what could have been done to avoid such a dreadful situation. It had never been in my hands to do anything, but in fairness to my father no dam on Myall Plains had been boggy for nearly thirty years. In 1965 he had cleaned every dam at great expense. The running of cattle on this continent may always be on the edge of calamity and short of utilising the land for other purposes we have to live with it.

We found a cow bogged in another dam. There was no need for the canoe. After her rescue Sal and I went home for coffee and I washed the 'Noosa sand' from my legs. In fact the mud was stinking and sticky. If I didn't have skin to worry about I would have used a wire brush.

I left feeling very uneasy. Three days was too long to be away. My parents were a day-to-day proposition. The ambulance collected my father if he was low and required hospitalisation, but he fought against it and we had to watch him closely. The only days we could relax were when the district nurse came. With the running of the property we were on our own. The tree lopper went home each night. He was a contractor and had nothing else to do with the running of the place. There were no men left in the small towns anymore. Those who wanted work had left long ago. The ones on the dole had slumped into the unemployable syndrome. Sal would be on her own.

CHAPTER 2

Reconnaissance

The first stock feed I had seen in months was between the border and St George. It looked dry and frost burnt, but the thought of the Myall Plains cows eating it made it seem like prime hay.

Once a sheep district, St George is now a major cotton centre. The town itself is most attractive. Two hotels overlook the Balonne river and offer patrons views across five hundred metres of water alive with ducks, cranes and pelicans. The river is famous for giant Murray cod, but environmental changes over the past twenty years have many of the locals worried. Some say that carp, an introduced species, are taking over and polluting the water. Others say it is to do with intensive chemical run-off from crop spraying. What *is* known is that the carp feed on a little bug which in turn feeds on blue-green algae, so at present the carp are flourishing. One of the great tragedies of our inland rivers is that the destructive power of the carp fish was recognised more than thirty years ago when the species was still confined to irrigation channels in southwestern New South Wales, but somehow the pet fish lobby managed to block any action.

St George held some old memories for me. In 1957 my father had taken me with him on a sheep buying trip to western Queensland, country that held all sorts of romantic visions for me in those days and I was looking forward to seeing it. When we got to St George, just seventy-five miles north of the New South Wales border, I thought I was in the never-never. We stayed at the Australia Hotel, nearly as grand in those days as its namesake in Castlereagh Street, Sydney. I threw some lines in from the river bank, tied them to trees and planned to get the fish early in the morning. The pelicans, however, must have been watching. They beat me and I was left with lines tangled beyond repair.

At breakfast Dad got talking to livestock agents and other travellers. The hotel was the communication centre and nearly forty years later perhaps little has changed, except the town is larger and some of the other hotels thrive as well. During the course of conversation it became evident (and very disappointing for me) that the road to Surat, our next destination, was just a track. I knew Dad wouldn't take it on. It was January and very hot. The Wet had already moved into central Queensland. One elderly man said the kangaroos were so bad that two or three travellers every week had their radiators knocked in and were forced to walk miles to a station for help.

For me such news was exciting. Dad, however, was a gregarious man and the possibility of a breakdown and being caught by rain was as unattractive to him as crowds of people were to me. We turned back and I didn't see the great downs country of western Queensland until I was a young man.

These days the track to Surat is a highway and it took me little more than an hour to reach Surat from St George.

The rolling open downs of scattered myall, box and brigalow in the east and gidgee and boree in the west are distinct from the famous Darling Downs of south-eastern Queensland. The vast downs of western Queensland extend for hundreds of kilometres to Longreach and way beyond. Broken only by low ranges, the fertile soils of the downs would be as productive as the North American prairies were it not for lack of rain.

It was sunset when I saw the Surat watertower in the distance. From the front gate at home I had travelled six hundred and eighty kilometres with just one stop, Before dark I wanted to stroll through the grass on the stock route.

The dominant grass was Mitchell and along a dry creek I waded through patches of Flinders. Flinders is one of the few tall grasses that cattle fatten on. In the west Kimberley the heaviest bullocks I have ever seen were fattened on this native grass. On Myall Plains we have a native grass called whitetop. In late summer and early autumn it will fatten stock faster than lucerne. But the king of all native grasses is Mitchell. In the dead of winter it can appear as lifeless as old stubble, until rain comes. Moisture stimulates sap from the roots and in just a few days the stems will appear green. The net effect is a thoroughly dead-looking grass transformed into first grade hay.

Much of the western downs is still covered with Mitchell grass. On the western plains of New South Wales the species has been a victim of the plough and the ever invading galvanised burr. Areas too far west for wheat production have become an environmental disaster due to the loss of this magnificent and prolifically growing grass.

I passed through Surat and went on to Roma, the heart of the southern Queensland cattle industry. A town of only eight thousand people, Roma is unique. Apart from all the rural back-up industries one would expect, there is a hint of culture quite unexpected in the interior. There are coffee shops as upmarket as the best in Double Bay, Sydney and exactly half the price. The town has a modern cinema. A live band, usually from the Gold Coast, will entertain you at least two nights a week. For clothes it is equal to Brisbane or Sydney and for the outdoor camper there is a shop superior to any I have been in.

Roma has some wild memories for me. The two-day picnic

races held there in the sixties were unlike any other horse-racing fixture in the world. The horses were known as grass-eaters. That is, registered thoroughbreds all let loose in a paddock for a month and mustered and dispersed to various stables about ten days before the race meeting. Some were not ridden before race day. My uncle who had a property near Injune heard I had ridden a couple of winners as an amateur jockey. He was a great sport and decided to arrange a full book for me over the two-day programme. The year was 1966 and I was still an apprentice amateur and an ordinary one at that. Dad was very worried, but there was no stopping me. I arrived in Roma the night before with Sal, then my fiancée. The horse owners had booked my accommodation and had already commenced a party in my room. Queensland hospitality can be very rugged. They allowed me to go to bed at 4.00 a.m., dragged me up to the track at 6.30 a.m. to give every horse a pipe-opener and at 11.00 a.m. I started riding them in a ten-race programme. Four threw me in the mounting enclosure, one fell after the start and in the Ladies Bracelet I forgot to pull my goggles down. It was a dirt track and I went the entire seven furlongs (fourteen hundred metres) with my head under the mane. I had to ask the other jockeys where I had finished. During the afternoon the stipendiary steward said I had no judgement of pace. 'You're dead right sir,' I replied. He looked at me strangely.

I won a race the second day and a lady complimented me for looking so neat and still. I thanked her profusely, because it was the only praise I got. I felt like telling her I was so stuffed that sitting still was all I could manage!

I pulled in behind the old Commonwealth Hotel. It had a bistro dining room with a bar, but the thought of a quick meal was secondary. I have a passion for old hotels. I love to walk out on the wide timbered verandahs and look out on the streets below. Sometimes I try to imagine what the scene may have been a hundred years ago—the sulkies and the drays, horses tethered on every corner and women in long frocks and feminine hats.

Today, however, was business. I booked in and before going to my room I telephoned Sal. She had received three phone calls in response to the ad in the *Western Star*. Two were from drovers and one from a farmer who had some feed. The farmer had some sorghum stubble which didn't sound adequate for a large mob. All three lived in the Roma–Mitchell districts.

I decided to have a meal first and then go into the bar and see if I could find a few cattlemen. If you ring someone for a reference they are often reluctant to say much. In bar talk you ultimately get the good or bad news. The most difficult part is introducing yourself to strangers without feeling like a pain in the backside. On this occasion I looked around the bar and saw mainly young people in large groups. There were some middle-aged men from the town, a few pairs of old men and not too many farmers. There was one group of three. They wore western hats and one was dressed particularly well. Another was tall, lean and sunburnt; he was a stockman. The third had his back to me.

I bought a beer and introduced myself. I explained I was from New South Wales and in urgent need of cattle feed. I didn't wish to raise the names Sal had for me immediately, so I asked them about the stock routes. They were very helpful. The well-dressed man owned two properties. He said the feed south and east of Roma was too frosted. He advised me to head west towards Mitchell. The district had received heavy rain in the late summer.

The four of us talked for a while. I steered the conversation to droving and got what I wanted. The first bloke to ring Sal was capable enough, but drank heavily. On one occasion he was sacked in the middle of a job. The other was thought to be southern Queensland's best drover. To allow drought stock unbroken access to feed he was known to supervise camp riding at night. That was the old practice, but stock routes mostly follow the roads and with bitumen and fast cars it takes a game operator to leave cattle loose overnight.

The farmer no one seemed to know. Or if they did, they were careful not to say.

I didn't stay too long. They were old friends and I was a stranger. I was travel weary anyway and when I woke next morning I walked out onto the verandah. There was a hint of spring. After the freezing tablelands several hundred kilometres to the south I felt keener than ever to place the young cattle up here. I telephoned the drover and he was available. The fee was $1800 per week. For a small mob that was expensive. He explained that whether the mob was small or large he had to assemble a complete droving unit and I accepted that. That left the farmer. I contacted him and he offered to show me the paddock as soon as I could get there. The property I went to was near Amby. It has since changed hands and to respect the privacy of the new owners I have elected to call it Amby Creek. The village of Amby is about twenty-five kilometres east of Mitchell on the railway line.

The spectacle that confronted me that morning was a mixture of Saltbush Bill and Ronnie Barker all wrapped into one. I picked my way through scrap iron, stripped engines and rusted drums to meet a short, white-haired man in his sixties. Despite his steel blue eyes he was friendly and smiled a lot; I warmed to him immediately.

We had to drive out to inspect the sorghum stubble. He told me to hop into what must have been Toyota's first model and while I waited he poured a little petrol directly into the top of the carburettor and hurriedly lowered the bonnet. To my surprise the old girl fired. The first kilometre out was red dirt and stone. All we had to do was put a bit of Mad Max gear on and we might have driven straight out of the film.

Much of the downs country has become the western sorghum belt. In marginal rainfall it is a high-risk crop, but if it fails to make grain it can be baled for fodder or eaten off with cattle. If the rain comes at filling time (when the grain develops) it's a bonanza—relatively small farmers have been known to harvest a quarter of a million dollars in grain.

We reached the sorghum paddock and the stubble was everything I had hoped for. The butts were still green and there were patches not harvested due to the small heads. Beyond the sorghum was a paddock of Mitchell grass. The Old Boy—that was instantly my private name for him—showed me how to assess the grass's value by scrunching the dry grass in his hands to shell the seed. If there's still seed in the grass it means protein for the cattle.

There was only one dam to water the stock. Considering the time of year it seemed to have plenty of water. If required, he said, there was a bore two kilometres away that only required a few minutes work to deliver water.

The Old Boy was naturally keen to get the cattle. He was a sheep man and wool prices were rock bottom. I had to make a decision on the spot. With the back-up of the Mitchell grass I had good feed for a month and maybe holding feed for another three weeks. In that time it might rain. The overall fee was approximately $750 per week, or more than $1000 below the cost of a drover. Reluctantly, I took it. If I went home empty-handed, the cattle would be trucked to Victoria and a bad sale was inevitable.

We headed back in the Mad Max machine and the Old Boy invited me in for smoko. He lived as a bachelor in the kitchen of an old neglected homestead. Living with him was a very smart rat. Everywhere I looked—kitchen table, plastic containers and old books—were signs of the rodent's teeth. Sometimes the rat shared his bed, he told me. He said he was beside himself and asked if I had any suggestions. I asked him for a rabbit trap and a piece of bacon.

During smoko I asked about neighbours. My father had sent cattle to the Bourke district the year before and we had lost cattle to a neighbour there. The stock squad would be the first to agree that ninety percent of all missing cattle go over the boundary fence.

The Old Boy said they were all good people. One man was very mean and I quietly asked him what he meant.

'You want to know how mean he is,' he said with a boyish grin. 'It's my guess he wraps a bandage around it so she only gets an inch.'

I had an instant picture of the definition being written into the English dictionary. There was nothing left to be said. He got me an old rabbit trap and I prepared the rat's execution.

CHAPTER

3

The First Lift

The most economic form of transport for stock is the road-train. A roadtrain is a standard semitrailer towing another equally as long. From bullbar to trailer end they are more than forty metres in length and therefore can only be safely used on major inland trunk roads with low traffic rates. In New South Wales, trucking firms cannot bring them east of Narrabri and Dubbo. Due to the tableland nature of the country, Myall Plains was out of bounds and I had to apply for special permission to bring the trains in from Gilgandra. Where livestock are concerned I find most people are very co-operative. Special permission was granted for daylight hours.

The other lucky break for the week was a man to help us. We had begun feeding grain to the cows and Sal and I struggled with the bags. Sal operated the silo chute and I lifted the bags onto a one-tonne truck. After about twenty bags my back would get that numb feeling and she would have to help me. This bloke from Mendooran threw them onto the truck like plastic bags full of paper. I could barely see his face for beard and had my reservations. He was a happy bloke. Nothing was ever any trouble and Greg remained with us for most of the drought.

The day the roadtrains arrived was cold and sleety. One Queensland truckdriver looking out onto the Warrumbungles thought he had made it to the southern alps. My sister Rosemary brought Dad down for his last look at the cattle and that was his last trip to the station yards ever. He was pleased and we all desperately hoped the next few weeks would be brighter for him.

The plan was for me to drive to Queensland ahead of the roadtrains and arrange a paddock for unloading. The Old Boy's yards did not have the facilities for a roadtrain. Instead, I had to find a spot where the cattle could be safely jumped off. Horsemen too had to be present. Cattle are very disturbed when they leave a truck in a strange place and the mob should be held until the last one has come off.

I figured I would have to tail the mob for two or three days before I could return home. Tailing is simply keeping the mob together and observing they all go to water. For this exercise I took the dogs with me. They sat in the four-wheel drive like people. Caramel always had the front seat. An aged half-dingo, he had a travel addiction. His only connection with livestock was eating them, but he did save me from severe hypothermia on one occasion. I had fallen from a kurrajong tree in the Capertee valley, and suffering from amnesia I wandered in the mountains for nearly two days. At night I held this fellow against my chest for warmth. Behind me was Millie, a type of kelpie known as a black barb. She hated travelling, but she was the lead runner and without her no control was possible. At the other window sat Ellie, probably one of the most beautiful black kelpies I have ever seen. She had never seen an emu and when one ran across the road near Mungindi her excited reaction was most amusing, her paws scrabbling at the dashboard as she tried to launch herself through the windscreen after it.

Two well-known cattlemen from Roma did the horse work. The three roadtrains were backed into a long ditch and the unloading was simultaneous. Immediately the last beast was off, the horsemen took the mob about three kilometres to the dam. The poor things were very thirsty and they gulped the water until their bellies spread beyond any shape of pregnancy.

When the cattle began to feed out, a problem emerged that I hadn't foreseen. On the red stony country there was a green pick. About ten millimetres of rain had fallen on the property the night following my inspection. The Old Boy had told me about the rain, but the possibility of a green pick had never entered my head. It was fresh, tasty and of little value, as the cattle would burn more energy chasing it than they could gain from eating such minute quantities. The senior stockman, a man older and more experienced than myself, thought they would rapidly lose weight. He advised me to employ a stock-man to camp with them for a fortnight and tail them onto the sorghum stubble. To my relief he agreed to do it for the first two days while I looked for someone.

It seemed the dogs wouldn't have to do anything to earn their holiday. They did at least save me the bother of travelling to Mitchell for accommodation. Being slight in build I feel the cold, so I had the three of them to warm me in the four-wheel drive. My dogs are never chained and therefore very clean. To keep the air fresh I fed them tinned food only once a day. My meals were no problem. The Old Boy had the kettle on twenty-four hours a day, and with the rat eliminated by the trap I had set, the kitchen table had everything from corned beef to scones.

Trying to find someone to camp with the cattle and tail them made me feel like a detective. I eventually found a bloke in Yuleba. Dick was in late middle age and out of condition. He had a broody look about him and he spoke with a quiet con-fidential manner. His horses were a mongrel lot and I won-dered whether his old Bedford truck would make the journey. He asked me in for coffee and I accepted as I couldn't make my mind up. His wife clinched the job for him. She was a strong, no-nonsense woman and I had immediate confidence in her. Men of the bush are often the reverse of what they seem upon first meeting. Invariably, their lives have been hard and disappointments frequent. They judge all strangers with great reservation. 'What's this bastard on about'; you can see the words written across their eyes. Their women, however, reveal the quality of their lives in a matter of minutes. With this family, life had been tough all the way.

I left the little farm, with hobbled horses all over the place, feeling a little uneasy. The dogs hadn't given their approval either. There was no tail wagging, just noses pressed hard to the windows and deep growls. Under normal circumstances I would have insisted on references and stayed another two or three days. Short of not turning up, I couldn't see how the man could fail to be of some help. The Old Boy offered to watch the cattle as well. I left uneasy all the same.

Buying a Coke at every truckie stop, I pushed it through the night and made it home about three o'clock on a Saturday morning. I stepped out onto the drive and the chill of mountain air hit me and my breath floated away. There was not a sound. No owls or night birds of any description. I left the door open for the dogs and there was not even a raised eyelid. The four-wheel drive was soft and warm and outside was only an hour from frost. I left them to it and walked carefully along the cement pavement. There was no moon, just the stars in a cold black sky, but so clear was the air the light permeated the atmosphere and I could see every door and window. I opened the back door and closed it quietly. Inside there was still some faint light. I removed my boots and tiptoed to the hall. Sal was waiting in the lounge room between the bedroom and the bathroom. Her long white nightie seemed to absorb light. It was as though the cotton garment was suspended by invisible thread. I couldn't see her. I simply extended my arms and she was there, hand against my chest and her invisible lips on mine.

'It's so quiet,' I sighed at last.

'Now you know how I feel when you're away,' Sal whispered, 'and soon you will be gone again.'

Sal let me sleep in for a while. I woke towards mid-morning to a cup of tea and toast.

'You and I feed today,' she said. 'Greg's got something on.'

'How's the lopping?' I asked.

'About ten days left. After that the trees are too far from water.'

I raised myself on my elbows and looked out the bedroom windows. There are three of them and a door studded with small square panes opening onto a verandah. The room was full of light and it seemed somehow wrong to be in a bed. Beyond the garden, frost-burnt and dry, the paddocks had a fallow look. It was as though it were late autumn and we were waiting for the big rain to sow wheat.

'Just to cross the border lifts your spirits,' I said, taking in the scene grimly.

'I know,' Sal said quietly, looking out the windows and onto the same scalded paddocks. 'Wait till we start the feed run.'

Sal is medium height and slim. She wears her dark brown hair to her shoulders and carries her age better than most women of her vintage. She is one of those women who left the teenage years a little on the plain side and with womanhood bloomed into beauty. So often the teenage beauties fade before middle age. Maybe it's nature's way. In a mystical sense I believe nature to be a great leveller, as though ordained by some intangible power.

I got up, pulled on some clean clothes and walked into the office to go through bills. Halfway through them I lost concentration and moved into the billiard room for no particular reason. It is a room so full of character. A man's room, yet designed by a woman, my mother. I always look on the room as her creative achievement in life. It wasn't because there was a full-sized billiard table dominating the room. Anyone could set that up. It was what she had done with the rest of the room. If I were simply to say there is a sporting bar at one end with high stools and a host of racing photographs it would conjure up an image of rakish masculinity, but it hadn't been finished off like that. With a painting here and there and some fine pieces of china, Mum had balanced the room with a feminine presence as well. When we moved in, Sal introduced her paintings and prints. We didn't change the room and never plan to. It did me good to walk around it. It made me feel, more than realise, there was so much to lose. Failure could never be accepted or entertained.

By late morning Sal and I were on the feed run. Sal drove the one-tonne truck and I unloaded the bags. Each bag I simply emptied onto the ground and within seconds several cows formed a ring around the little pile of wheat. The trick was to get the feed out as quickly as possible. While I emptied one bag Sal drove forward about ten metres so that each pile had that space in between. Some of the cheeky cows kept following me. They would take a mouthful and then run with me to the truck, the grain spilling out of their mouths. We take for granted the huge variation in human intelligence, but I have no doubt the same extremes apply in the animal kingdom. In this instance, a handful of cows had worked out that pushing and shoving for a few mouthfuls was not the way to go. Instead, they were first upon every fresh pile and had the last two or three piles to themselves until their cousins down the feed line followed through.

There were four mobs to feed and it took us about three hours. The slowest part was the travelling back and forth to the depot. The property is about two and a half thousand hectares and one feeding spot was four kilometres from the depot.

Feeding the last mob I felt a push against my backside. I turned and saw at once the cow had no fear of me. There were just those lovely, soft, expectant eyes. I moved to her side and glanced at her rear legs. One leg was distinctly bowed. In 1992 a large heifer calf had attempted to jump out of the calf crush leading up to the marking cradle, and she had twisted her leg so badly she was unable to stand for three weeks. I erected an umbrella over her and watered and fed her for that period. She came to accept me as her protector, and now she was coming to me again for help. There was milk in her udder too. 'Where's your baby?' I said. She just flicked one ear and slapped her tail backwards across her thigh, as though to say, 'Where do you think?' Along with all the other newborn calves, it was planted somewhere up in the basalt ridges. A lot of calves had been born and they were left in little groups, always near a tree. In most instances one cow remained as a minder.

'We should give her a name,' Sal exclaimed from the cabin of the truck.

'I wouldn't,' I remember saying. 'She'll be lucky to survive.' My subconscious mind had already named her though. She became the Bow-Legged Cow and during the next two years I often found myself looking carefully through the mob until I saw her.

The worry now was the rapid disappearance of old dry grass. The kurrajongs had not only provided nutrition, but roughage as well. I knew a few kilograms of grain each day would not hold the cattle together for more than a month. The drought had already proved to be a freak climatic phenomenon and no one could have any confidence in a spring break. I began to plan a mass move to Queensland. Some of the calves would die in transit and many would die on the stock routes, but I had to have a plan or I feared they would all die. Sal and I discussed the grim prospect at great length. There had to be a thorough reconnaissance of the stock routes. If we could drop off near Roma and overland to central Queensland, the breeders might be saved. Billy Little, the drover who had answered our ad in the *Western Star*, was the man I wanted for the job. But first I had to see the stock routes for myself.

It was mid-September when I loaded Circus and twelve heifers onto the old farm truck. Circus was an aged gelding with a few tricks that made him a bit special. The naughty one was gate-opening. The good trick was his ability to turn a rogue beast on a loose rein. On such occasions he had made me look like a super horseman. He could turn and shoulder with extraordinary speed and all the rider had to do was lock in with the knees and watch his ears. If you lost sight of his ears he'd leave you in mid-air. I remember a rogue bull bolting for freedom one day and when Circus wheeled him I turned to look at the men watching and every mouth was wide open. They thought it was my riding. It never was.

The plan was to inspect the agistment country, assess whether the tailer was still needed and then head out to Black-all with Circus. At frequent intervals I planned to unload him and just ride about. I have always been of the belief that feed and country can only be inspected from horseback. In this day and age, my view would be seen as very old-fashioned.

Circus had a whole partition to himself. If I had let the heifers in with him he would have bitten their ears off. The heifers were to be let loose with the young cattle at Amby Creek. Since I had to take the truck for Circus, I might as well put it to use—it was twelve less to feed at home.

I would be away about ten days. Greg had proved to be a good strong worker and with Sal driving the feed truck nothing would be any different in my absence. One of my boys, Nicholas, was giving up his job in Sydney to come home. The contract lopper had left for another property and Nick was going to continue with the lopping. We were down to two hundred trees and only the strongest of the cows would walk the three kilometres to the higher ridges. Every cow that went Nick's way was one less to feed.

The drive to Amby—eight hundred and twenty kilometres—took fourteen hours. Circus was very fed up. I backed into the loading ramp at the railway yards and as I inspected the yards for gates left open he was stamping his front hoof. He came off with a snort and submerged his muzzle in the water trough. I had some lucerne hay bales stacked in with him which he had pulled about. I stacked the hay in a separate yard and let the heifers off. I let them have a drink and fed them in a separate yard as Circus had no intention of sharing the hay.

My own bunk for the night was a small tarpaulin on the ground and a sleeping bag. With the torch I found enough wood to boil the billy and cook some steak on the griller. I was dog tired and must have been asleep by eight o'clock. A couple of trains rumbled past through the night, but the real disturbance was a damp nose in the face about 4.00 a.m. A mob of horses were loose on the stock route and they would have heard Circus blowing and snorting his disapproval of being locked in a strange yard.

Camping in the bush will always hold romantic connotations. The one moment that definitely isn't romantic is the chill of a spring dawn. I invariably find myself stumbling around for twigs and little dry sticks to light a fire and boil the billy. For me life doesn't begin until that scalding liquid is going down my throat. Even if a stampede was imminent it would make no difference.

I had some toast heaped up with blackberry jam and washed it all down with the tea. Then I loaded Circus and the heifers and drove out to Amby Creek.

I arrived at the cattle tailer's camp about an hour after sunrise. For a few minutes I thought it was deserted. There was the old Bedford truck I had seen before, plus a battered-looking trailer. Smoke still rose from the ashes of the night cooking fire and in a hastily made yard of ringlock and steel posts stood two old ponies. Then a face appeared from the rear of the trailer. The man was grey with deeply lined skin. From the back of the truck I could hear a lot of movement, a few coughs that only smokers can make and presently Dick, the tailer I'd engaged from Yuleba, climbed down a little ladder.

I apologised for arriving so early. Dick shrugged and said he was normally up and saddled by this time. He stoked the ashes, threw a few sticks on and when flame burst from nowhere he placed a large billy. It looked like being a day of sitting around the camp fire. Among bushmen it always seems impolite to get quickly to the point. We chatted about a number of things and slowly we got around to the cattle. By this time his brother had emerged from the trailer. He was stooped, stiff, bandy-legged and more haggard than I first thought. Dick said he had asked his brother to come out because the feed was so scarce we would have to go onto the stock route. The news came as a shock. The cattle had been here four weeks and I'd thought seven weeks feed was conservative.

They were busting to go, these blokes. Droving had been their life and they knew every inch of the big stock route that cut through the heart of Queensland. They wanted to go to Tambo, some three hundred kilometres to the north-west. I questioned them about water and it was immediately apparent they knew it all, right down to the bog holes in creeks. I looked at the two old ponies and wondered whether they would survive the muster, let alone the walk to the first watering point. Dick assured me he had plenty of horses left at home. Next question was a third man for moving camp, and then there was the wages. There was an old bloke they could get and they wanted $700 a week each. Dick had put himself on the top money with a third-rate droving unit. I didn't have any enthusiasm for the project and it must have showed.

Next thing Dick told me someone was making a habit of appearing from nowhere on a red motorbike at the crack of dawn. That the bike rider was cutting steers out into a paddock to the north. Dick said he and his brother had put them back each time, but any day now cattle would be stolen. He said bad things happened here. He got very confidential and his voice became little more than a whisper. What gave him away was his eyes. When he looked at me he was trying to assess whether I had fallen for the bullshit. It was in his own interest to persuade me to put the cattle onto the stock routes. There was no employment left here. On the stock route he could earn good money doing the job he loved. However, he should have credited me with more intelligence and attempted to market his capabilities rather than issue a lot of bullshit.

It wasn't long before the question of supplies came up, and money. Dick was due for a cheque. I had paid him a fortnight in advance when I engaged him. His brother I had never engaged, but Dick asked he be paid a couple of days wages. I was in no position to question anything and wrote the cheques out immediately. Within minutes they were preparing to leave for town and I decided to leave them and drop the heifers off at the dam. It was bare around the camp site and I was keen to drive the next kilometre or so to the dam and see how the feed looked.

The picture Dick painted appeared to be spot on. There was no feed in the vicinity of the dam, but the cattle watering there looked full enough. Beyond the dam I had no access in the truck; it was a horseback job. I remembered the best of the country was north of the dam and I desperately hoped the feed had hung on there. There was only one way to find out. After unloading the heifers in a ditch I drove back to the railway yards and loaded Circus. He was pleased to be on the move again and in no time we were together striding out over the downs dotted with scattered myall and brigalow.

We had not been going long when an emu burst out of the brigalow and in long bold strides came straight for us. Circus must have thought his worst nightmare had become reality, for I had no say in what happened next. We made good time over the next half kilometre. There are no emus left on Myall Plains and after that ride I plan to buy a handful just for the horses to look at.

The further I rode the better the feed seemed. But it was the dust that alerted me. There were little groups of cattle scattered everywhere and when they walked the dust drifted up through their legs. I dismounted and rubbed bits of grass through my hands. It disintegrated into powder. The days were already hot and it seemed the sun had finished the old grass off. The cattle too looked dry in the coat. Dick was right—we needed to get out, but Billy Little was the man I would be looking for.

I reached the boundary on Circus and noticed the cattle had worn a pad along the fence. It was a sign of restlessness and concerned, I rode along the fence heading east. Very soon I found the fence down and tracks going in and out. Another kilometre and I saw some of my steers in the adjoining country. They had mated up with a couple of Santa Gertrudis bulls that looked a bit wild. An hour later I found a gate open into a small access paddock with a dam. Some Myall Plains weaner heifers were lying down in the shade of some brigalows and I rode over to them. They looked terrible. They had walked into the paddock days ago, watered, and for no accountable reason had not fed out again. Bewildered young cattle will behave in this manner. The infuriating fact was that no one had checked. No one had bothered to repair the boundary fence either.

When I got back to the camp Dick and his brother had returned and had the big billy on. I took them on quietly. I explained I had a prior commitment in regard to any droving.

They seemed to take it alright and after a couple of pannikins of coffee they loaded their belongings and left. I had fallen in badly, but at the time of engaging this man I knew the risk and I have never been afraid to take a gamble.

I gave Circus some hay and for my lunch opened a tin of lamb stew. The steers outside the fence had me worried. Sometimes they form a strong attachment to bulls and if those bulls were scrubbers Circus and I would hear the slap of leather and suffer a few scratches. If I could get them back in I would strain the fence. I had a set of strainers and pliers in the truck which I put into a haversack. When I reached the boundary I cut the loose wires and pulled all the material back to make a gap in the fence. Circus and I had to get out and I wanted a wide gap for the steers. Rogue cattle will walk through fences in disrepair, but when it comes to going back they are smart enough to run past their point of entry and pretend they don't know about it.

I rode out into country that was no longer open downs. The timber reined in the visibility and from the north emerged a high rocky spur. Where I had cut the fence the ground sloped towards a dry creek. Pushing unwilling cattle along a fence with the slope running away was a distinct disadvantage. Beyond the creek the scattered box gave way to thick scrub. The last line of defence was the spur itself. Quietly was the way to go. If there was to be a chase I needed to win it before the scrub.

The cattle lay under a big tree near a dam, so boggy that two of the Old Boy's ewes were stuck and crows had pecked their eyes out. I carried a knife on my belt and performed the sickening task of cutting their throats. I wiped the blade on the wool and walked slowly back to Circus who I had tied under a tree.

The steers had taken no notice of me. It was the bulls that were wary. They were on their feet and one had the eye of a wild animal. Scrubbers are bulls that have escaped the castrating knife, but these had quality. It wasn't the country for spelling your herd sires. They may have been missed in a muster or just abandoned. The trick was to edge the steers away on their own.

One steer wasn't going to have a bar of it. Each time I poked him out he promptly ran back to the bulls who became more and more agitated. It was just a matter of minutes before the bulls would cock their tails and bolt for the bush, with the steers in hot pursuit. I would have to take the bulls as well.

It went well for the first kilometre. I began to think it was going to be a rocking horse job. The trouble began when the slope fell away from the fence towards the creek. The wild-eyed bull led them and he kept angling towards the creek. Twice I turned him back towards the fence, but on the third occasion he broke for the scrub on the other side and the others took off with him.

Circus always knew before any signal came from me. Within three seconds we were at full gallop to head him off. The bull showed a great turn of speed and knew where the scrub was thickest. Worse still, the other bull had switched course and one steer swung and went with him. The wild-eyed bull burst into a clearing and instantly there was an opportunity to cut the steers away to the left and head them towards the other steer and bull. Then from the corner of my eye I saw him and so did Circus and if he hadn't spun side-on, the charging bull would have knocked us down. The bull caught Circus in that first fleeing stride and I felt his whole body being carried underneath me. In a split second it was over and Circus was in full flight for the second time in just hours. I shudder to think of the damage if the wild-eyed bull had carried horns.

We stopped a hundred metres away and both Circus and I breathed heavily. We needed a few minutes to take stock of the situation. The cattle had gone into the stone country which

I was told sometime later to be the most southern spur of the Carnarvon massif two hundred kilometres to the north.

I could only follow at a walk. I had never ridden in country so inhospitable to a horse. In the southern alps or the steep country of the Warrumbungles, there is always some dirt for a horse to get a foot in. Not so here! Just millions of round-shaped rocks piled on one another as though the devils of hell had been given a picnic day. In fact the low range was once a reef in an ancient sea.

Poor old Circus picked his way over the top and on the other side below the stone I picked up the tracks. Soon I caught glimpses of cattle rumps sliding through the timber ahead. The only hope was a hell for leather ride. The bulls would tire, drop out and ultimately the steers would run themselves out. I yodelled my head off and on a loose rein Circus threaded his way through the box timber. There were patches of sandal-wood and wilga and I crouched low. Jagged branches ripped at my shirt and if it were not for a chin strap I would have lost my hat in the first fifty metres.

The bulls had quickly found each other after the first break and were already knocked up. They ran no more than three hundred metres before they swung sharply to the right. The steers were in full flight, their tongues out and bubbles of froth clinging to their mouths. I began to ease down. From past experience the steers would slow to a trot and then stop. At that point it was vital to keep clear and allow them to cool off. I was so confident of success I must have lost concentration. Circus stopped with a jerk at a fence. It was a new fence with high tensile wire. A beast can hit a high tensile fence and its weight alone will take it over. The fence will bounce back as though nothing happened. A few minutes tracking and I found where the steers had hit the fence and gone over. I had left my haversack with the pliers at the other fence, but even if I had the equipment I had no right to cut this fence.

I don't think Circus minded seeing the fence. It was the end of the day and he knew it. A fast walker at the best of times, his stride lengthened when I turned and headed back.

I loaded Circus and took him back to the railway yards. I gave him more hay than he could eat, set up a bit of camp and drove the truck into the village where there was a hotel. The position with the steers was serious now. They were worth about $350 per head and with the drought expenses compounding I had to get them. On the way back to the village I had stopped at the homestead to see if the Old Boy was about. The place was deserted. It was said he had a girlfriend tucked away somewhere. A young one. He had a bloom in his cheeks for a man of his age and when he told me it takes a young one to fire old hormones I disagreed, but it worked for him.

At the hotel I made enquiries about stockmen and who owned the property north of Amby Creek. The publican couldn't have been more helpful. He telephoned the property and within minutes I had permission to go in and get my steers. Half an hour later he had arranged for a stockman to come to the hotel and meet me. We agreed on a wage for the day and planned to leave Amby at daylight.

CHAPTER 4

The Forbidden Mare

The stockman liked to be called Smokie. He looked like one of those blokes Hollywood would grab by the shirt collar if he went near the front door. You can't create men like Smokie. Life moulds them. How many mustering camps he had been on and how many bad horses he had ridden was written on his face. His features were hard and his eyes a little sunken. God only knows what he had smoked in the last half century, and when he dies the directors of every tobacco company should be at his memorial. The smoking and his numerous accidents had wasted him. He was gaunt and in the mornings the stiffness gave him pain. In the past, men have fought for this country, returned as heroes and more often than not settled down into comfortable lifestyles. Our stockmen of the deep interior live their whole lives on the front line and I have not seen an aged one yet who was not scarred and busted up. And make no mistake, it still is the front line against nature. The only difference between the present and the previous century is that you won't get a spear through the thigh and you drive to town instead of ride. The devastating droughts, the great floods and the bush fires disrupt our lives as much as ever.

Smokie lived in Amby and he had a few hectares to run his horses. When I arrived in the truck to pick him up he was bent over examining the hoof of his horse. I went over to the old stable and I knew before he spoke something was wrong.

'She's lame,' he said. 'My other horses are on a property miles away. It got too dry to keep them here.'

The news posed an instant problem. The paddock the steers had jumped into was a big one, split by the uplift of a long wide escarpment. I hadn't tracked for years and I didn't think I could track over stone. I needed Smokie's help. Two riders could head off in different directions, cross-tracking, searching for the sign of a hoofprint. We would have to anticipate the lay of the land and any breeze. Even if a breeze is too slight to stir the whisker tops of old grass, cattle will walk into it, so they smell danger long before they see it. It's a survival instinct developed over thousands of years.

'How good's your tracking?' I asked.

'I've done my share.'

'We've got to get a horse then,' I said. 'Every day counts with me. My father's very ill and my wife's left to run all the drought feeding.'

'Mine are just too far away. By the time we get back the day's shot.'

'Who owns the horses on the stock route?'

'Dunno. I first saw 'em a fortnight ago. Drovers drop horses here at times in between jobs.'

'Come on,' I said. 'We'll grab one.'

Smokie didn't comment. He lived here. Next week I would be in New South Wales. He picked up his saddle with the leather lunch bag attached and put it in the truck cabin. Next thing he began rolling a cigarette.

The horses had been near the yards most of the night. I think Circus had been accepted and they were waiting for him to come out. When I drove back they hadn't moved far. Catching one could be a problem. I didn't want to feed them into the yards. Their owner would see the tracks and know something had gone on. If they were drovers' horses, oats in a bucket would do the trick.

I had an old milking bucket for this job. Plastic buckets are useless in the bush. All I had to do was shake the oats in the bucket and the response was simultaneous. The one I liked just on appearance was a brown mare of fifteen hands. She had a kind eye and walked up to me as though I had ridden her all my life. I let her smell me for a while and gave her a free go at the oats. The others all wanted some too and I could see if I didn't soon get the bridle on she might be bossed out of the way.

I led her to the yards and let her carry on eating out of the bucket while I unsaddled Circus. I told Smokie to put his saddle on Circus.

'No, I'll ride that one,' he said, 'you stay with your own horse.' Then he smiled that cheeky grin that was so much part of him. 'I'll call her Sarah-Jane.'

I thought about it for a moment. Pinching a horse was serious stuff. I didn't expect to be caught, but there was a risk.

'You can name her, but I'll ride her,' I said at last. 'It's a hundred to one anyone's going to give a damn about this mare being ridden for one day, but if there is trouble it's straight and simple if I am the only one to touch her.'

Smokie didn't care much either way and we loaded her. It was about forty kilometres to the paddock. A gravel public road followed the eastern boundary and there was a gate. I backed the truck into a ditch and before leaving on horseback each of us had a long drink of water.

Circus thought Sarah-Jane was alright. He smelt her bottom and she squealed and flattened her ears, but there was no time for horse smelling. The tracks were right at the gate. The steers had evidently run onto the fence and followed it. The tracking was easy until they veered left and headed into the paddock. The country was heavily grassed with scattered brigalow. Everywhere I glanced I saw groups of emus and mobs of kangaroos. The stinkers too were prolific. Stinker is the local name for a little fellow we call the swamp wallaby in New South Wales. They do stink too, the little rotters.

Despite the grass, we were able to track just walking along on the horses. We both knew it wouldn't last. Ahead was the low range and the stone country. Perhaps they turned and kept to the low plains, I thought—although in vain. Where the stones started the tracks stopped. We talked for a few minutes and agreed to split up. I would ride due north for half an hour or five kilometres and then swing westward. Smokie would ride north-west for an hour and wait. I would cut his tracks and meet him. If one of us didn't cut the cattle tracks they had crossed the range and swung west or south-west.

Tracking is fun if you're good at it. At the age of six I could track just about anything. I carried a hessian bag for rabbits. In the heat of the day I tracked them to their squats and with a stealth that comes only from running wild I grabbed them behind the ears. The Aboriginal trappers taught me so much, but when my parents sent me away to boarding school I lost it all. Today I can track a little, but whatever developed in the eye through to the brain never came back.

I had only ridden for twenty minutes when I cut the tracks. I began to feel excited, as though I was on some hunt. The steers had been running, tightly bunched. Something had spooked them on the range and they came back off it. Smokie would have crossed over by now and I felt his ride was going to be a dead end. But bewildered cattle on the run are very unpredictable. They ran north-west for only half a kilometre before they turned and headed straight over the low range. I couldn't see a single track in the stone, but when I reached the crest there was a slight breeze. I rode down the other side keeping it into my face and within minutes I had the tracks again.

Probably ten minutes later than me Smokie had cut the tracks too. At that point he waited for me. He knew if I didn't find the cattle tracks I would find those of Circus.

West of the low range the brigalow had been poisoned. We rode through dead timber and fallen logs. I found the tracking very hard and at times Smokie had to dismount and drop to one knee. In tough going you sometimes have to ride ahead and attempt to re-cut the tracks. On one occasion the steers did a full circle. Smokie never lost the tracks.

By midday we were both very thirsty and it was pure joy to ride onto a broad expanse of water. Queenslanders don't mess about when they sink a dam. Most dams are at least fifty metres across. This one had beautiful clear water, and humans so seldom came here the birdlife had no fear of us. The ducks watched us for a few minutes, then carried on with their feeding.

The horses had a long drink and we tied them up where they could pick at some grass. The tracks of the steers were everywhere. They had taken a long drink and we knew they would not be far away. We had no billy. I missed my tea so much a saddle quart pot was the first item I purchased when I next reached town.

There was nothing spectacular about the dam. Throughout Australia there are thousands of peaceful water settings. Yet here was a tranquillity I had not seen for a long time. I thought of the mud and the smell and then it hit me—the boggy dams at home had no life at all. The ducks had gone and not even the parrots came in for a drink. I could have stayed there for hours.

We swung back into the saddles and found the steers just a few hundred metres away. They had mated up with several crossbred bullocks and all were lying down in the shade.

Smokie wanted to cut the Hereford steers out immediately. I told him it wouldn't work; that there were two rogues and we would end up tracking them another ten kilometres. He was insistent and I reluctantly agreed to an attempt. I am a loner by nature and don't like to argue for long.

We walked them to an area of open ground not far from the dam. Smokie rode in quietly and eased the bullocks out, one at a time. He cut them out on the dam side, hoping they might simply walk to water. For a moment I thought it was going to work. It was the red steer with the horns, the troublemaker, that spoilt it. He dashed past Smokie back to the bullocks. Smokie tried again and after each failure the cattle were more stirred. I had trouble holding the mob together. It was inevitable they would break, and they did. By luck alone they bolted south and we followed in lethal country for horses. The timber was dead and much of it lay twisted in heaps. At the best the horses would get lacerations to their legs. It was the possibility of a serious stake that bothered me. But our tracking time had run out. We had to keep them in sight.

The cattle went all the way to the southern boundary. Sarah-Jane was a lather of sweat and so was Circus. For the first time I began to feel some guilt about the mare. To borrow her for a quiet ride was reasonable. To give her a hard workout and risk injury was plain tough. I told Smokie we would take the lot and float the bullocks back next day.

We had to go over the stony spur again and I elected to ride ahead and wait on the other side. There was no dead timber here. It was more like an open plain compared to what we had just left. I had a premonition the steers might have one last burst for freedom. There was a lot of low scrub on the spur itself. Animals sense freedom in rough terrain and will use it to advantage.

I heard the stones before I saw them. They had switched direction to the north and Smokie was helpless to do anything.

No horse could gallop downhill in that stone. I cantered out onto the plain to give myself more room. It was vital every beast had reached the plain before I attempted to turn them. The troublemaker with the horns came straight at me. He had no intention of charging. The beast was a rogue and he knew front on was the way to beat me. I moved to the side and let him go. When the others drew level I cantered in behind and waited for them to bunch their rumps. They spurted into a gallop and I followed, waiting for the plain to open up into a treeless expanse. The horny was only thirty metres ahead and if I'd had Circus he would have been well covered. But Sarah-Jane was slower and I had to be patient and wait for the opportunity.

There was a thundering of hooves and as we broke out onto the open plain I had a pang of nostalgia for the racetrack. Sarah-Jane rose to the occasion and as we neared the tail of that horny rogue I whooped like an Indian. The startled steer spun on his hindquarters and without knowing it he was once again on course with the others following. I glanced back and saw Circus and Smokie gallop onto the plain. Smokie turned to the east in case the cattle swung back towards the range.

That was the last bit of drama. We put them through the gate where we had left the truck and Smokie walked them along the fence towards the Amby Creek yards. I loaded a tired Sarah-Jane and followed in the truck. It was a long walk to the yards, through another two gates, and the shadows were long when Smokie shut the stockyard gate.

I fed Sarah-Jane a big lump of hay in the yard and planned to release her into the stock route mob later in the evening. Circus had to be fed on his own as usual.

It had been a long day and I didn't feel like camp cooking. Smokie said the little pub served meals and a few beers to wash it down sounded pretty good. There were several men in the bar and a couple of women. It was a friendly atmosphere and

Smokie saw that I met them all. One was a horsebreaker at the crack of dawn and tractor driver in the sorghum belt for most of the day.

It was going to be one of those evenings where the sinking of a few beers would be expected, so I slipped away and made my phone calls. Sal was just back from the hospital at Coonabarabran. A blood transfusion had become urgent for Dad and the doctor had put Mum in as well. Sal said they were both in the one room. I asked her about the cows and she thought they were holding, but the calves were looking more and more lifeless. The cows were only making a little milk. When I said I would be back the day after tomorrow she seemed very relieved.

During the day I had made a decision to move the cattle from Amby Creek. It was about a ten-day walk to Roma and when they got there I would sell them.

Drover Billy Little's number wasn't answering so I contacted the head stockman at Dalgety's. Billy had taken delivery of a big mob on the upper Warrego. I had missed him. I realised now I should have given him the cattle to start with. The thousand dollar cash saving per week was peanuts compared to loss of weight. Action on the stock routes had been quiet since the summer wet. Most of the feed was just as dry as the adjoining paddocks, but it was along the creeks and the flats where stock did well.

I went back to the bar and started making enquiries about drovers. Smokie had begun to spark and said he and I could walk them in. The stock route to Roma didn't offer much excitement, but he assured me his poetry and singing would fill the gap. I had heard of a boss drover who employed only young women for the horse work. He had been quoted as saying the women were far more caring and looked after their horses better than men. I put it to Smokie and he said it would kill him and if they failed his wife would not. The conversation got more ridiculous as the evening wore on and I enjoyed many of Smokie's tales about the wild country of the Carnarvons. It sounded like a huge blank space on the map. There were too many stories to remember, but the best was the tale of the riding constable. The constable had arrived at a station looking for a valuable thoroughbred mare. As usual the bush telegraph had alerted the manager. Before the policeman arrived they saddled the mare, rode her until she sweated (to make it appear she'd been ridden all morning) and resaddled her with a wide saddlecloth that covered her shoulder brand. The manager pretended to take the matter very seriously and offered the constable his own private mare to ride out and inspect the station horses. A man was sent with him to give any assistance that might be required. The constable rode for three hours on the stolen goods! I couldn't help feeling sorry for the constable. I am sure I wouldn't have woken up to anything as daring as presenting the stolen mare for him to ride.

Fortunately I had walked from the camp to the pub. I knew I wasn't going to escape with a couple of beers. Smokie didn't have to walk far either. When I got to the camp I let Sarah-Jane out. If I had known the steers were going to run into some sensible old bullocks I could have gone out alone and Circus and I would have got them unaided, but in fact meeting Smokie was a positive twist of fate. In the next few days there was to be a run on drovers almost unprecedented, so without Smokie I don't know what I'd have done.

Next morning I took the bullocks back to their paddock in the truck. The rogue steers I took to Roma to be sold at the next fat sale. Roma sells fat cattle every Thursday for the meat trade. I arranged for a Dalgety's stockman to feed them hay until sale day. I had a great sense of relief when they ran off the truck at the Roma yards.

The inspection of the stock route out to Tambo could wait

until I came back. Maybe no drovers would be available! I couldn't leave Sal at Myall Plains on her own while I overlanded the herd to central Queensland. I had a sickening feeling that day that all options for the Myall Plains cows and calves were running out. We were heading into a dead end.

I left Circus with the Old Boy. I hated doing it, but to get him back across the border I had to obtain health papers and I was coming back in a few days. Smokie would keep an eye on the cattle and sort all his old gear for the droving. All I had was the truck and a bit of camping gear.

Both my parents were still in hospital. It was late afternoon when I walked into their room. Dad was dressed, sitting in a chair. Mum was in bed. It was a pathetic and moving scene. They had loved life and they had lived it. Now it was all coming to an end.

I couldn't find the words to tell Dad things were no good in Queensland. They had just completed his blood transfusion and for two or three days he could expect to feel well. Bad news in Queensland would spoil it. We talked about characters and places and I felt guilty when I left.

While I was away Nicholas had arrived home. He had already started lopping and like me he enjoyed it. If I look at a photo of myself at twenty-two then look at Nicholas we are almost identical, except he is taller. He has the same passion for solo sport as me. I always feared it might be rockclimbing. Despite all the technology, I still think mountaineering is the most dangerous of all sporting activities. Instead, Nick chose to be a surfboard rider and skier.

Having Nick home was a breath of fresh air. It was as though we could put the drought behind us for just a few days. We loved the same videos and Sal would find herself going to bed early to get away from the stuff we watch. For me it was bliss— anything to take my mind off the nightmare around us.

Both Mum and Dad were discharged from hospital a couple

of days later. There was no way of avoiding it; Dad had to be told. As sick as he was, he owned the cattle.

Dad was in his usual chair by the fire when I went over to the cottage.

'We'll have to walk the cattle to Roma and sell them,' I said without any preamble.

He nodded and gazed out the window for a while.

'The bank overdraft's getting away again. There's no choice.'

Then he asked, 'Why not float them? The market's worse every week.'

'They've slipped. The stock route might pick them up.'

'The feed didn't last long.' His voice had that irritable tone.

'The feed's there, but it's too old and sour.'

'Who will you get to walk them?'

'There's no one available,' I said reluctantly. 'I've got to walk them in myself.'

I could see the alarm spread across his face. His one dread now was being forced into hospital. While Sal and I were on the property he felt secure.

'There must be drovers about.' I saw at once he was becoming breathless.

'None in Queensland. But it's okay,' I said, trying to be reassuring. 'Sal's not coming and Greg's doing a good job with the feeding.'

The oats had run out and we'd been forced to buy wheat. The grain is toxic if not initially fed in small quantities and we began feeding it with great reluctance. There was no sickness and we quickly increased the ration. We knew it was never going to be as good as oats, but by this time the stocks of oats in eastern Australia were exhausted.

'It's been a dreadful turn-out,' he said at last. For forty years he had used that expression when he was displeased.

'I should only be away a week.'

He said nothing for a while. I found myself in that unreal,

chilling situation of looking at my father for maybe the last time. I was to leave in two days and I didn't expect to be back in a week. If the job dragged on for a fortnight I could expect to be called back. I decided I would help Smokie set everything up and arrange for Nick to go up on the overnight bus.

The day I departed again for Queensland was a sad day. It was the last conversation my father and I ever had. He was in bed with nausea. He had a handkerchief opened up under his chin.

'I think I am finished,' he said quite clearly. There was a pleading in his eyes. All my life I had a misconception that the aged face death with resignation. It's not true. Life is all we have. To go swiftly and suddenly is a blessing akin to birth.

I don't know what I said that day. Very little I think. As I turned to leave his room he asked me to say goodbye to my mother. In my distress I had completely forgotten about her. That was the last thing I ever heard him say.

I loaded the three stockhorses we had left. The previous two years had been tough, no spare cash and we had made do with the old horses.

Mrs Brown was the first up the loading race. Dad had raced the mare in partnership and had allowed his partner to pin (register) the name. I always thought it sounded boring called out in a race, but ever since the film *Her Majesty, Mrs Brown* came out, I've wondered if I was missing something ... I had ridden her in a race and won. I thought she had a lovely disposition and one autumn I was asked to join some southern highland graziers on a ride over the Victorian alps. I took her and Circus. I was told we would ride along vehicle tracks, take it easy and be sure to bring seven bottles of whisky. With eight riders that made a total of fifty-six bottles of whisky. I have always told myself I have no brains, because that was the signal to pull out. Despite a premonition on the very first camp, I stuck with them out of loyalty to the bloke who had invited me. The track we followed was the one the brumby catchers used in the early days. At the notorious 'staircase' (an exposed, very steep spur) Mrs Brown became very frightened and I refused the group leader's order to dismount. Everyone else had, but I have a deep love of horses and if the danger was indeed extreme I believed I had an obligation to stay aboard. The poor mare had never seen much else but a racecourse. She fell and we parted company in mid-air. I don't recall any part of the fall. I remember picking myself up and on the very steep slope below me Mrs Brown struggled to her feet. She shook violently and she had lost some skin. The next few hours remain vague in my mind. There was a heavy fog and the mare was very lame.

The whole ride was a nightmare and haunts me to this day. To save the mare I had to hunt her down the mountains with a stick. The group leader carried a revolver for horses that didn't make it. I got her home and after a month's veterinary attention she slowly recovered.

The next on to the truck was Malameen—an eight-year-old retired racehorse. He was seventeen hands and a big sook. All the ladies loved him and there were frequent offers to buy him. I told him often he had the looks that befit a Melbourne Cup winner, but alas he had little heart for racing. Malameen won six races on the flat and in 1992 I took him to Adelaide to go over the hurdles. I think the decision was doomed from the first day. The old station truck broke down in the desert between Broken Hill and Peterborough. In desperation I tried to hail the Indian Pacific Express. Seeing me there, holding a horse beside the railway the train driver probably thought I was a madman. I simply wanted him to telephone the Adelaide trainer. Needless to say, the train didn't stop. Perhaps it was an omen: he jumped beautifully in pre-training but then pulled a tendon.

Last on was old Yarramin. A bay like Malameen, he was twenty-six years old. He was the only one left from our packhorse team of the 1970s. When the cattle industry crashed in the 1970s, Sal and I ran packhorse tours into the Warrumbungle Mountains. Yarramin was so quiet he may have tolerated a cracker lighted off his rump. Half Clydesdale, he never greeted the judge on the racetrack, but he was a character. He had an insatiable taste for bread and became so frustrated on an overnight tourist camp he picked up a pack, in which he smelt bread, with his teeth and dropped it on the camp fire. One could not assume it was his solution to getting at the bread, but it can't altogether be ruled out.

It was after midnight when I arrived at Amby Creek. I bypassed the railway yards as too much hay had to be given to the horses if they were locked up. The Old Boy had let me put Circus in his ram paddock. There was only a pick, but at least they were free and I carried enough hay to feed them properly once a day.

The ram paddock joined the cattle yards where I had to unload. Before I even stepped from the truck I could see Circus coming in the half moonlight. There was a chorus of whinnying and Mrs Brown nearly knocked me down in her rush to leave the truck. I fed all four in a large holding yard. There were only a few hours of the night left, so I slept in the truck. I woke very stiff and tired to the sound of the Old Boy's voice. He had bacon and eggs on and never had it smelt so good. I drank the scalding tea I love so much and listened to his latest jokes. An hour after sunrise there was a breeze coming through the front door.

'I am sick of this easterly,' he said. 'It blows up their fannies and puts them right off.' I was getting used to his sense of humour.

It wasn't until after breakfast he told me the big news. 'The police have been here Mick.' He looked concerned. 'They got nothin' out of me. I was away.'

'Someone must have seen me with the mare.'

'They grilled Smokie for an hour. Evidently the drover bloke came next day to pick them up and that mare was lame.'

On the way to Mitchell I dropped in to see Smokie. He had told the police he didn't know anything about the mare I rode. They knew he was lying, but were forced to accept it as no charge could be laid against him.

In Mitchell I went to see the herdsman and got more bad news. (In Queensland the herdsman is the person in control of travelling stock within each shire.) Five thousand head of cattle had been dropped on the stock route west of Roma. Another four thousand were still to come. Grain in northern New South Wales had become temporarily unavailable. In desperation, cattle owners had pooled their herds and contracted drovers to walk them on the best available stock routes. He said the mobs were all heading west and if I went onto the stock route I could be up against a tide of cattle.

'Try the back roads,' he suggested. He was a very decent bloke and I discussed with him the various camps and watering points. He warned me, however, that one day's walk from Amby took me out of his territory and from that point he could do nothing.

I left the herdsman's place and parked the truck in the main street. I felt exhausted and totally indecisive. There was a sign 'Coffee' and next door a newsagent. I thought if I read the paper and had some coffee things might get better.

A young woman with long fair hair brought the coffee and sandwiches.

'Sorry I've been so long. Been so busy this morning.'

In the adjoining room was the bakery, which was the principal business.

'Time's not a problem for me today.'

'You're lucky. In this shop there's never any time.'

'I am just stalling,' I said, forcing a smile. 'When I leave here I'll probably be arrested.'

'Oh God, what have you done?' she asked with a burst of laughter. She had such laughing eyes I couldn't resist saying it, although it was mischievous.

'I borrowed a horse.'

'Well it's not every day I get to serve Ned Kelly!'

She confirmed my impression that Mitchell is a friendly little town. If a lonely stranger chose to settle there it would be their fault if they were not accepted in the community within days. The town nestles into a bend on the Maranoa River and has one of the river's largest natural waterholes, free of all the carp problems now so chronic in western New South Wales.

Reluctantly, I left the town before lunchtime and went back to Amby Creek. Before leaving I collected my travelling stock permit from the Shire Office. If I waited, the stock route would be eaten out.

I was having that long cup of tea with the Old Boy when the police arrived. It seemed the Old Boy had a horror of them and he half fell over leaving the kitchen for the rear of the house.

I walked outside and the police officer asked me if I was Michael Richard Keenan. I wanted to say I was William Munny from Missouri, but I realised the occasion was very serious and simply nodded.

'I have a warrant for your arrest,' he said soberly.

'What for?' I asked.

'Using a horse without the owner's permission.'

'You can arrest someone for that!'

The officer explained to me that the charge under law was similar to taking a car. To me it seemed like taking someone's lolly and getting six over the backside.

No bail was required on the condition I didn't leave Queensland before the court case. The officer thought I would face the magistrate at Roma on 18 October.

5 The Grass Generals

To call upon any experience that may have helped me predict the rigours of droving I had to go back to 1958, when my father had sent me out with an old drover known as 'Senator' Cooper. He was a big man with a beard. It was difficult to tell where his tangle of white hair ended and his beard began. On top of this lion-like spectre sat a high top hat. I never saw it off him. He travelled about in a double-harness horse-drawn wagon. With the canvas pulled over the top, it was straight out of Arizona, 1885. The one thing which destroyed such a colourful fantasy was the sheep. We were droving sheep and snotty-nosed crossbreds are the pits on the road.

In those days the stock routes of New South Wales had big reserves and we had settled into one called the Bluebush on the Castlereagh River between Gilgandra and Mendooran. The place teemed with wildlife and I loved every minute of it. The big black goannas fascinated me. They would come creeping into the camp like miniature dragons drawn by the smell of cooking. Every day Senator said we were going to have one for dinner. I didn't know whether to be pleased or revolted. He must have had a chuckle or two, the old-timer, because I never woke that he was pulling my leg.

Senator not only knew the history of the river, but he had been a part of it. Just near the camp was the shell-like remains of the Mawby homestead where the Breelong blacks had slaughtered nine women and children. The chief of the band, Jimmy Governor, proved to be the most elusive Aboriginal outlaw in Australian history.

'Every man that could ride a horse was looking for them,' Senator stated from his bed in the wagon, probably about one o'clock in the morning. 'They killed them with tomahawks. There was real fear in the countryside. You see they could run fifty miles in a day. Drop a roo and eat it raw. White man was no match for them.'

Wide-eyed, I would ask Senator many questions.

'In 1925 I saw Roy Governor shot at a thousand yards. Wounded, mind you. He was a nephew of Jimmy. They hated the whites, them blacks.'

'What happened to Roy?' I asked.

'Released after a few years. There was a bit of sympathy, believe it or not. Some reckon homesteaders brought it on themselves.'

Jimmy Governor had been educated and very well brought up by a childless white couple. He was torn between two societies, and finally rejected by the white people.

'They say he tried, poor bugger,' Senator would mumble on. 'Even married a white girl. It was when they rejected her he went berserk. And of course the young Aborigines living on the missions saw him as a hero. They were oppressed and given no future. That's why a handful jumped the mission and followed him.'

One by one the murderous band was either shot or hung. The manhunt for Governor went on for three years. In the peaceful bush setting I found it difficult to imagine such violence.

Senator rambled on about the past well into every night and one morning we both overslept. The sheep had gone, pushing down the night break. The whole three thousand had crossed the river which never carried much water and headed south along a creek into the Goonoo forest. It took days to find them all. I remember the heat and the long hours in the saddle as easily now as old Senator remembered the events of 1901. Any romantic notions I had about droving were destroyed when I was just fifteen.

There are no wagons today. The modern drover has a lorry with a stock float, a caravan towed by a small truck (usually a diesel-powered Toyota or Nissan), a couple of motorbikes and several horses. Depending on the size of the mob, most units are operated by three people. Two do the stock work and one cooks and moves camp. Women have become just as much part of the scene as the men. In some cases family units do the lot.

The big droving outfits are elaborate and fascinating to observe. The first sign of movement on the horizon is the horses. There may be up to twenty of them. They precede the cattle, as they must have the best of the feed to be kept strong and in good physical shape. A man will be seen riding along with the horses and he is known as the horse-tailer.

Perhaps half an hour will slip by before the first beast appears. If you watch a mob over a few days a leader becomes apparent. A sensible leader is a blessing; a rogue a nightmare. Within a minute of the leader appearing the whole horizon will transform into a dark mass. When four thousand head converge over a rise in the distance it's like the advance of a giant army. If the mob comprises steers and bullocks a horseman on either side will be seen near the lead. On a stock route there won't be much excitement for them. But in the big mustering camps of the Gulf Country these men are hell riders. If the lead bolts they rein in at nothing. In the west of the USA someone, a long time ago, wrote a song about the lead riders— 'Ghost Riders in the Sky'.

Behind a big mob will be four or five horsemen. One of them will be the boss drover. He's usually last and in the middle. Most of them become legends within their own life-time. They are the grass generals of the interior.

For the first six days we walked the cattle due east to the village of Muckadilla. Nick had arrived on the bus with a friend, Rupert. The young man had never ridden a horse. I put him aboard Yarramin and he was riding competently within twenty-four hours. He was tall, strong and very willing. The questions were never-ending and when he met the Old Boy on the first day I knew he was in for it. I was holding a mug of tea and cringed when one question came up.

'There's no toilets out there.' The Old Boy's eyebrows shot upwards. 'Never been in the bush before son?' he said knowingly.

'No.'

'Just go behind a tree. Then when you get back to the truck you'll see a rope hanging off the side. Everyone uses it.'

Smokie wasn't much better. Rupert's initiation with him was in a pub at Mitchell. Smokie started with the blokes he'd punched out over the years. After several beers the bars from Muckadilla to Quilpie had been awash with blood at one time or another.

'I've never heard people talk the way they do out here,' Rupert said to me quietly that evening. I could see he was quite distressed. He was a gentle young man who never once became agitated or even irritable.

'It's a lot of hot air,' I remember saying to him. 'There are some terrible fights over women. The rest of it's just grog talk.'

It was at the Muckadilla bore we struck the first lot of trouble. Three kilometres from the bore I rode ahead on Circus to see if we could go in for water. I knew there was a boss drover ahead of me with two thousand head and on the limited intelligence available I thought I could get to the bore first, let the cattle have two hours on the fifty-metre trough and

pull back onto a road running south. While waiting for Nick I
had done some reconnaissance in the truck and found magnificent feed south of Muckadilla. If I could slip in for a drink
twice a day the cattle would freshen up before the final stage
to Roma. I had wanted to go the back way to Roma, but three
graziers had denied me water. In 1991 and 1992 we had
Queensland stock all over New South Wales and I know everyone helped as much as they could. The saying 'The further
west, the friendlier the people' is a myth.

When I got near the bore there were cattle as far as I could
see. The reserve at Muckadilla is one of the best on this great
arterial stock route. Five hundred hectares in size, it comprises
mainly creek flats. It was every drover's dream to camp here
and be left in peace. The one condition not found on stock
routes, however, is peace. By regulation cattle must walk six to
ten kilometres a day, depending on availability of water. The
local herdsman monitors every mob and if a drover fails to
comply he can be ordered off the stock route. To spend a few
days feeding on a non-stock route road I had to obtain special
permission.

Circus was very thirsty and he had a long drink while I
thought the position over. By the creek I saw a truck and two
caravans. Four saddled horses were tied up under trees. With
some misgiving I decided to ride over and discuss the possibility of a drink for the cattle.

The dogs let everyone know I had arrived. The stockmen
were all having a midday camp. They had probably started
moving the cattle at 4.00 a.m. Presently a tall swarthy bloke of
about forty stepped out of one of the caravans. I made some
effort at a greeting, but none came from him.

'I've got thirsty cattle,' I said. 'Can you clear me a passage
for about an hour?'

He just looked at me—a stern, summing up sort of stare. I
was instantly pleased I hadn't dismounted.

'You won't tell me what to do,' he muttered in a threatening voice.

'I don't intend to. Just want a drink.'

'I'll be leavin' in the mornin'. You get yer drink then.'

The other stockmen had appeared by this time. They all came out and just stood, eyes to the ground. To my right was another caravan and beyond it the fireplace. An iron tripod had been erected and some billies hung over the flame. An older man had appeared from nowhere and he lifted a billy off a hook and poured the hot water into a large dish.

There was nothing to say in the face of such hostility. On the bush telegraph they knew all about me. An owner on the road with his cattle. A little mob—less than six hundred head— just enough cattle to be a nuisance on the stock route. And here he is in person, the little bastard, asking us to get on our horses and move the cattle away from the water.

Only a kilometre from the water I found Smokie at the lead. Sometimes cattle can smell water over a long distance. The leaders of our mob were mostly rogues and too smart for their own good. If they knew about the water Smokie may not have held them. In fact all the cattle had their heads down in the grass.

'They won't shift,' I said.

'The bastards.'

'He said they'd leave in the morning.'

Smokie took a long draw on his cigarette. He was a wild-looking man when he was cranky.

'They'll go for a dry camp tomorrow. That means a dinner-time pull out.'

'We can't wait that long,' I said, alarmed. It was already mid-afternoon. 'We better go back.'

'Be two hours into the dark. No hope of gettin' them tapes up.'

The tapes were the electric fence. One man would hold the

cattle together in a confined space while two ran out the electric tapes which were supported by plastic posts. The posts have a spike and are simply pushed into the ground with a man's boot.

The cattle were in no danger. They'd had a lengthy drink about mid-morning from a lagoon. A dry camp was within reason, but on this stage of the walk I wanted the cattle to gain weight. On one drink a day they would lose weight. If we had to wait until lunchtime tomorrow they might suffer a setback that would negate the whole exercise.

The cattle were feeding across the southern road. It was a gravel surface used by no more than ten cars a day. The drivers were invariably farmers and only for the restless rogues we need not have taped off for the night.

Smokie started turning the leaders down the lane and I rode down to the tail where Nick and Rupert were waiting. The cattle were scattered over four hundred metres. Nick was on Malameen—a tall young man on a big tall bay horse. It made me think of an old Texas song.

'We'll hold up here tonight,' I said to the boys. 'About half a mile down, the lane opens up into a reserve. Good camp for the cattle. We can camp this side in case the rogues want to walk back towards the highway.'

'We going in for a drink?' Nick asked, worried.

'They won't let us in. Got to wait till the morning.'

'What about the herdsman?'

'We're out of his territory now,' I said. 'I don't know the Roma bloke. He might instruct me to go back.'

'I think you should ring him just the same,' Nick went on. 'He might get the drover to leave early in the morning.'

I thought it was an excellent idea. We allowed the cattle to feed for another hour before walking them into the reserve area and taping off the northern end. The road had to be left open, so we set the camp up near the gap. Sometimes the horses were a nuisance in these situations. Unlike the cattle, they had no fear of the camp and would walk out of the break if not sent back with the crack of a stockwhip. Once this camp was set and the horses had been given a drink from the truck's water tank, I left for the Muckadilla pub. Smokie stayed to mind the camp. I promised him a couple of stubbies when I returned.

The village of Muckadilla has several houses, a service station and the grain silos. If it were not for the hotel, with its motel-style accommodation, the village would have been a speck on the wide open plains where no one ever stopped. The pub, however, had defied the modern trend of village disintegration near major towns, for few locals could resist its temptation. The bar had an atmosphere I have never seen anywhere else. All the patrons drink and talk as one group, irrespective of whether they've ever met before.

We walked into the bar and the woman serving caught my eye immediately. It was a friendly come and have a drink look and nothing more. She stood so straight and her eyes, which were green, never moved from your own. Her red hair was everywhere and some of it fell on bare shoulders. I quietly made a decision to drink only beer—the ale that quenches your thirst and leaves the fantasies of the mind buried.

The sun had gone down and the regulars were on to their third or fourth beer. I looked across the angle of the bar and saw a bloke with a reddish tinge in his hair and beside him a woman with grey hair. She had gone grey before her time and her skin was dry. I looked away too slowly and the bloke gave me a wave. I had never met him, but that's the way it was in this bar.

Between the boys and me and the couple, two farmers were in earnest conversation. One was already under the influence and talking loudly. Someone hadn't drafted his cattle correctly for sale. In other words, he had copped a bad sale. As the drink

flowed, I felt the sale might get worse as the evening pro-
gressed. To our right were two young blokes. One was taller
than Nicholas and had a friendly open face, but a shifty eye.
The other boy just sat on his stool with a bemused expression.
Nick and Rupert struck up a conversation with them almost
immediately. That left me with the bar lady. Her name was
Donna. She told me it was a good business. The motel wing
was full on weekends and in the summertime people stayed
every night and took advantage of the swimming pool. The
down side was the exhausting hours. On weekends farmers
drank nearly all night and most of them had dinner. While she
was talking she dropped a beer herself.

I contacted the herdsman in Roma and he promised to
come out and see what was doing. He thought the drover
would move at daylight and make for the Amby reserve some
twenty-five kilometres to the west. We had come from that
reserve in two stages; midway a farmer had let us into a dam
for a drink.

There were few opportunities to use a telephone. Sal
sounded flat this time. When the night nurse wasn't available
she was sleeping at the cottage. She said the nights were the
worst for Dad. Angina came on suddenly and she frequently
had him on oxygen. When would I be home?

Back in the bar the boys were playing pool. There was laughing and ribbing and I could see a move to the camp would be
unpopular. I bought another drink and when I turned the
bloke with the red tinge in his hair was behind me.

'Mick is it?' he said with an outstretched hand. The locals
all knew me by now. The eccentric on the road from New
South Wales. I was being kind to myself, for in western Queensland the word 'eccentric' is not in the vocabulary.

We shook hands and he introduced himself. 'I'm a dingo
shooter and got a fair bit of country too,' he said. I later found
out that he was a crack shot, taking bags of dingo scalps to the

local shire council to claim the bounty—a modern-day bounty hunter. So I gave him the nickname of 'Scalp', which he seemed quite pleased about.

Scalp took me over to his grey-haired lady and introduced her as his woman. I shook hands with her in the manner my mother had taught me forty years before.

'I haven't got a redback spider in me palm.'

We shook hands again. This time I took her hand as though it belonged to a rugged stockman.

'How yer gettin' on with yer cattle, Mick?'

'Water's the problem. They reckon there's more mobs on the stock route than watering points.'

'We heard they held yer out,' she said.

'How?' The speed of local gossip in small communities never ceases to amaze me.

'The cook was in for a beer. He was goin' off about the pain in the arse. Bloody Mexicans, he said.'

She laughed and there was a glint in her eye. Jenny was her name and there was a time when the grey hair might have been black and the dry skin soft and moist.

'Mexicans! What do you mean?'

Scalp giggled. 'Up here youse blokes are called Mexicans.'

It was not with any affection either, but I didn't say it. In Texas and New Mexico they are not popular either.

'What are you goin' to do about the water?' Jenny asked.

'Wait till they go.'

'You could hang the washing out.' When she smiled it was wicked.

Scalp laughed and shook his head. 'Oh Jesus, don't tell him to do that.'

I looked at her, really puzzled this time.

'You got a couple of boys with you,' she said, poker-faced. 'Cut a couple of saplings about ten foot long and tie on your sheets.'

'We don't have sheets,' I said. I knew something shocking was coming.

'Anything, just as long as it flaps when you wave the stick.'

'The good old rush,' Scalp piped in. 'Jesus, the bastards go. I reckon this mob would pull up at the Maranoa.' He started to shake his head and look elsewhere, even behind him. 'Sneak in behind 'em and wait till the boss drover comes out for a piss, which is often after they've been here. Then up 'em.'

'Take him too,' I said aghast.

'Oh shit no,' he giggled and drained his glass. I looked to the bar lady as I was going to get another into him. It was better than stage entertainment. 'Make sure he sees all his cattle piss off.'

With that he doubled up and was not composed until the next beer had been poured. The bar lady didn't speak much. She didn't have to. Most women mirror their thoughts in their eyes, but this one spoke with them.

His woman didn't laugh. Jenny just smiled.

'Would you do that?' I asked.

'He would,' she said softly. 'Mischief to him is like ice-cream to a kid.'

'You ever hear of stampedes?' I asked the question seriously. It was part of droving folklore, but I had never heard of one.

'The big bullocks are dangerous,' Scalp said soberly. 'I never seen it happen. They reckon when the buggers go real quiet, you can't hear a pin drop and it's very dark—watch out then. That's what they reckon.'

I enjoyed Scalp's company. He was well dressed for a bushman and wore a wide western hat. The dingo shooting kept him in good physical shape. He told me he had a twenty thousand hectare property a hundred and sixty kilometres from Roma and if rain fell he could give me agistment.

The boys would have liked to stay, but we had to get back

and put the camp oven on. I was the cook. I made a camp casserole most nights and occasionally grilled some steak. Lots of spices went into the casserole and the boys ate a tin plate full and never forgot to tell me what a good cook I was. I might have made it with the casserole, but in general I am a terrible cook, limited to the making of tea and coffee and once in six months an omelette.

Smokie ate very little of anything. I often wondered where his energy came from. He was sitting by the camp fire when we got back that evening. Cigarette butts lay on the ground near his feet and the one in his mouth was nearly spent. His eyes lit up with the stubbies and while I mixed the casserole ingredients I asked him about stampedes.

In the 1890s there had been a tragic one only a few kilometres west of Mitchell. He said he could show me the exact spot where the wagons and drays had been smashed. There were eight hundred bullocks from the Channel Country. No one knew what started it because there were no survivors. He said it was usually the dingoes. In the old days a pack might follow a droving unit for two or three days. When the night camp was vacated they searched for scraps. Still nights with a wind blowing up after midnight would put drovers on alert. A leafy branch from a gum tree—that's all it took. It seemed on this fatal night the night riders had come in for coffee. The boss drover and stockmen were all found dead within thirty metres of the camp fire. One body had been skewered by a bullock's horn and possibly carried for twenty metres. Even the dogs were killed.

By the camp fire every night each of us would sit on our private log. There was always something that could be picked up and used as a seat. Sometimes it might only be the remains of a stump. Smokie often lay his oilskin on the ground. I think he was always more exhausted than he ever cared to admit. With the coffee mug in one hand we would discuss plans starting from sunrise.

The two young blokes from the pub destroyed any privacy that night. We saw the lights and instantly noticed the sway of the vehicle. The nearest guide post to the camp was taken out and the vehicle stopped. The tall boy emerged from the driver's side and I have never seen anybody so drunk.

By this time I had formed the conclusion that a frontier culture exists in some parts of Australia. It has both refreshing and depressing elements, as I believe all past frontier cultures had. The usual constraints of western society today are still not properly enforced in these places, and on rare occasions it can be like breathing in fresh air after leaving a stuffy room. Weighing against this is the entrenched rawness and insensitivity. East and south of Roma is no different from the southern farming communities and many of the old family holdings west of Roma have never changed—quiet, law-abiding and conservative. But beyond the invisible boundaries are communities that live under a different, new code of ethics. It is an expression of deep frustration, as though the modern world has passed them by and underneath lies an anger that doesn't rise and fall, but burns like a smouldering log that defies even rain.

Our camp in the lane was about three kilometres from the bore. I saddled Circus at daylight and rode along the lane until I reached the reserve and then took a short cut through the timber. The belt of timber in the reserve was the only one for miles. Before white settlement the Aborigines systematically burnt the dry grass in winter to stimulate fresh growth following the first rain. The green grass attracted kangaroos and when they wanted meat the Aborigines drove them towards barricades made from brush, which they carried in. It was the Aborigines who created the vast open downs of Queensland.

The boss drover had given the word. I hung back in a patch of sandalwood and watched the men ride away towards the southern boundary of the reserve. There were cattle all around me, feeding. They were principally shorthorn and Santa Gertrudis-cross cows. The calves were half the size of their mothers. A late summer calving and under normal management conditions the calves would have been weaned weeks ago. They were pulling their mothers down now and some of the cows were weak. The hide clung to their ribs and their hips revealed the exact nature of the skeleton underneath.

Circus began to strain on the bit. He was thirsty and I let him have his head. The equipment on the bore was powered by an engine. The water itself was pumped into a giant earthen tank known as a turkey's nest. From the turkey's nest the water was reticulated to a trough. To safeguard the water supply the turkey's nests were fenced off. So huge were the mobs coming through, the supply to the trough was inadequate. The fence around the turkey's nest had been cut to let the cattle in. The boss drover would not have wanted to do this. In a small area cattle can be drowned and the carcass must be removed from the water. I rode round the banks of the turkey's nest and found two beasts hauled from the water. They were bloated, legs hard stretched and in a couple of days they would stink. The general mood of the men was understandable. There was no joy in overlanding weak cattle. Without even waiting to watch I knew what their long day would entail. The weakest of the cows would have to be driven, mile upon mile. Every time a rider left to push another obstinate one, the cow would stop. The worn-out cows would just stand, holding a baleful eye on the nearest horseman. For the stockmen it is exasperating and they become more and more irritable as the day drags on. Some crack their whips until their arms ache.

It was the crack of the whips I was waiting for. The sound heralded the start of the mustering from the southern boundary and a company of forktailed kites heard it too. The caravans were parked near a dry creek, some three hundred metres from the bore. The cook had thrown his kitchen scraps into a gully and the big brown birds had wasted no time. When they heard the whips crack they flew up and slowly wheeled above the camp. The kites are harmless scavengers, but in trigger-happy communities they learn quickly to identify sounds that resemble a rifle shot.

The boys were relieved when I got back to camp. The sun was an hour up, but the cattle were not feeding. They hung on the electric fence and their mooing was so persistent anyone from a distance would have thought it was a mob held in a yard.

To be safe I suggested we wait another half-hour. I wanted to be sure the boss drover and his mob were well clear. Smokie and the boys would steady the lead, but they would not be able to hold them. Smokie had already nicknamed some of the rogue leaders. They were all steers and the names he gave them were unprintable.

When we did release the mob I remained at the camp. As well as being camp cook, I was camp cleaner and camp mover. It was a one-man job and I didn't mind as it broke the monotony of the stock route. In one of Mary Durack's books (her most famous is *Kings in Grass Castles*) she quotes her father as saying the great overland drives through the Northern Territory conjured up only one memory—monotony. That was through hostile Aboriginal territory! God spare us. Our walk to Roma was going to be like delivering the papers.

I was about fifteen minutes into the job when the Roma herdsman arrived. He was a stocky man in his late fifties and had a kindly manner for the sort of job he had.

We shook hands and talked about the drought for a few minutes. Then he said, 'There's about four thousand in the next mob. They'll camp tonight in the big box reserve about ten miles from here. One stage after them is Terry Hall. He's got two thousand now and there are more roadtrains coming from New South Wales. South of Roma three thousand have been dropped on the southern stock route. They're headed this way.'

'The route's going to be eaten out,' I said, and he would have sensed the alarm in my voice.

'I suggest you get through to Roma as quickly as you can. I'll put you on an untouched reserve about ten miles east. I can give you a week or ten days. We make special allowances for sale cattle.'

I thanked him and asked him what the feed was like on the reserve. He said it was the best dry feed in the district and if we fed the cattle along the highway in the daytime they would find green spots in the hollows and along creeks.

We yarned for a while and he left. I found out later very few mobs ever get onto the country where I was now headed. Someone had helped me and to this day I am grateful.

Spurred on by the prospect of fresh country and no boss drovers, I tossed all the gear into the back of the stock float, took down the electric fence and drove the truck to a clump of myalls about three kilometres east of Muckadilla—the site of the next camp. I left Circus tied up to a fence in the shade.

It was nearly smoko time. I don't know what it is about horses, but when you are riding them up goes the appetite. The boys would be looking out for me. I packed two billies into my haversack, the pannikins, a loaf of bread, some cheese and fruit cake. In separate jars I had coffee and tea.

The walk to the bore didn't take long. I lit a fire and pushed the billies into the flame. The water was out of the trough. Provided the brew was strong no one cared. Smokie always drank coffee. He took the change of plans soberly. Slipping through the big mobs would have us on our toes, day and night. There would be more dry camps. For the boys it was music to their ears. The previous day two girls, sisters, had walked from a homestead near the stock route to meet the boys. Someone had seen these strapping young men from a car. In western Queensland there are countless young boozers—pig and roo shooters by the dozen—but company that may interest a young lady is lacking. The girls told the boys Roma was an exciting place. The prospect of packed bars and live bands just five days' ride away was enough to prompt wide smiles.

The tea-leaves had not long settled in the tea billy when I heard a car. I turned around and a four-wheel-drive police wagon drew up beside us. An older man emerged this time. I had never met him, but he knew me. He had the summons in his hand and gave it to me with a solemn 'good morning'. He made no comment. I thought he seemed more interested in the cattle. Some of them hung around the trough, tossing the water in little splashes with their noses and half curious at the morning tea proceedings. He commented on their quality. Members of the Queensland stock squad are respected for their stockmanship. It was a comment I took warmly.

After the policeman had left Nick confronted me.

'What was that all about?'

I hadn't told him. I hadn't told anyone. I briefly explained the situation to him and he looked very worried. Nick had studied law for a short time, passed a couple of subjects and then decided to change courses. He was now thinking like a lawyer.

'You can't plead guilty!' he said, aghast.

'Be hard to convince a magistrate I wasn't.'

'You'll end up with a criminal record. No passport for one thing.'

I had reached the half century and never been past Darwin. However, in principle he was right and I agreed to consult a solicitor when we reached Roma. There was going to be a lot doing when we got to Roma.

The questions went on and on. Did Mum know? Mum will

freak out. When will you tell her? By lunchtime he had my whole defence worked out.

I left the food and the billies with the boys and set off for the new camp. Circus gave a whinny when he saw me. He didn't like being left on his own much. On our way back to the bore we saved a precious life. A plains turkey had himself caught in a fence. The bottom two strands of wire were twisted on his leg. He had been there a day or two. Another day may have been too late. Literally thousands of kangaroos, wallabies and emus die every year on fences. The fatal twist of wire is always the same. A leg goes between the wires, the head goes through the fence first and when the leg follows the bottom wire kicks upwards locking the leg in a perfect trap. It's not that they die, these poor animals. It is the way they die. The dreadful constraints of our civilisation are a sad defiance against the law of nature and in the passage of time will fail.

About mid-afternoon we gathered the cattle in a tight mob and drove them towards the railway bridge. We had to go under the bridge and the clearance was barely enough for a horseman. The cattle were spooked and to make it more difficult the highway ran parallel with the railway. Nick and Rupert held up the traffic and Smokie and I pushed hard against the reluctant mob. We spun on hind feet and galloped after the breakaway beasts. It may have only taken ten minutes, but when the leaders finally went under the bridge our horses were a lather of sweat.

For the night camp Smokie suggested we tape right across the stock route, fence to fence, on the eastern side. The cattle would be free to feed over a large area and he thought they were so spooked by the railway bridge none would go back. There was a vehicle track along the stock route and it did cross my mind the boss drover east of us might want to bring his men in for a few beers after dark. I mentioned it to Smokie and he said they would use a nearby lane to gain access to the highway. What both of us forgot was the highway patrol. Drovers don't have just one or two beers—they drink a skinful and no matter how rough the bush track is they will take it every time rather than risk meeting the highway patrol.

By late afternoon the cattle were spread over fifty hectares, heads down in thick dry Mitchell grass. The previous mob had made little or no mark on this part of the stock route. They had already walked several kilometres since the last water and they would have been thirsty. The tracks indicated they simply walked through the grass. On the other hand our cattle had been on water for half a day and were keen to tuck in. They had a healthy full look about them and I may be biased, but a line of five hundred poll Herefords grazing on an open plain should inspire any bush poet.

I cooked an early dinner. I had a sneaking suspicion Smokie was eyeing the pub off and I knew the boys were. They'd had a lot of fun on the pool table the night before. Smokie decided to ride his mare to the hotel. Old stockmen never walk, he told us. Also I think he wanted to give her some more education. He had only broken her in the week before we left Amby Creek. She was more of a pet than anything and one evening caused Smokie acute embarrassment.

Smokie was a great one for washing and cleanliness. What the boy's mothers failed to do over the years, Smokie achieved in just one week. The mare was always hanging around the truck. A dipper of grain, an apple, a piece of bread—almost anything would please her. On this occasion, as though to demonstrate her dissatisfaction, she lifted her tail and urinated over the table. No laugh from Smokie, but it was the boys' turn to offer hints on hygiene.

'You want to tell her we got our own dishwashing fluid,' I heard Nicholas say.

The boys and I walked briskly along the dirt track with

Smokie riding ahead of us. It was already quite dark and the mare's dark form and the sound of her hoofs on the track allowed us to talk among ourselves and not have to concentrate on the road. We were all relieved the cattle were full and contented and if it had not been for the worries down south I might have been in a buoyant mood myself.

Directly opposite the hotel and across the railway was a set of stockyards. Smokie shut his mare in one of the yards and walked over with us. The bar was deserted. I glanced through a window at the far end and there appeared to be no guests at the motel wing. It was one of those quiet nights and Donna said she was delighted. It gave her a rest before the weekend. We had beers all round and Smokie settled into the right-hand corner. On the L-shape we were at the lower end and behind us was the pool table, which the boys immediately put to use.

Donna had a smouldering look about her. She was one of those women who always looked attractive, even if she was cranky or tired, and no matter what she was wearing. With plenty of fresh air and heaps of good bush tucker a man could find his principles had a shallow base out here. Worse still, there were not many places to duck. With the second beer gone and a harsh word to the devil down under, I didn't even hear them. Suddenly the long bar was full of the hardest and meanest looking blokes I had ever seen. The one nearest me on the right-angle turn of the bar would have blunted barb wire if he ran it down his cheek. His weather-beaten face suggested an age beyond sixty and I got the impression violence would be the only occasion for a mirthful response. His stained hat was full of holes around the top crease. On his left stood the boss drover, a big man. His face was flushed and there was a belligerent glow in his eye. Only for a bushy moustache, speckled with grey, he would have reminded me of Clint Eastwood in the film *Pale Rider*. The brim of his hat on either side almost touched the crown. He was in his forties and I observed almost instantly he had the absolute respect of his men.

To his left were four stockmen. There was one that caught my eye. Tall, dark and angry. Black hairs bristled out of the vee of his shirt. His arms had sinewy muscles that might have made a gorilla baulk. He wore a black western hat and a black jumper. If there had been a bookmaker at my side I might have taken fifty dollars at 2/1 on that his belt was black too. The others may have been less forbidding. The fat one had the steady, no-one-at-home eyes of a cane toad. The type that would make even a prostitute jump through a window.

The boss drover drank his first beer as though it were a glass of water offered in a heatwave. Then he fixed me with his eyes.

'Who the hell do you think you are?'

I just looked at him. I could feel the blood draining from my face.

'No one tapes a route off. Unheard of.'

I tried to explain. I thought he would come via the highway. I told him I was sorry and that I hope no one got an electric shock.

'Three shocks,' the old bloke growled. 'Balls 'n' all.'

From the corner of my eye I saw Nick put his hand over his mouth. I thought if he laughed openly we wouldn't make the door.

'Did you leave it up?' Smokie asked, a little too casually I thought.

'Only because we would have had a box-up come mornin',' the boss drover said angrily.

After that I thought it might settle down. We'd just mind our business and they mind theirs. Donna put a tape on and turned the volume up—'Heaven is my Woman's Love'. There wasn't much love around that night. The drovers had nothing to say to each other. They had been together all day. The only other people in the bar were us. It was inevitable someone would become the source of entertainment. Donna hung back. She served the beers promptly and found jobs for herself.

'If I see that fence come mornin' I'll hang you with it,' the boss drover said harshly. He had dropped three or four beers in ten minutes and his eyes already had a glaze.

'I'm sorry it happened,' I said, ignoring the threat. 'I'll turn the power off when you go out.'

'You may not be on your feet.'

The music was loud and the boys were preoccupied with the pool table. Smokie sat quietly, pretending to hear nothing. He was a veteran of bar trouble and knew that stillness and a sealed mouth were our only chance.

'Ever seen a human torpedo?' the boss drover said to his men, an evil smile lingering on his mouth.

'Sure like to,' the old bloke replied.

'You got to get out of here,' Donna whispered. 'He's thrashed men from Moree to Winton. He loves it and he's merciless.'

'If there's any sweet nothin's to be muttered about here,' the boss drover had stood up, 'it's to be our side of the bar.'

'Go,' she said urgently. 'You haven't a chance in hell. The boys will be okay.'

I quickly told Nick I was going to turn in early. If the boss started to pick on them they were to leave immediately.

The sky was ablaze with stars and I had no difficulty following the track back to the camp. The boys stayed on for about an hour. No one bothered them. I asked Nick from my bed-roll how Smokie was getting on. Nick said he was very busy when he last looked at him. He had a cigarette in his mouth, his hands were rolling another, and in between puffs he got a glass to his mouth. God help anyone who interrupted him, even the big fighting boss drover.

With the boys home and safe I fell asleep. About 4.00 a.m. I woke to the smell of leather and something on my face. It was darker than before, but I could just see the outline of a horse's head. Smokie's mare was standing over me and the leather I smelt was the reins. I got up, took the mare in charge and said Smokie's name several times. I didn't want to wake the boys as we had a big day ahead. When there was no reply I unsaddled the mare and let her go, which in her case was freedom to smell around the truck for food.

A saddled horse returning without the rider is cause for alarm. I tossed some sticks onto the camp fire coals and began searching the truck cabin for a powerful torch I kept as an emergency. I searched the whole camp area and was about to wake the boys for help when Smokie limped in.

The police from Roma had finally put the boss drover and his men out of the pub. Smokie said there had been no trouble. He had no idea why they were called, except they were all drunk. The officer said they had to be driven back to camp. They waited until the patrol car left and drove out onto the stock route. Smokie didn't know who drove, because in the meantime he rode his mare out to the electric fence to let them through. He said he was half drunk himself and had great difficulty finding the battery. He had dropped the reins somewhere and the mare left him. After the swaying Toyota truck lurched through, with three drunks hanging on desperately in the back, he tried to find his way back to camp. He lost all sense of direction and finally tripped and fell. He said the grass was soft and he had a warm coat on. It was bed time.

It was times like this I wondered where the hell Smokie had been trained. He rode to the fence in near pitch darkness to make it easy for them. The fence was his suggestion and he paid for the mistake. He never admitted it, but he would have been frozen with the temperature still plummeting to zero every night. A pocket of very dry air had drifted east from Sturts Stony Desert and in the slight uplift of Queensland's central highlands the night temperatures have been known to drop to minus ten degrees Celsius. In the spring both extremes apply.

We began that day huddled over the fire, as though the plains were smothered under snow and at 2.00 p.m. the radio station in Roma recorded the old hundred (38 degrees Celsius). The extremes sapped our energy and in the morning the oncoming heat affected the cattle. They were thirsty—more so than normal, and to make it worse we had to drive them ten kilometres to a holding lane in order to let the big mob through.

There was no shade in the lane. Rupert held them at the southern end with the railway behind him. I anticipated the railway to be the safe end. Nick and I held the other end where the lane merged with the stock route. Smokie I had sent to the drovers' camp. They had accepted him. I was confident he would get them moving so we could have our turn on the water.

Rupert had done a long stint and I waved him in for a lunch break. When he was halfway in I rode out from the truck to take over. While Smokie and the boys were driving the cattle I had driven the truck ahead to the lane. Circus always just followed along with the other horses with the reins tied to a stirrup.

I stopped to talk to Rupert, mainly to explain what was on the table for lunch. I remember saying Smokie had ridden ahead to try and persuade the alcohol-sick drovers to move on. Our attention must have been diverted only two or three minutes. Rupert gave Yarramin a little dig in the ribs and when I straightened Circus I was stunned at how quickly the cattle had scattered. There were cattle trotting in both directions on the railway and some had followed the track over the line and were on the highway. Rupert and I took off together. Nick saw it all at the same time and galloped a kilometre. Trains frequently used the line—heavily loaded goods trains unable to stop suddenly.

The older steers were tonguing from the heat and gave us hell. Some of the road traffic stopped and watched. Urban people often have a serene image of drovers, as experienced bushmen in total control. Watching these loonies with cattle all over the rail track must have been like a preview of the *National Lampoon* family on an outback holiday.

It took a lot of hard riding to get them all back into the lane. I was worried I might lose them again when Rupert and Nick left, but Rupert hadn't had a drink for three hours and Nick had to hurry back before the cattle at the other end woke up there was no horseman to hold them.

The afternoon dragged on with no sign of Smokie. Some of the steers kept looking for the break. With the heat and the constant turning back of the rogues I became over-anxious. I thought maybe we would have to let them back on the stock route and head for water. Stock route box-ups are never very serious. Like most animals cattle have a natural instinct for bonding with their own herd and are easily sorted out on horseback. The big deterrent was the drovers. I visualised the need for an ambulance if we did that to them.

I was debating whether I could risk a very fast pee when twenty or thirty horses appeared on the horizon. Only ten minutes behind were the cattle—a mixture of every colour and breed imaginable. It was the largest herd I had ever seen and unlikely to be seen again in southern Queensland. The long column of bovine flesh proceeded past me for half an hour. With the backdrop of the vast open downs it might have been a migratory column of buffalo in another land, in a previous century.

When the tail of the great herd had gone we let ours go. Smokie had been helping them muster and with a final nod to the boss drover he turned away and rode in behind. The leaders broke into a trot and then a canter. By instinct they knew where the water was. I suspected they could smell it all along as the railway line was only a kilometre from the dam as the crow flies.

The reserve vacated for us was the largest reserve east of the Chesterton Ranges. In the southern corner the dam resembled a mini-lake. The cattle wallowed in the shallows and so fascinated with it all was Rupert that Yarramin caught him unprepared. The old bay thought he would have a wallow too.

We camped there that night and during the next few days there were more mobs and more frustrations. It took a week to pilot the mob to the untouched feed the herdsman had set aside for me, east of Roma. With the cattle up to their knees in feed and fresh water from a creek, the boys made the most of the bright spots in Roma.

My trips to town were of a more serious nature. The solicitor advised me I could have the hearing transferred to the border town of Goondiwindi and that would give me time to go home. His professional advice, however, was not to do so. In his view it was important the matter was dealt with in the local court.

It was during this period I got the dreaded message. Dad had received a transfusion and it failed. He might survive for another three or four days. In three days' time was the court appearance. I had to tell Sal and it was moving she had such confidence in me. My mother and sister were not told.

CHAPTER 6

The High Plains of Death

If I were to plead not guilty the case would be adjourned and I would be tried by a jury. I was appalled such a petty offence could reach such a serious level. If I were to plead guilty the magistrate had the power to discharge the case or impose a fine. Bound in with a fine was a criminal record. My solicitor thought the charge was trivial in light of the fact I had returned the mare the same day and had there been a serious injury to her the prosecution would have obtained a veterinary report. He advised me to plead guilty.

To fuel my unease about the matter, a carload of rough-looking young men had come looking for me on the reserve. I was in town seeing my solicitor. Nick said they arrived in a sixties model Holden with half the paint off. He said they were up to no good and he wouldn't tell them where I was. I asked Nick if they went back to town. He said he watched the car after it left. When they reached the highway they turned towards Miles.

I realised at once it was the Yuleba mob—friends or family of Dick the cattle-tailer. He knew he had been sacked at Amby Creek and I'd thought he'd left just a little too quietly. The drovers all knew each other. I was yet to meet the owner of Sarah-Jane, but it crossed my mind he might be a mate of Dick's.

'Don't worry about them,' I said. 'The court case is only a couple of days away. Be all over then.'

'No Dad.' Nick was always firm in his opinions. I respected them. 'They'll be back. There were five of them.'

'I'll stay in town then.'

Nick nodded in agreement. 'If it's only fists we can hold our own. They had guns in the car. Maybe roo shooters. Maybe not.'

I knew I had to take the trouble away from the camp. Problem was I didn't know what this mob looked like. They could be on top of me before I could even turn around. Yet I didn't feel nervous in the street as I couldn't visualise such a blatant attack. It was in the hotel I felt nervous. The Commonwealth has long corridors and my room was near the old wooden stairs leading off the verandah to the rear courtyard. Late at night, when the bars were finally closed, I missed the smell of the camp fire and the security of all being together. It was a state of mind of course. If there was any danger, it was less than from a bolt of lightning.

To speak to Sal every night I had to telephone the Coonabarabran hospital. She was very calm. Most of the time she just sat by the bed holding Dad's hand. My mother was very ill as well and my sister had to give as much time to her as to her father. At the time Sal spared me the sad details of Dad's last days.

On Tuesday morning, 18 October 1994, my solicitor and I walked into the courtroom about 9.00 a.m. We were informed at once that my case was second on the agenda and would commence any minute.

The courtroom was impressive with its beautiful timber beams and old wooden benches. I wondered whether anything had changed since the court opened in the early 1860s, more than one hundred and thirty years ago. I was snapped out of my dreams by being asked to stand in the dock. The police prosecutor read out the charge—unlawful use of a mare.

I was shocked at the wording. The court was packed, not for my hearing, but other matters to follow. The magistrate seemed to hesitate, in fact I thought he passed his hand across his mouth. He asked the prosecutor to read the charge again. Mercifully, the details of the charge were then read out and there was probably a sigh of relief from some and a groan of disappointment from others. Some people were in for a long wait and if they could be entertained along the way I am sure they would have been grateful.

My solicitor then took the floor and spoke at some length about the circumstances surrounding the use of the mare. He explained that while my plea was guilty, the circumstances were exceptional. Reference was made to the severity of the drought in New South Wales and the great strain of looking after cattle a long way from home. He stated that I was a registered amateur jockey and if I were to receive a criminal conviction the Australian Jockey Club would decline to renew my licence. In conclusion he asked the magistrate to also consider that I'd had no previous brush with the law.

Both my solicitor and I stood for what seemed a long time. I felt my pulse racing. What if I was convicted and jailed! On the day of my arrest I had asked the officer straight out if that were possible. He said it was, but he doubted that would happen. The magistrate had opened a huge book, I think the thickest I have ever seen. I noted too how old it was. Instead of being a clear white, the edges of the pages were black, a soiled sort of black. Then the magistrate made a strange comment which was barely audible. He said he was examining a reference from the previous century.

I began to think the worst. This was going on too long. My solicitor kept his eyes to the front and his face was expressionless.

Suddenly the magistrate closed the book and looked at me. It was not an unkind look.

'You needed a horse to get your cattle back,' he said quietly.

'Yes your Honour,' I said enthusiastically. 'I thought I might lose them.'

'Charge dismissed,' he said and nodded to the prosecutor.

Outside the court I asked my solicitor if he knew the reference the magistrate was consulting.

He smiled, tickled by the humour of it. 'Harry Redford, 1873.'

'How do you know?' I asked.

'That old record book is living history. Any local lawyer with a love of this area has been through it. I knew exactly where he was.'

The Roma Court is of great historical significance. In colonial times it was far more than a district court. Offenders were brought hundreds of miles to appear at Roma, including the famous boss drover Harry Redford, immortalised as 'Captain Starlight' in Rolf Boldrewood's *Robbery Under Arms*.

In 1870 Starlight lifted a thousand bullocks from a station called Mount Cornish on the upper Thomson. That entire region of Queensland had only been settled for a few years. The headquarters of any station would have been only a base camp and there were no fences. It was therefore feasible to steal such a large mob and the theft be undetected for some weeks. In her book *The Territory*, Ernestine Hill claims that Starlight's duffing raid is the biggest in history.

There are two conflicting accounts of what became of the cattle. What's factual is Starlight's crossing of the eastern Simpson Desert. Normally impossible, it was a wet season and lakes that have been almost continually dry since the retreat of the Ice Age were full.

Starlight was arrested not for the historic theft, but for the possession of a white bull. The bull was not wanted and several attempts were made to drive him away. Finally the animal, which had been reported missing from a station in South Australia, was recognised in the Adelaide saleyards.

The bull saw more of Australia than most people did at that time. He walked to Adelaide, was then shipped to Rockhampton, walked to Blackall in central Queensland and as evidence before the jury had to hit the road again for Roma. For some weeks he was fed by the local constabulary in a yard outside the courthouse.

In modern times a jury's verdict of not guilty has rocked a nation. Starlight's acquittal may not have rocked the colony, but for a man who was truly guilty to be carried from the court shoulder-high was one of the rare lighter episodes of a miscarriage of justice.

The judge's concluding remark to the jury has been recorded. 'Thank God, gentlemen of the jury, that it is your verdict, not mine.'

My moment in common with Starlight was so minor that it is my loss. I would love to be remembered as the first man to overland cattle onto the Barkly Tableland. To be remembered as the man who founded the famous Brunette Downs. Starlight was a colourful character who broke the law, but never harmed anybody. Trying to cross a flooded river on the Barkly, he died as an old man with his boots on. His grave is on Brunette, simply marked 'Starlight's Grave'.

Far from carrying me out shoulder-high, Nick's opening comment was, 'Now that you're acquitted they'll be really pissed off.'

But we never saw any of them again. There were no drovers at the court. Nick, Rupert, Smokie and I discussed it at some length by the camp fire and we concluded someone with authority played a hand in the matter.

The eighteenth of October 1994 is a day I will remember for its enormous relief. The nineteenth of October 1994 I will remember as one of the very sad days of my life. It was the day my father died. Dad and I parted with no warmth. That was the sadness. Through no fault of his I was reared in extreme isolation. I related to what I knew and in my early world there were few people. He never understood.

The passing of my father prompted the same halt in time that occurs in any family the world over. For perhaps a week time stood still. The good times were remembered and the bad were mercifully forgotten. Only when faced by death does everyone show, no matter how deep they may have to dig, that there is some compassion in them.

Dad was interred in the family vault at Orange. When the undertaker padlocked the door it was to be for the last time. To me Dad was the last of the Irish Keenans. The first interment had been in 1856, of James Keenan who'd landed in Sydney with his wife in 1828. It was said he broke in horses for William Wentworth, but no written record emerges until 1851 when James Keenan purchased Cheeseman's Creek, a property of twelve thousand acres near Molong. In 1854 he slaughtered a neighbour's heifer and the case was heard in the Bathurst Court. He was exonerated, but it appears we always had that wild gene. The family remained in the Bathurst–Orange district until 1923. For more than half a century the property known as The Bridge was the family home. My father was born there and despite heavy subdivision within the Orange district, the property remains today as it was in 1923.

The scene at Myall Plains at the time of Dad's death can only be described as one of lingering despair. Each day two or three calves died from malnutrition and most of them looked dry in the coat and were tucked up with hunger. The cows too were deteriorating. The value of the wheat fed to them each week exceeded two thousand dollars, but it was nothing like enough.

Even if the finance and the feed were available, a doubling of the ration would have been of little benefit to the calves. Their mothers needed fresh green grass or quality lucerne hay to make milk. Neither was available. The whole lot had to be moved and it had to be done within days. But to where! The Queensland stock routes were eaten out. There were rumours of agistment in South Australia, but the cows and calves would not survive such a journey.

I had been following the rainfall reports every week and a small pocket of country in the upper Murray had received about fifty millimetres. The western foothills of the alps were in the middle of spring. Clutching at straws, I thought maybe the stock routes there had fresh green feed. To save myself a trip I could have contacted the local Rural Lands Board, but with the drought so widespread I didn't expect any encouragement. I decided to look for myself.

In the meantime Nick had passed the cattle over to the Dalgety drovers. They took them to the Roma saleyards and drafted them ready for sale. Nick and Rupert stayed on. They set up camp near the yards and waited for the sale. On completion of the drafting there were some rejects and Nick loaded them onto the truck and took them out to the Old Boy's place at Amby Creek.

There was no work for the horses anymore. The boys rode them around the outskirts of the town and little by little, usually from a slip of the tongue, I began to realise there was no shortage of female company. A month later the manager of the Commonwealth Hotel left me in no doubt. He gave me the restaurant bill. I was delighted to pay it. The boys were not on wages and had worked hard. Following the handover, Nick took Smokie and his mare home to Amby. The night before, the boys had bought a carton of XXXX beer and Smokie entertained them with his mouth organ. They said he was fantastic.

The next morning Smokie warned the Dalgety boss drover

about the rogues. He didn't listen too well. Those smart rogues made the professionals look like another episode of *National Lampoon*'s Australian outback holiday. Nick and Rupert were called upon for help and things must have been desperate for that. There's no prouder man than a drover.

The trip to the southern highlands was little more than a reconnaissance of stock routes. Sal and I had been apart for two months. We both needed an escape from the nightmare world of drought. It was only four days. Four days of green pastures, fast flowing mountain streams, hospitable people and magnificent walks. On the third day we had an argument about the compass. I had locked it in the car and had the haversack on my back. I didn't want to open up the vehicle to get it. I told Sal it was impossible for me to become lost. She should feel safe with me! We planned to hike to the summit of a giant monolith and photograph the spectacular uplift of the alps on the western side.

After some discussion, I gave in and retrieved the little compass. An hour out from the car the fog from the river drifted onto the mountain and we had to abort the climb. Stepping carefully, we slowly descended. We entered thick fern growth, which wasn't around on the way up. Being just another obstinate man I still wouldn't look at the compass. On the valley floor we walked through a eucalypt forest and I expected to reach the road any minute. We walked on in gathering gloom and I eventually consulted the compass. I think that little pink object saved a search party being mounted. If only our problems at home could have been so easily solved.

We hated leaving Kosciusko, Corryong and Tumbarumba. It was a world so far apart from the one we'd become used to. To have been able to walk our cattle on those southern stock routes would have been a privilege. No dry camps, holding paddocks every eight to ten kilometres, affable people and scenery at every turn in the road. But we were too late. Several droving units were already on the move and there was clearly no room for a big mob of cows and calves.

The day we returned home was sale day at Roma. Nick was jubilant when he telephoned me. The Roma district wheat crops had been written off and farmers wanted steers to turn onto their crops to salvage what they could. The day before the sale there was a storm in Roma with forty millimetres of rain. It all combined to produce a reasonable sale. I estimated the steers made a hundred and thirty dollars a head more than corresponding sales in New South Wales; the heifers about fifty dollars more. What would have been the conclusion of a drought analyst? The markets had fallen since mid-August, anchored downwards by the drought, and circumstances had forced me to leave home at a critical time. I think the conclusion would have been that I'd given too much attention to the young cattle at the expense of the cows and calves. The sale at Roma may not have been any better than a Wodonga sale in mid-August after all expenses had been added. Working on the land will always involve timing and anticipation. Nothing will ever change that.

The best news was the rain. Nick said there were big storms in the Injune district, dropping up to a hundred millimetres in isolated pockets. Injune is only a few kilometres south of the northern cattle tick zone. For most overlanders the area was a dead end and one to be avoided. British breeds are highly susceptible to tick infestation and the cattle on the move from the southern drought were predominantly British—Hereford, shorthorn or Angus-cross. To move cattle back out of the tick zone they must be dipped twice.

With the cattle sold there was nothing to keep the boys in Roma. They were booked on the Toowoomba bus and would be arriving in Coonabarabran at midnight the next day. They had taken the horses out to the Old Boy. That meant they would run with the brumbies. Nick had seen Mrs Brown. She towered above the half-breeds, he said, and he thought she had already usurped the stallion's control. I told Nick there would be no doubt.

To leave the soft green countryside of Corryong in Victoria and wake up in western New South Wales was a depressing experience in the spring of 1994. The great deserts of the interior had temporarily expanded to the dividing range. Not even the butts of dead grass remained.

At least Greg had done a wonderful job with the backbreaking work of lifting wheat bags from ground level onto an old one-tonner and carting them to the starving cows. On my first day back from the Murray I went out with him and saw at once time had run out. The calves were going to die. During the past month some of the old cows had perished while giving birth. The ground was so bare the dead cattle stood out starkly—crumpled heaps of hairless hide, like a plangent reminder of impending calamity. A cold wind crept over the plains and it cut through my clothes as though I were standing naked. These high plains of my childhood had become a place of death.

CHAPTER 7

Race Against Time

It was a sobering homecoming for the boys. Drought and war have a chilling element in common. Under siege, cities may hang on for months. In drought, property owners will hold on and on. Then quite suddenly it all compounds. The battle's lost. Death pervades the whole scene and every breeze carries the smell of it.

Following the death of the head of the family there are always estate matters to be settled. I was left sole executor of a highly complex estate. But I couldn't give it a moment's consideration. Nick, Sal and I sat down to discuss the plight we now found ourselves in. We decided that we would split the herd into three. The cows with the baby calves would stay as there was no hope of little weak calves surviving an eight hundred kilometre trip. To provide urgent green feed Nick would stay behind and lop the kurrajongs that had been pruned back in a dry spell in 1991. It was premature for the trees, but fortunately I had done the lopping myself and left all the small branches which had since grown out. The grain feeding would be cut to every second day to encourage the cows to go looking for kurrajong.

We anticipated the size of the mob staying at about two hundred head. Whether they would survive with summer around the corner was pure speculation. The only thing certain was the commitment of Nick and Greg. The bulk of the cattle would be roadtrained to Queensland. Including the calves, that was about nine hundred head. Nick was in charge of the loading and Rupert and I would receive them at the other end.

Still unknown was the destination. There was a bus to Too-woomba that night and I would take it. Rupert had only just arrived. I told him to come up with the roadtrains.

I had never undertaken anything like this before. The risks were enormous. How many cows would die in transit? Would they mother the calves at the other end? Would they survive the inevitable dry stages? With the heavy storms widespread throughout the Injune district I felt confident I would find somewhere suitable to unload. I would need three or four days to settle the cattle down and I thought the local herdsman would agree to that.

It was a hard couple of days for Sal. She was brave and said nothing, but she knew when I left it might be for months. The new territory had no bush pubs with handy telephones. Trips to town from the cattle would be rare.

From Toowoomba I caught the connecting bus to Roma. I arrived late in the afternoon and booked in at the Common-wealth. The truck had been locked up in the Dalgety merchandise yard and I thanked the manager.

I hadn't slept much on the bus. The hotel gave me the same room I'd been in only ten days before. I lay down on the bed and felt a deep sense of loneliness almost smother me. So much had happened in a narrow space of time. The future was bleak. If the cattle perished it lay on my shoulders. The estate would be bankrupted.

Next day Jim Scott generously loaned me his Toyota to go out to Injune. Jim owned Scott's Roadways and had organised the lift of the five hundred and sixty head of steers and heifers from Myall Plains. He owned a property near Roma and had a great knowledge of the district. With each lift of the mobs from Myall Plains I always consulted him before making any decisions.

About five kilometres south of the town I found a suitable reserve for unloading. It had green feed boot-high and there were ducks and ibis feeding in the billabongs. From the reserve there was little choice in direction. The tick border ran north and east of Injune. The south road went back to Roma and the eaten-out arterial stock route that I had just vacated. To the west and north-west rose the massif of Mt Hutton in the Great Dividing Range. The only passage out was to the south-west. I would have to walk one stage south and pick up the stock route that on the map zigzagged across the range to Mitchell. I decided to inspect the first few stages for availability of water.

The strike and miss pattern of the storms became evident on this drive. There were bare patches, dry and drought-stricken. Other patches were still wet causing the rear wheels of the Toyota to spin. The surface water was disappointing. Dry creeks cut across the narrow stock route. Some of them had run water, but there were no natural holes on the stock route. Every watering point was a bore and that meant stages of twelve to sixteen kilometres—too far for weak calves. I would have to ask for water; if necessary, buy it.

Back in Roma I discussed transport arrangements with Jim Scott. He was in the middle of a job. Cattle stations on the Gulf of Carpentaria watershed had missed the late summer Wet and were short of feed. Some of the station managers were de-stocking and transporting their stock to Roma for sale. The Roma saleyards had developed into the largest cattle turnover centre in eastern Australia. Jim expected two roadtrains in the next day and a third the day after. It looked like three road-trains would head south to Myall Plains in two or three days. I telephoned Nick to see how he was going with the herd splitting. He told me it was painfully slow. The cows had their calves planted all over the place. Not to worry though. He would have the job completed before the roadtrains arrived.

While I was waiting I decided to go out to Amby Creek the next day and collect the horses. I would drop them on the reserve and while they were consuming a big feed of oats I would put some wire netting and steel posts around a couple of bags on the ground. Old Yarramin would never stray far from the oats. But with other horses this trick didn't always work. In the past I'd had horses clear out on me.

On the way out I couldn't believe the transformation of the big stock route. There wasn't a blade of dry grass. The big droves of cattle had got their teeth to ground level. The heartening sign was the new shoots. The storms had been generous to this stock route and a burst of growth was already on the way. There were no cattle. The big mobs had all moved west.

At Amby village I stopped and walked over to the bank of the local creek. The telltale mud along the rim of the bank was the mark of a full flow, what they call out west a 'banker'. The same creek shared its name with the Old Boy's place. There'd been big rain and if he had that storm I might be spared a stock route unloading.

The show of green grass improved as I drove north and by the time I got to Amby Creek there was cattle feed along the creek flats. Most of the property was still bare. The Old Boy had a few thousand sheep and rather than feed them he had opened the gates to let them have the run of the place. I still had eighty head of young cattle there and he had them in a good paddock of about eighty hectares. The creek country was unstocked, made up of three long narrow paddocks. The total area may have been only about one hundred and fifty hectares. But it would hold them for a fortnight, long enough to recover from the trip before I ventured onto the main stock route again.

'It stayed hot and humid,' the Old Boy said. 'The grass has grown overnight.'

The Old Boy had made a go at just about everything through the course of his life. He had a wealth of experience and was worth listening to.

'I think those cows would bolt on you if you unloaded on the stock route,' he said, sitting by a steel pot bubbling on the stove. 'They'll be spooked after a trip like that. Your biggest problem will be the mothering. When we unload here we'll place the roadtrains so that they jump off and run to a corner where there's water and feed.'

I went back to Roma and discussed the change of arrangements with Jim Scott. The three roadtrains would leave the next day for Myall Plains. The only reservation Jim had was the border crossing at Hebel. The office was closed between 5.00 p.m. and 7.00 a.m. With strong cattle it didn't matter. The drivers arranged loading so that they arrived at the border some time after midnight. It suited them to stop and have a rest. When cattle were weak Jim liked to keep moving. The less time on the truck the better.

When the first two hundred and fifty cows were unloaded the drivers would rest for a day and return for the second lift.

I telephoned Sal with the good news. Once the cattle had mothered, I told her, I would come home for a few days. She said we had to do something about the racehorses. We only had enough lucerne hay left for the bulls. Over the telephone we decided Dad's two horses, Vodka Jack and an unnamed three year old, would come back with me on the truck. The yearling we would take to a horse handler for education. His name was Wonderous. The existence of Wonderous was one of those delightful stories which too rarely occur in a lifetime. In 1990 I had accepted a mount in the Macquarie Picnic Race

Club Cup at Dubbo. The horse was called Stride for Glory. We went out onto the track at 20/1 and won by half a head. It was the most gruelling head-to-head struggle I can remember. The owners were stud breeders and gave me a free service to their stallion Wonder Dancer. Little Wonderous was the manifestation of that gift.

Everything was arranged. I could do nothing but wait. I had told Nick to keep Rupert at home. The cattle were going to be in small paddocks. For a couple of weeks there would be little to do.

I set up camp near the creek, not a camp site I would normally choose. The creek water was brown, full of fine silt and everywhere I walked clumps of galvanised burr caught my trousers. This time I put up a tent. The days were hot and nights sticky. Mosquitoes pounced on me from sunset. The storm season had started and would last until March.

The horses were running in a big scrub paddock on the eastern side of the property. The Old Boy had been a keen horseman in his day. One had thrown him some years before and he was left with an injury that made horse handling impossible. The horses had been bushed and they ran as a brumby mob. Under the umbrella of Mrs Brown, it appeared Circus and Yarramin had been accepted. Malameen they held out. He looked poorly and I fetched the bridle the moment I saw him. The horse too knew he was sick and led away from the others without hesitation. I loaded him onto the truck and took him to Mitchell. I didn't know anyone in Mitchell and looked on the poor lady who owned the bakery as my information desk. Her adjoining coffee lounge was an added bonus. I told her I had this seventeen-hand horse who needed a special caring hand. She told me her name was Annette and introduced me to Brooke who served at the bakery counter.

An hour later Malameen was in a twenty-hectare paddock

with two mares. I bought a few bags of oats and chaff at the local produce shop and Brooke agreed to feed him each evening. He became the most pampered horse on the Maranoa.

It was only mid-afternoon and the night on the creek would be long enough.

'Now what do you want?' Annette asked. 'If coffee was even slightly poisonous you would be dead.'

'I need someone to look after two racehorses.'

'Old Bill Anderson is a trainer,' she said. 'I think he's retired, but he might stable them and look after them.'

Bill and his wife Mary lived on the edge of the town, near the racecourse. He was a big man in his mid-sixties and when I got to know him I found him always good-humoured and ever ready to offer sound advice. He had four stables about fifty metres from his house. Each stable opened out into a yard. There were also small paddocks of about a quarter hectare and a sand yard. Most impressive of all was the shade. There were plenty of trees.

Bill was lukewarm about the proposition for a while. He said his health had slipped and he wasn't very active. The more he talked the more the idea grew on him. By the time I left he said he would train them if I could find time to do the track-work. I told him nothing would give me more pleasure, but the cattle situation would need to change. I offered him a fee for the stabling and he cut the figure in half.

I reported back to Annette. To myself I called her the 'switchboard', but I never told her. Over another cup of coffee I told her about the cattle. There would be calves left unmothered. It was inevitable they would have to be shot or picked up. She said her father reared poddy calves. Across the river she and her husband, also named Bill, had a farm and her parents shared with them the big old homestead.

I left Mitchell thinking what a fruitful day it had been. Three horses bedded down and someone to collect the calves rejected by their mothers. I had no trouble with shooting a diseased animal, but a calf that someone might rear was another matter.

The next day was a long one. I had no further business in Mitchell. The country didn't invite any bushwalking. About 5.00 p.m. the Old Boy arrived in his Mad Max jeep to tell me Nick had telephoned. The first lot of cows was on its way.

The onset of the stormy season had driven out the last vestige of spring. Only three weeks before I had woken to a light frost, a film of frozen dew on the sleeping bag. Now at the crack of dawn the sun rose with a different shade of orange. I left the tent with a jumper on, but by the time the billy boiled I had tossed it back into the tent. Two hours after sunrise I could feel the first trickle of sweat from my armpits.

I expected the roadtrains about 2.00 p.m., the hottest time of the day. A hold-up at Hebel was the last thing a cattle owner and a roadtrain operator needed. Why arrangements have never been made to facilitate twenty-four-hour border crossing at Hebel is a matter of concern that strikes deep within the work psyche of this nation. If cattlemen were asked to pay a night-opening fee they would do it gladly to spare their stock. The stock inspector merely examines the health papers, the travel permit, and with a torch it only takes a few minutes to establish whether the cattle on board correspond with the papers.

The day dragged on and the absence of news seemed to add time to every hour. I had established my camp close to the unloading point. The public road hugged the creek for some kilometres and I knew I would hear the roadtrains some minutes before they arrived. They would cross a culvert and at my direction swing off the road onto a claypan, dropping the rear wheels of the second trailer into a shallow drain.

I had worked myself into a state of anxiety when they finally arrived. It was 4 p.m. The drivers were exhausted. Their eyes were bloodshot and faces drained of colour. From midday on they were forced to stop repeatedly and try and get the weak cows to stand. They said the six-hour delay at Hebel had been disastrous. It forced them to travel in the heat.

It took about two hours to unload the trains. When the last live one was off we started with the dead ones—six cows and seven calves. The calves were dragged off easily enough. The cows we had to roll over and over. At the rear of each roadtrain lay a pile of dead cattle. The drivers were becoming used to it, but they still hated it. The only job satisfaction available for a truckie is to deliver goods in the same condition as received.

From the trucks the cows trotted away until they reached a long narrow billabong. They drank and then commenced to swallow watery green grass like a child might gobble marsh-mallows. The calves walked around in a daze. Some tried to bleat, a muffled sound that was neither a calf bleat nor any sound I had ever heard.

The trucks left and I found myself alone with four hundred and fifty miserable animals. The cows had skin off their hips from hours of standing and rubbing. A few swayed when they walked. Some of the calves began to orientate themselves and walk among the cows. But for the first hour not one cow was interested. They would feed with a feverish urgency, then simply stop and look around in bewilderment.

I lit my fire and just before dark I drove down the creek to the Old Boy's place to use the telephone. I knew an anxious little group would be waiting to hear from me. Nick came on and told me he thought the second lot were slightly weaker. When I told him storms were brewing in the west and we may have to delay a day he said he didn't think we could wait even a day.

I telephoned Jim Scott next and discussed the possibility of crossing the border at Goondiwindi where the office is open twenty-four hours a day. The problem was roadtrain access.

The trains were not permitted through Coonabarabran and down the Oxley Highway. If we decided upon Goondiwindi we had to use a back road from Coonamble to Narrabri and travel more than one hundred and fifty kilometres extra.

We adopted a different plan. The drivers would stay at the homestead with Sal and the boys and start loading at 4.00 a.m. The loading would be completed about 8.00 a.m. and they should reach the border at Hebel before 5.00 p.m. The cattle would be unloaded about 1.00 a.m. I didn't like the night unloading, but having already observed the disinterest of the cows towards their calves I conceded it would make no difference.

A storm lashed the tent in the early hours and in the morning the wood was too wet for a fire. I walked out among the cattle and took stock of the calves yet to mother. A dozen or so hadn't moved a hundred metres from where they'd been unloaded, but apart from these pathetic creatures the mothering seemed nothing short of miraculous. Most of the cows had a calf. Four cows were bellowing around the dead cattle. Another two cows were down, lying on their sides. The crows had already gathered and I knew I would have to deal with them before breakfast.

With dead cattle, crows floating overhead and already a stale smell in the air it was difficult to weigh a loss in realistic perspective. In prosperous seasons many a farmer has lost cattle to clover and lucerne bloat. Unexpected losses are a reality of the industry. To have shifted nearly five hundred head in drought condition for a loss of fifteen plus poddies was a fair result. Sometimes the business side of farming is ugly because we are forced to look upon death as an inevitable statistic.

I needed the early morning tea badly and walked down the creek to the Old Boy's house. The mud on the road stuck to my boots. The humid air hung like some invisible weight and soon my shirt sleeve was damp from wiping my forehead. The storms had cleared away for now, but high above the western horizon I could see a haze that was neither cloud nor smoke. Storms would regather, if not today, then tomorrow. I had to find a new unloading site on hard ground. On most properties in Queensland it would have been a simple matter of unloading at the station yards. On this place the unloading ramp was in a yard, giving access only to small trucks.

Below the Old Boy's house a stony slope fell away to the creek. It was hard ground scalded from overstocking and diagonally across it a shallow gully had formed. The drivers of the roadtrains could drop the rear wheels into the gully. The cattle would jump off into a small bare paddock without water, but a gate led out into one of the creek paddocks.

I discussed the plan with the Old Boy over a cup of tea and he thought the calves would walk out with the cows. In theory it seemed a good plan and better than the only other alternative, which was to unload directly onto the big stock route near Amby. The water trough was almost in the village and we both felt the cattle might shy off it. The creek downstream formed a much bigger watercourse with steep banks and the Old Boy thought some of the weak cows would slip and become cast.

On my way back to the camp a Nissan four-wheel-drive truck pulled up. I looked through the windscreen and saw it was Scalp, the red-haired bloke I had met in the pub.

'Hop in, I'll give you a lift,' he said cheerfully.

I scraped the mud off my boots with a stick and got in. We slipped around a bit despite the four-wheel drive.

'God, ya cattle need some decent feed in a hurry. This green stuff's goin' to run through 'em.'

'How's your feed?' I asked.

'Goin' up now to have a look. Reckon them storms would have hit my place.' He paused and looked at me. 'Why don't yer come? I got a spare paddock. It's yours if yer want it.'

I hesitated briefly. I didn't want to be stranded out there if storms blew up and closed the road.

'Be back this afternoon,' Scalp added.

Back at the camp three cows were still bellowing for their calves. It was too soon to contact Annette. Another two calves at least, I thought, would be claimed by their mothers during the day. The odour from the dead cattle was gathering potency and it was still too wet for my truck to grip and tow them away. The decision was easy.

I had to share the seat with Scalp's guns. There were two of them, both with telescopic sights. Scalp said he had shot two dingoes during the week. The pups were starting to venture out on their own and he expected to increase his weekly tally. He said he lived in Injune and had a scrub-clearing business. The loss of natural habitat flushed the dingoes out and sometimes he would shoot up to ten in a week. The bounty was $25 per head.

I asked Scalp if he ran any cattle himself and he said about seven hundred cows. There were several dams scattered around the property and the cattle free-ranged. He had two round-ups a year; one for branding and one for trucking and selling the weaners.

Fifty kilometres north of my camp we crossed the dingo barrier, a two-metre high fence with the netting dug into the ground. It's known simply as the 'dog fence'. More than a barrier for wild dogs, it's the final division between sheep farming and cattle raising in the vast rangelands.

Scalp had a Queensland road map in his glove box and immediately north of where we crossed the fence lay a huge blank space. Some three hundred kilometres to the north-west was the little town of Tambo. Due north not even a village clung to the map south of the tropics. Far to the north-east and beyond the great gorges of the Carnarvons was another small town called Springsure. In the south-east corner Injune appeared as the gateway to one of the most uninhabited regions in eastern Australia, which I named from that day the 'Blank Space'.

The country changed rapidly. Basalt hills rose steeply out of the undulating country and like an ant trail through high grass the road meandered through forests of brigalow on the darker soils and box in the lighter country. The whole area had a different atmosphere and I began to feel the wild stirring in my veins. The steep hills gave way to high tablelands and the air was distinctly cooler. I felt a twinge of disappointment when Scalp stopped at a cattle grid and said we had reached his boundary. The first paddock was the one I could have.

At this point we left the road and followed a track up into a valley where ranges on both sides closed in to form a gorge. The Nissan churned the mud.

'Got the storms alright,' Scalp exclaimed with a smile. 'Your cattle'll do well here. Wait till I show yer the real feed.'

The valley country had been lightly ringbarked many years before. The dead timber had fallen and protected a whole range of grass species, but it was country that in the best of seasons would still only handle light stocking rates. At the entrance to the gorge we stopped.

'We'll walk from here,' Scalp said. 'I want to show you the tableland country.'

He walked about fifty metres and stopped near the foot of a low sandstone cliff. 'Take a look at this.'

In the dry interior permanently flowing springs are rare. Judging by the size of the cavern from where the water flowed this one may have been in existence for thousands of years. The flow would not water a herd; maybe sixty to eighty head. Sometimes springs can be a nuisance, tempting the weaker cattle to hang around for water instead of walking to the bore. What fascinated me was the geological formation. The cave itself was eroded out of the sandstone and just above the cave began the basalt. The basalt layer embodied the blackest rock I have ever seen.

From the cave we walked through the gorge, ascending gradually as we went. The passage to the top was more like a long defile. Before reaching the plateau rim we must have gained about two hundred metres in altitude.

The scene before my eyes would have excited any pastoralist. The bluegrass tableland seemed to stretch to the edge of the world. There was a soft breeze and I watched in disbelief the wavering tops of a grass knee-high. It looked excellent cattle feed. I plucked some and chewed it. It tasted sweet. If something tastes bad in the bush you can be sure cattle won't touch it. I kept a handful of grass to show the local Department of Primary Industry officer in Mitchell.

What struck me most was the lack of trees. Below the plateau rim the country lay under forest to the horizon, with some thinning of trees by ringbarking. On the tablelands it appeared no axe had ever been swung. It crossed my mind Aborigines had undertaken frequent burning up here. Fresh sprouts of bluegrass would act as a magnet to kangaroos.

The frustrating reality for me was that the cows were not strong enough to feed up onto the tablelands. They would need to gather considerable strength before I could use the paddock to any advantage. The big valleys had pockets of summer grass which were inadequate.

I explained to Scalp it would be a month before the cows and calves would be strong enough to follow the game trails up the various defiles. With the wet season only beginning I thought the tableland country would carry more than seven hundred head until autumn. Scalp thought that was a conservative figure, saying there were more than fifteen hundred hectares of bluegrass. I wanted to clinch the deal immediately. I have never been particularly religious, but to me fifteen hundred hectares of bluegrass were beyond the normal expectation of coincidence. I told Scalp I would make immediate arrangements to transport a semitrailer load of heifers from Myall Plains. The line of heifers had been fed separately all through the winter and they were in reasonable condition.

We turned back and upon reaching the vehicle the next stop was the bore. Another track led off from the road to a little holding paddock of about four hectares. At the opposite side to the entrance gate a huge diesel engine marked the site of the bore and nestled in among the timber, thirty metres away, stood the supply tank.

'A hundred thousand litres of water there,' Scalp said proudly.

'How many litres an hour?'

'She pumps three and a half thousand.'

I pulled out my notebook and did some quick calculations. At the height of summer a beast consumes forty to fifty litres of water a day. The bore pumped about three and a half thousand litres an hour. For eight hundred head a full tank would last about three days. To keep ahead of consumption the bore had to run for twenty hours each second day.

'Looks like I'll be taking up residence here,' I said half jokingly. Even for a bushie like me it was going to be a lonely old camp. But compared to the hassles of pushing cows and calves along a stock route it would be like a beach on a tropical island.

The water trough was about twenty metres down the slope from the tank. Someone had gone to a lot of trouble with this trough. Stout wooden rails had been secured to posts at four-metre intervals to prevent any animal damaging the fibreglass surface. I couldn't have been more impressed. Scalp must have noticed my mood and was keen to show me more. He told me there was a pinnacle called Mt Kennedy and that the station consequently carried that name. The surveyor Edmund

Kennedy had been with Mitchell on his expedition in 1845 and they passed through here.

It was some kilometres to Scalp's camp. The dirt road led over a pass onto a tableland of sandy-loam heavily timbered with cypress pine. We turned off to the east and a couple of kilometres off the road the track passed the stockyards. A big solid loading ramp stood at the front of a large set of timber yards. There was enough space to yard a thousand head and roadtrains could use the ramp. Beyond the yards and half hidden among the trees was a hut with hitching rails out the front. The hut had the quaint style of early settlement—a high pitched roof and a tin chimney. The walls were pine slab, severely cracked and weathered. In the old days they had little choice with timber. A dwelling constructed from hardwood would draw the white ants.

No one lived there, but there were signs of men coming and going. A two-hundred litre drum with the top cut out overflowed with empty stubbie bottles. Inside, discarded clothing lay on the dirt floor and the fireplace had become the rubbish can for empty food tins.

'The horse runners,' Scalp muttered, a little embarrassed. 'They party on a bit up here. Hit the grog bad.'

'Brumbies out here?'

'No, no. I got this real good stallion. Me mates. Me draftin' mates, they let mares loose with him. Foals comin' all the time, so they run 'em all in from time to time. Everything's done here. Breakin'—the lot.'

'Where do these horses run?'

'All up through them ranges.' He waved his arm out towards the main divide, blue in the distance.

'That all your country?' I hadn't yet become used to the rangelands.

'Abandoned pastoral leases,' he said, his eyes to the ground.

'Well, more or less abandoned. Some blokes run a few cattle up there.'

Everywhere I looked were bullet holes. Several had penetrated the front door, but it was in bad shape anyway. There was a shed with just an iron roof. An old truck had been parked in it for years. The windows were shot out and probably bullets hastened the collapse of the tyres. For an Australian outback camp scene it was not, however, particularly abnormal. Only a year before while walking in the Warrumbungles I had stumbled onto a deserted timber camp where goat skulls and empty shells had been used in bizarre decorative forms. I remember lengthening my stride considerably.

Much to my relief Scalp kept tea and coffee in the hut. He set the fire in a rough fireplace outside and placed the billy.

The timber encroached upon the little hut from every side. I had just seated myself on a wood block when there was a rush of wind in the leaves. I turned and watched a whirly-whirly advance, collecting dead grass and bits of paper. It passed over a dog kennel; the scrap iron roof creaked in the updraft and then it was on top of us. The soot of old fires blew all over us. Scalp cursed and dusted himself. I looked back at the dog kennel and saw it for the first time. The corrugated iron sides were not merely riddled with bullet holes, but shot out leaving gaping holes. A shiver crept up my back, my neck tingled and slapping the soot from my shirt I looked to see if the billy had boiled.

Scalp dropped me back with the cattle about mid-afternoon. I did a count of the unmothered calves and there were six left. The road had dried out enough for my small truck and I went down to the Old Boy's place to telephone Annette. About an hour later her father arrived in a little truck with a calf crate.

Like Smokie, Noel Hamilton carried the scars of a lifetime of chasing scrubbers in the Blank Space. His sleeves were rolled up and I doubted whether there was any original skin left on his forearms. There was a gauntness about his frame and he had gone snowy grey, but unlike most men in their fifties his stomach line compared with an eighteen-year-old's. If I had detected a weariness about him I was soon mistaken. We ran the calves down and loaded them within ten minutes. If I needed a hand he told me to telephone him and I knew he meant it.

The roadtrains arrived at 1.00 a.m. The quick passage through Hebel probably averted heavy losses. Only four cows perished. With the calves it was a different story. They were in a pitiful state. Seven died in transit and at first light it was obvious many more would die. Some lay on their sides, beaten. Driven by thirst, the cows had bolted through the gate to the creek. I knew none would return for some hours, but fifty calves at least appeared too weak to follow. Against the mothering too was activity near where we unloaded. A bloke had arrived to work on a harvester in the little paddock and I think some of the cows were spooked.

Within a week of the unloading of the mob sixty calves died. The clouds massed again and dropped a deluge of a hundred millimetres. For some of the calves it was the final death knell, for their bodies had no resistance and they died of exposure.

8

The Black Hole

The scene at Amby Creek was dismal and deeply distressing. We humans hold the key to the welfare of animals. Whatever the circumstances, these things should not occur. Looking around, I resolved for the rest of my life to stock well below recognised carrying capacity.

The rumours of disaster were now common. A whole herd from far western New South Wales was unloaded on a stock route and virtually buried at the site. Shire bulldozers were used to dig the trenches. A huge mob of cows and calves after walking fifteen kilometres for water floundered in thick mud; the holes left dry by the previous mob. These sort of stories reached Mitchell nearly every day.

Very little could be done to assist the mothering. Calves that were too weak for Noel to try and rear I loaded onto the Old Boy's jeep and dropped them among the bulk of the cows. Only one of these found a mother and survived. After the storm there were no weak calves left to worry about.

It took only a week for the cows to eat the first creek paddock to a level where a shift was urgent and it took another two days to gently move the weaker mob into another small paddock on the creek. Both mobs were too weak to go on the stock route, which was disappointing because the Mitchell grass was superior to the explosion of nutritionless summer grasses in the creek paddocks which had been so heavily stocked for years the Mitchell grass had petered out.

Following the shift of the cows and calves onto fresh feed I took the opportunity to go home. The first mob was doing well and the Old Boy had opened the gates into some escarpment country which gave me a few more days. Nature had total control for the next two or three weeks.

I had planned a ten-day break. There were urgent estate matters to be resolved. The family accountant had a number of issues to discuss with me and I was hoping to catch up with my other boys. My eldest son, James, an auctioneer in Sydney, had become engaged to Kari while I was away. The next boy, Richard, I hadn't seen for several months. He was in his second year of law at Southern Cross University, Lismore, and the baby of the family, Tom, lived in Sydney with his grandmother pursuing a Business Studies course at the University of Technology.

I got no further than signing a few papers for the accountant. The Old Boy telephoned with bad news. The pink-eye virus had hit the calves. Within forty-eight hours every calf was blind in at least one eye.

The pink-eye virus severely affects the eye for about two weeks. In chronic untreated cases it can result in death. The calf, stumbling around unable to see, walks into trees, logs and fences. Unless the mother is very attentive with regular feeding the calf becomes a skeleton of its former self within days and remains stunted for the rest of its life. The only treatment is penicillin ointment administered directly to the eye. I had to load the two racehorses and leave next day.

Old Bill Anderson took over the horses and for the next week I threw the blind calves and treated them. A horse was no use to me for this work. I had to sneak up on the badly affected calves and get them. If I missed the first time I would have to leave the calf and come back. To chase a blind calf in timber caused more damage to the calf than the virus. Sometimes the bigger calves would rear and fall on top of me and when the struggle was over we would both just lie there, panting. If my left hand missed the ear on the strong calves they might half drag me for ten metres and that was when I copped the kicks. At the end of the week I wore a multiple of colours from my ribs to my shins.

The pink-eye battle is one that I did win. Mercifully, the cows were unaffected. The local vet explained that high humidity and almost zero resistance to the virus had led to the outbreak in the calves.

The virus left as suddenly as it had arrived. Over the years I have observed a number of outbreaks and they usually drag on for weeks. It appears almost every calf was hit at the same time and their sight recovery was almost simultaneous. If the herd had to accommodate the virus, then the circumstances were the best possible. The virus slowed the recovery of the calves from drought, but the cows had gained strength rapidly. Two weeks after their nightmare journey I could see they were on target for Mt Kennedy. The Old Boy did everything possible to make the feed last. He moved his sheep off all the creek country, from one side of the place to the other.

After the pink-eye outbreak I shifted camp to the Maranoa River outside Mitchell. I pitched the tent only a hundred metres from the caravan park where I could have a shower and wash my clothes. I had been washing myself in muddy creek water and when I soaked soiled clothes in a bucket I removed the sweat and compounded the stains.

I set the camp up among weeping myalls overlooking the river which had wide sandbars and a meandering flow of water. There were hundreds of birds, including many species I had never seen in New South Wales. At night the river became a world of murmurs, shrill squawks and little growls.

Although this period lasted less than two weeks, it was the

only peaceful time I had during the drought campaign. I would breakfast at 5.00 a.m.—a few sticks, strike of a match and I had a billy of tea as quickly as in a modern kitchen. Then there was cereal followed by toast and I would drive to the stables, saddle Vodka and ride over to the racecourse. The air was cool at that hour. I would trot him around the circuit once and then drop over his neck and do pace work. Bill had a few horses running in the forest country around the racecourse and I had to be careful some mornings I didn't run into one. Vodka behaved in the initial stage of his preparation and I found it a refreshing start to the day.

When I returned to the stables, I would release Vodka in the sand yard. He would pigroot and half buck and then down he would go for a roll; three or four rolls one side and the same on the other.

Often Bill and I sat down outside the sand yard and yarned. He had owned and managed stations in the Blank Space all his life. I could listen for hours to his stories about the post-war years. Brumbies galloped along the tops of every range—from the Great Divide to the Chesterton and north to the Carnarvons. Men in those days rode after them, jumped from their horses and threw them. I used to watch Bill walking sometimes and I reckon that body had taken a thousand more knocks than a veteran league player.

Sometimes, he told me, danger came from unexpected quarters. As a boy Bill had the job of taking the meat out to mustering camps by packhorse. Packs of dingoes would follow him and on one occasion the dogs began to snap at the heels of the packhorse. The load and distance were too much to outrun them. Slapping at the dingoes with a stockwhip he managed to unsaddle the horses and release them. The numbers increased like a pack of hyenas and forced him to scale a tree. He managed to pull one bag of meat up after him with the stockwhip. The dingoes tore the packs open, ate the meat and hung around the base of the tree. In the end he had to give them the lot, for they had no intention of leaving while they could smell the meat.

The most dangerous activity was probably the bull running. Most of the vast range country was under forest. Cows and calves would be missed in the branding muster and the bull calves would grow into scrubbers. When the horsemen returned, these fellows bolted for freedom. The riders pursued them, one horseman to each bull. They clung close to the bull's rump until he overheated and got the staggers. Then the rider jumped from his mount and threw the bull by the tail. It's a highly skilled, split-second manoeuvre. If an untrained novice were to try he would probably get a horn through the belly. Once thrown, the bull's legs are strapped. During a muster several wild bulls might be thrown. After the cattle had been mustered into another paddock or taken to a set of yards, the musterers would come back and release one bull at a time. If he didn't trot along as required, he would be thrown again. In other words, the bull was broken in to human handling.

The paddocks were huge, measured in thousands of hectares and riding back later in the day to find those scrubbers and unstrap them would seem impossible, considering the thick cover of pine. For the bull catchers however it was simple: they just followed their own horse tracks.

In western Queensland and the Territory the term 'tracking' is as common as 'mustering'. The highly skilled Aboriginal tracker has faded into history, but most station people can track a little.

It was about mid-December when that short period of peace was shattered. At the camp in the evening I would cook a simple meal in the camp oven. I'd pour some olive oil into the old iron camp oven, cut up a little meat, some carrots, potatoes and a small onion. While dinner was cooking I would have a shower at the caravan park. The meal took about forty-five minutes to cook. I would wash it down with a billy of tea, clean up with some river water and walk across the bridge and up to the pub. It was never hard to strike up a conversation and while I had a couple of beers I waited for the weather report on the television. Before I left the hotel I telephoned Sal. In both states we had at last got on top. There were no more losses at Myall Plains and the cows were feeding out onto the scattered kurrajong. What we both hated was the enforced separation. Once the cattle settled down into their new home at Mt Kennedy I had in mind to employ someone to run the bore every second day.

On this particular evening I was back at the camp by eight-thirty and went straight to bed. I didn't worry about gas lights. My days started so early I was happy to be in bed by nine o'clock. About midnight I woke and heard something moving through the grass outside. For a while I didn't pay much attention. Sometimes cattle would come around at night and I would hear them eating. But I soon realised this thing was a human. The leg movement through the grass was slow. The last sound was beside the tent, to the right of the front flaps.

There are unwritten survival rules if you are camped alone in the bush. You never put your head out of a tent at night if someone's around. If you do, you may be struck on the head. As quickly as possible I felt for the rifle and cocked it. I always left the magazine in. Then I groped around for the torch. Outside there was no sound. Finally I said, 'I know you're there and I am armed.'

I lay there waiting, rifle butt in my left hand and the barrel across my thighs. In my right hand was the torch. I began to wonder whether I might have imagined the whole thing. Finally I fell asleep and didn't wake until the morning. The first thing I became aware of was the extra space in the tent. All the food was gone and items such as toothpaste. The thief had even zipped back the insect screen. Nothing of any value was taken. I found the nature of the robbery disturbing. Rather than a common theft for food, it was like a message—leave. If he was only motivated by hunger the thief could have got the food without any hassle while I was at the pub.

No one goes hungry in Mitchell, as it is such a small caring community. With the sort of life I was leading I came in contact with a lot of people. I spoke to a lot of women as they ran the business world in Mitchell. Sometimes I had coffee with one or two, but I never made a pass and was always mindful of what a close community existed in the little town.

I decided to leave town and camp on Mt Kennedy. The station was more than an hour's drive from Mitchell. A burst of very hot weather had taken its toll on Amby Creek. Feed that was fresh and green in November had burnt off. The cattle had gained weight and calves for the first time had begun to play. But it was time to move again and it would have been straightforward if it were not for the necessity of branding the calves. In the rangelands an unbranded calf becomes a clean-skin and cleanskins belong to the first person capable of planting a brand on the rump. That wasn't the law of course and never will be. If someone brands a calf that you can prove belongs to your cow the offender can be charged. In the range-lands the problem is to prove it.

The question plaguing me now was where to brand. Due to the high risk of infection, calves cannot be castrated, branded and then loaded onto cattle trucks. Trucking operators do wash their trucks out but it's very difficult to remove all traces of manure. The cows and calves had to be dropped into a set of yards with a calf crush, so that I could brand immediately. The yards at Mt Kennedy were several kilometres from the bluegrass paddock, but if we started at first light and split the mob into three the horses could be saddled early and the cows and calves on their way by seven o'clock. I discussed the plan with Richard and John Hamilton and we decided upon a three stage lift from Amby Creek.

Those pleasant mornings on the Mitchell racecourse came to an end and not altogether through fate. Vodka had started to misbehave. The oats and corn had him fired up. At first it was only a few pigroots. On the last morning I rode him I put the stock saddle on. No particular reason, other than instinct. I have been riding racehorses for more than thirty years and instinct has become a part of my decision-making with horses. It was as well I did. That morning he dropped his head and threw a couple of good bucks into me. He was strong and went high. In the racing saddle I would have been pelted. I made him move along to try and get his mind off it, but down went the head again. Cranky now, I sent him along and into the timber. We cleared logs and ditches and leaves of trees were scattered. Over a high bank and down went the head again. I drew the whip and we were nearly flat gallop. One and a half kilometres out I came upon drovers with a huge mob of Santa Gertrudis steers. Mouths open, they gaped at this madman on a horse. We went flying past the cattle and when Vodka saw the drovers' horses he let out the boldest whinny I have ever heard. The rotten thing was loving every minute of it and I was breathless.

Anderson's son Peter was an experienced rodeo rider and he agreed to take Vodka over. Typical of the bronc riders, he was about ninety kilos, strong and game. Next morning he put Vodka in the sand yard and gave him a workout. Vodka bucked until he was too exhausted to keep going and has never bucked since. A horse that may drop the head on a racetrack is extremely dangerous. In a racing saddle you are perched right up on top of the horse's wither and if you are covering the ground at sixty kilometres an hour and your mount props, chances are you will be speared to the ground head first. It happened to me once. I lay in hospital semi-conscious for a week and didn't stand straight for three months.

The three year old I didn't ride. He had been broken in and not ridden for months. Peter offered to try him out one day. Not far away, across the railway line, Malameen had settled in well with his girlfriends. From the stable I took some oats and fed him out of my hat on slack days. He didn't need the oats of course. Brooke fed him every day.

To impose as little stress as possible on the cattle I planned a three-stage move to Mt Kennedy. I also only used single-deck trucks. Jim Scott provided a semitrailer and Scalp had a truck similar to mine. Richard and John Hamilton helped me and we mustered early in the morning to the Amby Creek yards, loaded and took the horses to Mt Kennedy and in the cool of the evening returned to truck the cows and calves.

The first cut-out took in a hundred and forty cows and about a hundred calves. Each truck had to make a second trip to move them all and it was after midnight when the last truck unloaded.

The Hamilton boys drove out early next morning and helped with the branding. We had a quick smoko and walked the cattle up the road to Mt Kennedy and onto the water trough at the bore.

The same exercise was repeated and had it not been for another onslaught of storms I would have moved the whole herd inside a week. All the gullies ran water, the creeks rose to bankers and for heavy transport the road was closed. Fortunately for me the storms struck at night when I was parked on the main road, not far from the bore. It marooned me for three days and I took the opportunity to establish another camp. During the four torrid days of moving the cattle I slept in the truck and cooked a meal when I had time.

The storms introduced a new problem. In a valley below the tablelands a run-off of water from the top had half filled an old dam with half a metre of silt. By watering there the cattle didn't have to walk the extra distance to the bore, through a pine forest.

The day following the storm I watched some of them water. Initially the water remained unaffected by the black silt underneath, but when the cattle waded out of this black hole they had a sticky black slime up to their knees. At some stage the water would turn putrid. My experience in the south was that cattle rejected bad water and without any prodding walked onto the bore. At the rear of the homestead at Myall Plains is a trough connected to the bore supply and a hundred metres away is a dam. If the trough is connected the cattle bypass the dam, even when it's been freshly topped up by storm run-off.

It was Christmas and I wanted to go home if I possibly could. We all knew Mum wouldn't see another Christmas. Yet I felt uneasy about going and the premonition proved to be correct.

Christmas time in western Queensland is not a time to ask for favours. The police call it the mad month. Before the New Year festivities had begun there had been a shoot-out in Injune and a Mexican draw near Yuleba. All involved had been drunk. One man was shot and barely survived.

Before leaving to go south I collected Yarramin at Amby Creek and dropped him and Circus at the bore. I knew they would never stray far from the water. Mrs Brown I left once again. She had adopted a brumby foal and made milk. I suspect she had hunted away the original mother, knowing Mrs Brown. Poor thing, she had roamed the paddocks at home wanting a foal so badly. I had a Christmas drink with Bill Anderson, the horse trainer, before leaving for Chinchilla and he told me he had observed such an occurrence several times among horses running in a wild state.

At Chinchilla I took on a load of lucerne hay—two hundred bales and half the price of quality hay in New South Wales, if you could get it at all. Sal still had her hospital paddock and the retired bulls had to be maintained in good condition for sale.

The trip south took a day and a half via Chinchilla. Myall Plains looked terrible and almost lifeless. Sal and I greeted each other as though we were to go on a honeymoon and then she said, 'The bulls! They're starving. Throw some bales from the top.'

Back five minutes and feeding stock already! Yet it was so good to be home. We knew the time was short. We laughed about it and called it R and R.

Sal had so much to tell me and we spent the first day sitting under the old kurrajong in the garden. Through the shrubs at the bottom of the garden I caught a glimpse of the tennis court. I hadn't played on it for thirty years.

'Nick and I have been lonely too,' Sal said. 'We've done up the tennis court.'

When I last saw the court it was a tiny paddock of grass and suckers. I had thought the surface was beyond recovery. It was all part of the little things of home and I tried not to think about the return trip.

Poor old Mum was sad that Christmas. She had lived and breathed through my father. The only respite for her was the absence of pain. With painkillers, her doctor had managed to control it. Our boys kept my three days at home bright, and when it came time to leave the only spark about the return trip was Richie coming back with me.

We left at 4.00 a.m. and by sharing the driving we covered the eight hundred kilometres to Muckadilla in about thirteen hours. I thought we should have a couple of beers before heading out for the camp. If I'd known a party was in full swing I would have kept going, but once we walked out of the harsh sunlight and into the friendly atmosphere of the bar there was no turning back.

I instantly introduced Richard to Donna.

She stood behind the bar in a two-piece costume and water from the pool dripped onto her breasts from hair that fell around her face in a wild tangle.

'There's a barbecue on,' she said. 'You better stay. I'm closing the pub and it's all down the back.'

I had every excuse in the world for saying no, but didn't. One drink led to another and for the first time in a year I had far too much. It was a night under a summer sky, with the trace of a breeze from a billabong full of noisy frogs. For most of the time the frog chorus was drowned by music blasting through a window. The smell of cooked meat from the barbecue permeated the air. The red juice from the meat stained everyone's lips and long after the sun had set the heat rose from the ground and saw to it that the beer cartons ended up in the fire, empty.

We danced in the paddock and made a pad in the Mitchell grass plain, and when most of us were down the strongest of all fired shots at the moon and declared he was immortal.

When Richie woke me I felt sweat all over me, as though I had stepped out of a sauna. There seemed to be a radiator against my cheek and after the waking moments and a clenching of teeth against a throb deep in my skull, I realised the sun had been up at least three hours.

'Where did you sleep?' I asked Richie, as I struggled to my feet.

'In the truck with a million mosquitoes.'

I looked at him and despite how I felt I realised he was exhausted. It must have been the last night out on earth he would have hoped for.

'We'll go to Mitchell,' I said. 'Book into a hotel and straighten ourselves up.'

'It will take more than a hot shower.'

We stood there on the plain, in the grass, like lost souls. I saw him gazing out towards the tree line that marked the twisting course of the creek. The kites were there again, slowly wheeling, hovering above some dead animal. That morning, I think he thought I had brought him to the edge of the world as we know it.

At Mt Kennedy we were greeted by a scene that made me feel doubly sick. The black hole had become a pond of soupy mud, the colour of oil. One glance at the cattle and it was clear fifty to eighty cows and their calves were not going to the bore for water. They looked terrible and some of the calves were near death. To add to the frustration two or three hundred were walking daily from the tableland to the bore and passing within two hundred metres of the black hole. That these cows, with stinking mud up to their bellies, didn't tag on and attach themselves to family groups on the way to water defied explanation, until I realised the presence of dingoes was the cause.

I had not realised the effect dingoes have on cattle never before confronted with them. Once the surface water dried out the dogs relied on the troughs too. In the summer they must drink twice a day. Cattle reared in the rangelands take no notice of them except at calving time. My cows were spooked by them. Even when they weren't around they could smell them, so they had been avoiding the bore.

In the stifling heat the cattle were reluctant to move. They would have just looked at a man on a horse unless he had a stockwhip. We broke branches off brigalow trees and with a lot of yelling we finally got them walking towards the bore. At the bore we found the storage tank nearly empty. It too had been neglected. The cattle drank until they looked like they might burst and before the last beast had buried its head in the trough, I heard the dreaded gurgling sound from the float valve. The tank was empty.

Dripping with sweat I walked over to the pump jack to start the big diesel. The fuel containers were gone and the fuel line to the engine's fuel tank was disconnected. There wasn't an ounce of diesel. Richie and I just stood there, saying nothing. In each of our minds was the dreaded return trip in the heat to Mitchell.

The return trip took three hours. I reconnected the fuel line, filled the fuel tank and swung onto the crank handle. The bore was two hundred metres deep and equipped with thirty lengths of rod. When the down stroke commenced you thought of crystal clear water, crossed yourself with your left hand and drove the crank handle. Halfway through the stroke you snapped down the compression lever. Bad timing means a broken arm with these monster pre-war diesels. I didn't get it quite right. A burst of blue smoke shot into the air and I hit the ground.

'It's going Dad,' I heard Richie exclaim. 'It's going.'

I don't think he could believe it. I caught him looking at that engine and then at me. He didn't hold out much hope.

I regained my feet and was about to walk over to the tank and wait for the water when the engine began to die. The rotten thing had air in the fuel lines. I had to bleed the lines and the injector and start it twice again. Water began to flow before dark.

We were filthy and I had no fresh food in the bore camp. Exhausted, we went back to Mitchell to the hotel. I was busting to show Richie the tableland country. He had only seen the brigalow and the pine and may have been wondering whether I had gone troppo in the heat and imagined all that grass.

McCafferty's ran a bus service from Charleville to Brisbane every day. The next day was a Thursday and Richie could stay only till Friday. But when we went to book a seat, the Friday bus was booked out.

'There's a bus due in half an hour,' the booking lady said. 'There is one empty seat on it.'

'I can't believe it,' I remember saying. 'All you've seen are drunks, scrub and half dead cattle.'

'The heat too,' Richie said dryly. 'I've never felt the bite of the old 110 degrees before. All part of the Maranoa experience.' He paused and braced himself to really rub it in. 'You know Dad, you really have found paradise out here.'

I felt it when he left. I never saw him much. Boarding school provides opportunities for children, but in many ways it shatters family life. The little boy who was always one step behind me had gone a long time ago and was nearly a lawyer destined for Sydney.

I had decided to fence off the black hole and had to wait in Mitchell for fencing materials sent specially from Roma. When I got to Mt Kennedy another mob of cows was standing in the stinking mud, trying to get a drink. I am sure what moisture they did get was toxic. Two calves were dead and more were going to die. The temperature soared that day, compounding the extreme dehydration. Some of the cows wobbled about as they walked to the bore. I was forced to carry a two-litre container of water. I drank every ten minutes and if a cow tried to break back and I had to run, I soon found myself doubled up, inhaling air that was like a blast from a furnace. I had to play games with myself: *hang in for another five hours,* came a voice from the white glare, *then that thing will drop out of the sky and there will be nine hours of no sun. Lovely cool hours of only 95 degrees Fahrenheit.*

For the next two days little mobs of cattle drifted in from the gorges and the high tableland country. They were famished and I walked each lot to the bore. The spring had also been turned into a mud pit, with too many cattle seeking a drink.

I had to move camp once again. Cattle I had already taken to the bore were reappearing at the black hole and that was when I woke up to the dingoes. Early each morning it was possible to see their tracks beside the trough.

There was quite a bit of company about. A dead calf nearby had attracted several goannas. I watched with interest the order of seniority. A big black goanna had first go after sunrise. Like a miniature dinosaur it would furiously tear the flesh out and swallow it whole in one gulp. Back went the head, neck muscles expanded and the rotten meat more or less fell into its stomach. When the black goanna left, a more slender sand goanna would run in. This fellow was very wary and if I appeared would scuttle away, whereas the black goanna would watch me, motionless, raised at full length on its front legs.

The other visitors were the rat kangaroos. The striped little marsupials would go into the mud for a drink and get stuck. Normally reliant on native shrubs for moisture, these creatures had been driven by the extreme heat to find water. To get them out I had to build log bridges across the mud. They growled when I grabbed them by the scruff of the neck. And odd as it may seem they were stiff, as though cold. Under the surface the black slime remained cold, reflecting the heat away. I had to wash them in camp water before releasing them. They are shy, elusive creatures and when the weather returned to normal I didn't see them again.

I managed to get the fence up in a day. In searing heat it is sometimes better to have something to do. Provided you drink plenty of water and keep your body covered, 115 degrees Fahrenheit will not do you any harm. It's just very uncomfortable. The following days I found more difficult. I went looking for cattle that might have needed help. In extreme temperatures the ground moves. It's an illusion of course, but sometimes my feet didn't seem to touch down when they should have.

There were tracks of a great variety of animals, some of which I never saw. The eastern scrub turkey I saw only twice, but I cut their tracks every day. Dingo tracks were everywhere.

It was the pup season and I would get glimpses of a bitch and two or three pups. The locals told me attacks on calves were rare at this time of the year. The pulling down of calves in the heat took too much out of the dingoes and they settled instead on the stalking of small game at night. However, I still had some weak calves and I heard them take a calf one night. The mosquitoes were bad after sunset and to get away from them I had to crouch almost over the camp fire and keep my face to the smoke. On this particular evening I was working on an early dinner so I could go to the tent and escape them.

The first sound seemed to almost grab me—a chilling primeval outburst in a gorge. Something had hold of this calf and it bellowed its heart out. I had lost my glasses at Muckadilla and I am nearly blind at night. I stood there helpless. It went on for five or ten minutes and then a cow—its mother—called all night for her calf.

It's hard to have a rational conversation with many people in the bush about dingoes. In the highlands of central Queensland the dingo is a vital component of the ecosystem. Remove the dingo and much of the area would soon be overrun by swamp wallabies, known locally as stinkers. They have no value in the meat trade and control rests entirely on the landowner. But if dingo populations rise too much they begin to hunt in packs and will do a lot of damage. It's not what the dogs actually eat. It is the biting. Their teeth are covered in deadly bacteria and the bites turn septic.

In an ecological debate perhaps the most important observation is the absence of foxes in the dingo habitat. In New South Wales the fox has wiped out every ground-dwelling bird except the plover, every small marsupial except the possum (and they now only exist in specific areas) and the once common goanna has become very difficult to find. In the dingo habitat many of the small creatures of the bush still survive. If our native wild dog causes losses of a million dollars a year in

Queensland, the combined effort of the fox and the feral pig in New South Wales would incur losses in excess of ten million. In addition to the export losses are the environmental consequences. Foxes are voracious eaters of frogs. Frogs in turn eat mosquitoes. The mosquitoes carry Ross River fever which is now endemic in the western river towns of both Queensland and New South Wales. There may be no connection, but the suspicion is enough for concern. A lot more could be done to eradicate foxes.

CHAPTER

9 The Wild Bunch

The old year passed by and the truck wireless kept me in touch with current news. It had taken about a week to educate the last of the cattle away from the black hole. I got to know some of the cows and I called them super-optimists. On the way to the bore they broke away from the rest and walked up to the black hole fence. They'd have a long look, nostrils flared for the smell of water and then with a flick of the tail it was back to the bore trail.

I moved camp back to the bore. The black hole camp I'd shared with the goannas. They have an extraordinary sense of smell and knew I had some goodies in the tent. I left a plate by the fire one morning and when I returned the boss goanna—the big black fellow—ran away with it in his mouth. I had to chase him and he only dropped it when he reached the foot of his tree.

It was about the sixth day of January, 1995, and I hadn't had time to check the boundary. At this time of the year even moderate days were still hot, but nothing like the heatwaves that came and went in cycles. With the cooler temperature it seemed a good opportunity. Diesel was low and the cows and calves at Amby Creek needed checking. If I checked the boundary at Mt Kennedy I felt I could leave for a day and a night.

Circus and Yarramin were never far from the bore and Yarramin made his usual camp inspection when I moved back. He would eat anything and to feed him was fatal, for he would wait outside the tent and get his legs tangled in the tent ropes. The boundary inspection would have been a lot more pleasant on Circus, but some of the country was so rough and steep it wasn't worth putting a horse through it.

Walking west from the bore the country was heavily timbered with lancewood and ironbark. The trees sucked the moisture and left little for grass. The only grass belonged to the wire grass family, unpalatable for cattle. I didn't expect to see cattle tracks in this country and when I did I stopped and examined them. A mob had gone through, probably thirty to forty head. They had been driven fast and ran packed tight, knocking down brush and snapping branches from trees.

I followed the tracks for about three kilometres, tracking backwards. I reached the western boundary and here the mob had been driven along the fence. The fence led over a sandstone ridge covered in wattle and dropped into a ravine, flat at the bottom and under head-high kangaroo grass. Halfway across this narrow strip I found the fence down, where the cattle had been turned in. I didn't see any horse tracks and didn't expect to. The horsemen would have crossed somewhere else and wiped the tracks leading to and away from the fence.

To confirm my suspicions, I had in the past few days seen some strange cattle among mine and simply assumed they'd got in from somewhere. They hadn't got in. They had been driven in.

Another two kilometres on I found the fence down again. Logs had been laid across the wire and a couple of wooden posts had been lifted out of their holes, which would not be difficult in sandy loam soil. Clearly men rode these ranges and stole cattle.

I moved slowly, looking for horse tracks, and by mid-after-noon had only gained the far north-east corner on the basalt tablelands. I saw no more tracks and in the high country the fence was in good order.

It was a long walk back to the bore. Half a kilometre out I could hear the labouring chug chug of the diesel engine. I had become fond of the noise and its echo through the timber, for it was more than an echo of sound; it was a vision of flowing water, healthy cattle and security. The sight of a strange vehicle by the tent was not so welcome.

It was an old model vehicle with a trayback and sides. Vehi-cles have never interested me much, but at a quick glance it might have been a Land-Rover, popular in the sixties. The driver stood near the front of the vehicle, looking down towards the bore where a group of cows and calves was filing through the gate into the access paddock. He didn't see me coming and wheeled around when he heard my boots crunch-ing the eucalypt leaves.

'Jesus—yer give me a fright!' he burst out, forcing a smile. He was about my height, but had a powerful look about him, a sleeveless shirt exposing deeply tanned, sinewy arms. There was a litheness, about everything he did, even when he pulled a cigarette packet from his shirt pocket.

We shook hands and I asked, 'You from about here?'

'Not too far away. I'm a station manager.' He made no further effort to introduce himself.

'Similar country?' I asked. With strangers it was always the weather or the country. I always prefer to talk about the country.

'Rougher,' he replied.

'This is better than it looks,' I said. 'The tablelands are covered with the biggest expanse of bluegrass I've ever seen.'

'Oh yes it's beautiful on top. The gorges that drop off it would worry me. Do you think you'll ever find them all?'

'I wouldn't like to leave them for long.'

'You can't leave them for a day.' His grim reply jolted me.

'What do you mean?'

'There's a bad bunch that come and go. The soft name given to 'em is the Wild Bunch. Other names are less flattering.'

'Sounds like they rob banks and snatch payrolls!'

He shot me a knowing look and smiled wryly. 'They're not much better. If it wasn't for air surveillance these blokes would be right into it, although none of them have Butch and Sundance's charisma.' He paused and looked at me steadily, his jaw set like a man about to deliver very bad news. 'There's no thanks for this sort of thing, but someone has to tell you. You're a deadset sitter. They hit Claravale station a few weeks back and not a beast sighted since. What was most alarming was their boldness. They cut out what they wanted and ran 'em straight past Scalp's yards.'

'How many?' I was truly shaken.

'Forty or fifty head.'

'That their biggest coup?' I was trying to convert the new threat into dollars.

'Oh no,' he almost moaned, shaking his head. 'They've knocked off up to a hundred head in a single raid.'

'Impossible,' I declared. 'You can't run off with a mob that size.'

'In the heavy pine and lancewood yer never see 'em. You might run a three-day camp before you know yer short. You'll learn. Wait until yer go to round 'em up.'

'Scalp should have told me,' I said. 'The stock route would be better than this.'

'My bet is he couldn't get you here quick enough. Once here yer stuck. Someone's gotta run that big old bastard of a diesel for water and he's away pullin' scrub. You've become his minder and he gets a cheque every month to boot.'

'Minder!' I exclaimed.

'Call it what you like. Big place north of here employs a gunman. Anyway Scalp's got a thousand head scattered about and while yer watchin yer own I guess he thinks his are safe enough and he can go pullin' scrub and forget 'em. They water everywhere on springs and dams. He's given you the dry country. But in a drought like this one yer lucky to get it.'

'I had planned to have a week or two at the bore and if there were no problems pay someone to run the engine and go home.'

'No one's goin' to come out here. Plenty of brave men around the pubs of a night. But try 'em next morning.'

'What about you?' I asked. 'I could make it worth your while.'

'It's hard enough watchin' me own back on forty thousand acres.'

I breathed deeply. This was bad news. Far worse than I could ever imagine—I could hardly take it in. 'It's that bad is it?'

'You ride with yer gun, sleep with it and when yer squat behind a tree you have it in reach. These blokes'd shoot a hundred cows just to get the hundred unbranded weaner size calves. They have credit on demand and use bills for toilet paper.'

For some moments his phrases seem to echo in my mind. It was as though I had slipped into a nightmare and was waiting for that jolt when you're suddenly conscious of your own snore and with that you're back in the comfortable, safe real world.

A sprightly bunch of cattle trotted through the timber to the access paddock and the water. They were led by a big framed cow. Her calf was one of those frolicking in the rear. She caught the scent of the camp fire and stopped. The calves, too, stood motionless. Their communication was instant. The discipline beyond the new world of humans. Then she swished her tail back over her rump, tossed her head once with delightful arrogance and walked on. They didn't trot again.

'You been under fire?' I asked.

'Yeah—twice,' he muttered and nodded vigorously. 'It's when they're drunk. They don't aim. Bullets skip on the dirt and slam into tree trunks. It scares the shit out of yer.'

'If you did that back home there'd be a squad of police on the scene in thirty minutes.'

'No police. Yer leave 'em out of it. They won't find 'em for a start and if they did they'd find unarmed stockmen looking very surprised and sympathetic.'

'I'd call them just the same.'

'That night they'd shoot yer horses. If you had a house they'd burn it.'

During the next half hour he related the little he knew about the Wild Bunch. The identity of some was so obscure they might as well have been faceless. The one feared most was 'Frankie'. Accused of everything short of murder he nursed a grudge against the world and drank heavily. By the time he had finished his story more cattle had drifted in. Some trotted and some walked. Each little group had a matriarch and she made the decisions. After they drank they wandered into a patch of brigalow and mingled with other groups. Some cows would lock heads, light-hearted gestures of territory—that's my shade, not yours. The little charades went on all day.

I had begun to feel very hollow in the stomach. I asked this bloke if he'd like to try a reheated johnny cake. He still hadn't volunteered his name and after all he had told me I gathered he didn't want me to know. The cakes were palatable enough with jam and fresh billy tea and we talked for a while longer. I listened to him carefully; for a comment, slip of the tongue—anything that might suggest exaggeration and rumour, but his story didn't change. I had to plan for the worst possible scenario. In fact I hardly noticed him go. He had left me with a lot of thinking to do.

After the visitor left I sat on my log seat for a long time and dwelt upon the unbelievable. Over the years I had heard about outlaw pockets in Queensland and the Northern Territory. It had always been my private belief that some men duffed cattle, resorted to shoot-outs where bullets were never aimed at human targets and plunged into pub brawls to fill a vacuum of loneliness and despair.

Outback Australia possibly comprises the loneliest landmass on earth outside the great ice wastes of the poles. There are vast deserts in Africa, but people live in them and have created culture going back thousands of years. There is no longer a culture in the remote areas of Australia. The Aborigines first lived on stations following the destruction of their own culture. And had the situation been left alone by bureaucracies and by people passing through this world who at the end of the day have acquired zero knowledge of any facet of human existence, I believe more of these people would today own and manage cattle stations in the outback.

The Aboriginal people today live in old mission camps and on the edges of towns and the majority survive in the cities. If it had not been for the opening of the live export trade, Top End cattle stations would have been reduced to lonely homes in a wilderness, for cash flows would not have even equalled the cost of mustering. An area half the size of western Europe may have become almost uninhabitable with a climate alien to all but the Aboriginals. The dark people belong there and will save that fragile land from the irreversible ravages of the southern arid zone.

The unbelievable was that I had blundered into one of the last remaining pockets on the edge of civilisation. For the cattle I had no regrets. The only mob not secure now was the two hundred cows left at Amby Creek. For myself I had to admit I had no regrets in the short term. I enjoyed the return to the wild. It is always nice to dream about a world that is a spinning nightmare, in which you alone can step off and on as you please. The reality is you only ever step off once. The fantasies soften the blows and those who can never indulge in fantasies grow old before their time. My immediate fantasy was to have Sal here with me. Together we could escape the world for a time, observe the cattle in this beautiful setting of forest, gorges and high tablelands, and at night listen to the possums squabble, the dingoes howl like the violin of the Dreamtime and wake to the shrill call of the curlew. But alas it was a fantasy. We were locked apart and loneliness would fall heavily upon her now.

Next morning, Saturday, I loaded the empty diesel containers and left for Mitchell. About sixteen kilometres down the track I stopped to watch a feeding frenzy. Seven or eight wedge-tail eagles had set upon a kangaroo hit by a vehicle overnight. They tore at the carcass with their claws and their huge beaks pulled the meat from the skeleton. I felt privileged to be able to watch. These birds are the lions of the sky—the largest eagles surviving in the world today. A larger bird in the Philippines is so close to extinction it may not be a valid comparison.

I observed no fighting among the birds. There was a total acceptance of one another and they appeared to have little interest in me. I had been watching for more than five minutes before I saw why. Perched in a tree high above them a pair of beady eyes stared down on the truck. This bird was the sentinel.

Throughout my life I have been saddened by the basic lack of understanding we humans have of all other creatures. We have become too removed from the natural world and basic commonsense. I have always defended this magnificent eagle and an Aboriginal whom I have employed on odd occasions told me of a white man in the Quilpie district who shot eagles relentlessly for forty years with no drop in lamb losses. The

Aboriginal shot a large sow one day and gutted it in front of this man. Its insides were full of young lambs. There is a tragedy in paradox here. The eagle was the only ally this man had. An eagle can swoop and take a piglet, whereas a dingo has to face mum.

What we have lost in the name of civilisation is difficult to define. While I watched these birds feasting I pondered over the millions of magnificent animals the white man has shot needlessly over the last hundred years. I didn't hear the vehicle coming from behind, such was my trance. The first warning came from the sentinel. The bird's huge wings expanded and those on the carcass responded immediately. With a beat of wings they rose into the trees. One only alighted to a nearby log.

Beside me a four-wheel-drive trayback had stopped. There were three blokes in it. The driver already had a rifle out the window. His hat cast a shadow over his face. The one nearest me I could see. He had heavy jowls and his scruffy face badly needed a razor. The life in his eyes had died long ago and he sucked on a stubbie of beer the way he might have thirty years before with a bottle and a teat.

'These birds are protected,' I yelled to the driver as I got out of the truck.

'Not here mate. We use 'em for target practice.'

The bird perched on the log didn't like me leaving the truck. It followed the others back into the timber. The eagles selected high trees and were already out of range for anything but a freak shot.

'You the Mexican?' the driver asked when the bird had gone. He moved the rifle back into the vehicle.

I nodded. I didn't feel like saying anything. There was no need for any introductions either. I reckoned the driver was Frankie of the Wild Bunch.

'None of my business what you do,' I said at last. 'But I was enjoying watching those birds feed. Nothing special to you blokes because you see them all the time. Where I come from they're rare.'

'That's alright mate,' the driver said in a tone that let you know it wasn't alright. He too hadn't shaved for a while. The stubble was slightly reddish on a belligerent-looking face. His hair was brushed back sharply revealing a broad forehead. The size of his arms suggested a heavy build and someone not too fit.

I stepped away from the vehicle and they drove off. The eagles were well away from the road now, maybe two hundred metres and when the vehicle drew level with them I saw a barrel emerge from the passenger-side window and a shot was fired harmlessly in the direction of the birds. The report was sharp and loud and the big birds rose into the sky and drifted away.

I drove on to Mitchell, filled the diesel containers and went to see how things were going with the horses. Vodka had run a good time and Bill, his trainer, was keen to start him. He had looked through the western districts programme and all the clubs had shut down for January. We had to wait for Wandoan at the end of the month. The story of the three year old was less encouraging. He had bucked like a veteran rodeo horse.

Mary, Bill's wife, always provided tea with some scones and in no time the morning had vanished. I look back on those morning teas with Bill and Mary Anderson as some of the best moments in Queensland.

The next stop was the Old Boy's. He had already moved the cattle onto better feed. His cultivation paddocks had exploded with summer weeds, some of which cattle loved. He said there was no need to move for two weeks, which was a relief. My calculations on the bore had not been quite accurate and I had to run the engine sixty percent of total time to keep ahead of the cattle. It appeared I might have to sell the remainder at Amby Creek.

After a drive out to the cattle in the Mad Max machine, a cup of tea, a report on the rats and the last lot of jokes he had gathered from various bars, I went on to Muckadilla. Someone would have found my spectacles by now!

It was late in the afternoon when I arrived and the hotel was packed. Donna was so busy I didn't get to speak to her for an hour. No glasses had been found to her knowledge. Ask so and so—they went to Roma, but should be back before dark. I decided to take the gamble and stay for a while. If I got the glasses I could drive back to the camp after a meal. If no one had them I had to wait until morning.

The hotel had a party atmosphere from the moment I walked in. There must have been twenty kids diving and splashing in the pool. The tables set around the pool, under umbrellas, were all taken by travellers. Those from Brisbane and Toowoomba on holidays stood out. The men wore shorts and short-sleeved shirts and the women soaked up the last of the sun in two-piece costumes. Inside, the locals hugged the bar. Caps never came off, but most of the women wore frocks and filled the long bar with a measure of femininity I had not seen before.

With a beer in my hand I began to look for faces. The young guide-post flattener Nick and Rupert had chatted to was there. He raised his glass. For the moment he was sober. I couldn't see anyone else I knew and must have looked a bit lost, for Donna appeared at my side and took me across to a table where four blokes were seated. They were drovers, enjoying a bit of a break from the cattle. I had not seen them before and I found them much easier to talk to than the bullies in October. They told me about the lady boss drover. She had cows with young calves and heat had caused havoc with the calves. The men had thrown it in and left. The stock route south from Mitchell had plenty of feed and little water. When they left Mitchell storms had filled every gully and ditch and no one had anticipated such a rapid evaporation of the water.

'She won't make it through if the Wet don't blow up again,' one bloke said. He had a moustache and a rugged face to carry it. His western hat had character, shaped for his head. So many of the hats worn by stockmen conjured up the brainless cowboy look.

'Make it where?' I asked.

'Down the dry track,' he said. 'It's like a desert to St George. Very little water. The Maranoa runs underground.'

News like this made me count my blessings. Two hundred and twenty kilometres of scrub and dry stages. One woman and two girls. I began to wonder whether the women in the twenty-first century might have to do the front-line fighting while the men managed the supply lines.

'She'll make it,' the drover with the long nose said. 'Stubborn bitch they say.'

We drank a round and conversation swung around to my cattle.

'Yeah, know the place.' He didn't speak much this bloke. Balding slightly, he spoke and looked at you with his head tilted back. Not the most friendly of the foursome, but the best of them if strength of character is indeed registered in a man's face.

'Bloke from Longreach lost fifty percent in there,' he said. 'What they could muster they walked out. They walked north.'

'North,' I said in disbelief. 'A couple of good stations and then the most hostile country in Queensland.'

'They slipped down through the Great Divide. Good belt of country there.'

'There was a fight at the yards,' the long-nosed bloke said. 'Some mad bastard said he was gonna shoot 'em all. So they went north to avoid the pass.'

The beers softened the reality of the rangelands and I resigned myself to at least two weeks of night blindness. The tall bloke whom I last remembered trying to shoot the moon after the barbecue had arrived with his woman. She had a pretty face but the muscles of a man. God help him if his virility failed.

The bar had become a sea of faces and hats. I excused myself to have a wander through the crowd. Near the pool table I found Scalp and Jenny. I made sure I shook Jenny's hand firmly. I wondered whether she had the same rule for kissing.

'Have a New Year drink with us,' Scalp said cheerfully. 'We missed the barbecue. Make up for it tonight.'

'Don't make up for the hangover.'

'My hangover's waitin' for the first beer.' Scalp wore mischief like some women wear cheap perfume.

'Met the mob up there?' Jenny asked.

'I've met them. Guns and a shot thrown in as well.'

'They're taken pot shots already?' She looked stunned and I saw a glimpse of the real woman.

'They fired at some eagles,' I said, forcing a smile. 'They have to drop their sights a fair bit yet.'

'Come on Jen,' Scalp laughed and put a beer in her hand. 'Make the man nervous, lookin' serious and all like that. They're just larrikins them blokes. Be here in a minute. We've got some musterin' plans.'

'Bit of bronco work too I suppose,' I said.

'I'm going up to keep 'em in line,' Jenny said firmly. 'The buggers get drunk and are rough on the horses.'

Four blokes had appeared on the verandah, through the open double doors. Three of them had been in the trayback. The one not at the eagle scene was Johnny. Short and dark, his face travelled from sombre to the widest grin I have ever seen. If he played poker he would lose every hand. He bowled up and shook hands with Scalp and gave Jenny a kiss and a squeeze. There were no introductions. He knew who I was and it was party talk as though we had known each other for years. He wore a red shirt with the long sleeves rolled up and a red bandanna to keep his black hair in place. Not a man in the bar looked as striking as this bloke. He had shaved and unlike his mates he had a strong face with just the faint crease of mirthful lines coming away from his mouth.

Frankie's entrance was about the reverse. Close behind Johnny, he sneaked in, his eyes working overtime to take in every angle of the big room within his vision. Ike had the big characterless cowboy hat on. He wasn't too worried who saw him enter. Tall and lean he looked the stockman only for the hat. Lenny slunk in like a mongrel dog. There are some men in this world that couldn't buy it, and if a woman did oblige she would deserve the community medal. Nature herself let the miracle of procreation down sometimes and one would be inhuman not to feel compassion for the victim. Yet these blokes had accepted him and I wondered briefly whether they were merely larrikins after all.

'Meet Starlight's shadow,' Johnny said suddenly and giggled. It was an infectious giggle and despite being the target I laughed myself. The others closed in and we shook hands as though the eagle incident had never occurred. 'There's some camp fire yarns in this bloke,' Johnny blurted out and slapped me on the shoulder. 'Steals horses and runs bank managers out of town.' Back went his head and he roared with laughter. Even Lenny smiled. I felt desperately uncomfortable. Some people had turned to take a peep at us. Then the girls arrived. They must have gone to the powder room first. Wherever they came from they arrived just in time. I almost introduced myself. Johnny's girl had a wave of blonde hair across her face. Soft and young with a rare femininity for this region, she would have adored a wild and colourful man like Johnny. Her name was Anne. Beside her stood Josie, a wild-eyed brunette. She had fun and naughtiness written all over her and I felt she might have been only Frankie's on a whim. Frankie had stopped glancing around the room and was already asking her about a drink. It was Dutch shouting which greatly relieved me. I had four on board already and a whole round with this group might not put me down, but I had become instantly nervous of Johnny's mouth. There had been an incident with a bank manager and I had been within my rights, although above the law. That Johnny knew about it was staggering and I decided to deny any knowledge of what he was talking about.

Ike's girl probably used horse sweat for perfume. Thin, dry skinned and with stringy blonde hair she was typical of those women who give every ounce of their love to horses. Not that I have contempt for them. These women set the standards for horse care and we need them. I can pick them at a glance and before I was married I steered clear of them. Their passion for horses is beyond the capability of the male. I once saw a mate of mine emerge from a stable pulling up his pants. It was an autumn afternoon, a long time ago.

'I don't believe it,' I said to him. I knew the girl.

'Bale of hay,' he grinned. 'Her horse had no hay.'

I eased myself out of the group and had a steak from the barbecue. I rang Sal and there was an atmosphere of strain between us when I hung up. The cattle were settled and the bore had proved to be reliable. Why wasn't I coming home? It was a fair enough question and I had to make up stories about mending fences and packs of dingoes. I couldn't tell her about a band of outlaws. I wasn't confident she would believe me. Who would in 1995?

I felt low in spirits after the phone call and had no desire to go back into the hotel. I couldn't see well enough to drive, so I pitched a small French army tent I carried as a spare. They were the most durable tents I have ever seen and this one I had carried around for twenty years. I walked across the road and over the railway line. On the second trip back to the truck I picked up a thin mattress and half an hour later I closed my eyes.

The first shot woke me out of a heavy sleep. With the second shot I even heard the bullet cut the air. Right over the top of the tent it went. I may not have moved if it had not been for the shouting, both male and female. During the next few seconds I absorbed a few jumbled words. He's this and that, roared someone. A woman screamed 'Don't shoot!' I had my boots on in a flash, but I fumbled badly with the tent's gauze zipper. When I got out I ran for a pile of railway sleepers and squatted behind them. The shouting had stopped and in the dim glow of the only two street lights I saw a small blurred figure walking back to the hotel. No one had emerged from the hotel. There was music from a tape deck and even if anyone heard the rifle shots they would be too drunk to care. I couldn't help smiling when I thought of the tourists lying in their little rooms. The party in the bar was in full swing and judging by the language I could hear, a rough one.

I couldn't stay outside naked for long. The mosquitoes homed in and I found myself slapping parts of my body I normally take good care of. I went back to the tent and slumbered fitfully until dawn. I must have felt safe then, because I fell into a heavy sleep.

CHAPTER

10 Stake-out

The tent was so hot I crawled out in the nude and had a look about. It didn't matter because there was no one around. Not even the tourists had stirred and it was after eight o'clock. The only sound was the crows kicking up a ruckus in a tree near the kitchen door.

I dressed, rolled up the tent and walked across the rail line and the highway to see about breakfast. Donna was behind the bar cleaning up. She had a sexy slip of a frock on. It clung to every curve and I felt like saying I would be more comfortable if she took it off. She looked exhausted and she mumbled something about never making it through the day. I was lucky to have a tent to escape to, she told me.

I didn't have the heart to say anything about breakfast. I found the cereal, made toast and drank a whole pot of tea. It was back to the camp and I hoped she might sit down for coffee, just for a minute. She didn't.

It took two hours to drive out to Mt Kennedy. The black hole was in sight of the road and I saw two cows hanging on the fence I had erected. Despite the distance I could tell something was wrong. Sick cattle have a way of standing. The back is slightly humped and the four legs are planted square, as though to steady themselves.

I stopped the truck and walked over. They were like skeletons. They had not drunk for days and they should have been dead. Only months later did I hear about the native pear trees. In the cool months cattle have been known to survive on these trees for weeks.

There were some in the paddock and they're the only explanation I can find for the survival of those cows. The cows didn't want to walk but were too weak to offer any resistance. One of them kept stumbling and I let them poke along in a general direction. The bore trail held no appeal for them and they ended up on the road, not far from the truck.

We had only gone a short way along the road when I noticed a lone calf sheltering in a clump of box suckers. I made it get up and saw it had a broken leg. The little steer had been hit by a vehicle and his mother had planted him while she went for water. He was a big calf though and in the heat milk from his mother would not have been adequate. Taking him gently, I made him hobble along with the cows. A few hundred metres on, the bore trail crossed the road and entered a thick patch of box suckers. The cows followed the trail this time. It was just a few minutes to the trough and I needed a drink myself, which I got directly from the float valve.

On the way back to the truck I followed the vehicle track to the main road. At the turn-off I found another calf, dead and soaked in its own blood. A robust steer calf, with a soft red coat.

I examined the road. There were no skid marks. The vehicle had hit him hard and the driver had meant it. Two calves within five hundred metres is not an accident.

The loss of income flashed through my mind, but it had nothing to do with the rage I felt at that moment. I thought about what this little calf had been through. Born on cold windswept plains with not a blade of grass, carted nine hundred kilometres in searing heat, stumbling around half blind with pink-eye and just as he begins to frolic and love life he's snuffed out by a vehicle, deliberately.

I walked back to the truck and drove it to the camp, which was only about two hundred metres from the calf. With my camp axe I cut down a box sucker and cut two pieces out of it. It would have been bordering on dementia to erect a cross on the side of the road. I simply laid it beside him.

Before the calf incident I had been content to mind my own business and look after the cattle. Now the problem of lawlessness in the rangelands was mine as well. The men who killed the calf had set upon themselves a relentless enemy. I would track them, watch them and when they undertook criminal activity, I would contact the police. Next day I drove one hundred and forty kilometres to Roma to discuss a stake-out with the stock squad. I wanted to get rid of the Wild Bunch and the sooner the better.

When I arrived the stock squad was out on a job and I was passed on to an officer of the CIB. I told him the location of my cattle and he immediately invited me into his study. He told me the region was of serious concern to the police, as there had been several reports of cattle theft during the past two years.

I explained my plan and I had a feeling he secretly liked it, but could not condone it.

'I can't give approval on the record,' he said. 'If you're shot and killed I am in big trouble. Furthermore, you cannot undertake a citizen's arrest with a rifle.'

'I can get myself to a station and use the phone.'

The officer wrote down three telephone numbers on a piece of paper.

'When are you going in?' he asked.

'Tomorrow.'

'If they find out and get hold of you,' he paused and looked at me with a solemn expression, 'I think you'll get a bullet and be burnt up a hollow log.'

We chatted for a while and he knew all about the cattle duffers' tricks. He told me the strange cattle in among mine were possibly 'coaxes'. Before the rustlers strike they pop a few very quiet cattle of their own into a herd. They are soon accepted by the herd and when the horsemen arrive for the raid the 'coaxes' lead the way. With good 'coaxes' a job could be done under moonlight.

I left the police station confident of support. Before I went in I'd realised official approval would not be given. This was a vigilante operation and if law enforcement authorities supported vigilante action the community would not know who was being protected.

The next thing was to purchase supplies. Dried packets of beans and peas, rice and pasta were the main items on the menu. My luxury was five tins of lamb casserole. A bit heavy for the backpack, but I only had the heavy load going in. I couldn't depend on any bush tucker. There were no foods I could collect and apart from the rifle shot giving me away, there were no animals I cared to shoot for meat.

It was mid-afternoon when I left Roma and by the time I got back to the camp it was too late to go up to the stockmen's hut. I had to start the engine and I wanted to check Circus and Yarramin. The country near the bore was eaten out and once I had found fresh tracks I followed them as far as the road. Circus was wary of strangers, but Yarramin would go to anyone with a piece of bread.

At the road the tracks simply crossed and the pair of them had kept walking. There was no need to track them any further and as I turned to go back I heard a vehicle. On the average three vehicles a day passed through here.

Frankie was on his own. 'G'day,' he said. He stopped in the middle of the road and I noticed his pupils were dilated and he had a stubbie in his left hand.

'Got a bit of mustering to do?' I asked, shaking hands

through the window. I wanted to be as friendly as possible.

'Scalp wants a few dollars. We'll run a few out of the hills for him.'

'I'll bet your horses need the work.'

'Reckon they'll be fresh,' Frankie laughed and took a swig. 'Johnny and Ike are up there now. I'm not much keen on the buckjumpers.'

There was a pause and it seemed a good time.

'I've got to go away for a few days. Reckon you could start the old diesel for me? Be worth a couple of cartons.'

'Be okay mate.' Frankie's glazed eyes suddenly looked normal and he nodded several times. 'We'll kick the old bastard up. Enough diesel there?'

'Got a fresh load today. Be enough until I get back.'

'Go home and relax,' Frankie said with extraordinary sincerity. He made me feel a bit of a bastard. 'When ya goin'?'

'Tomorrow.'

He left and I walked back to the camp. I didn't feel tired for hours and must have stared into the red coals for some time. At heart I didn't much like the job I had set myself. I'd been out of money and run a cleanskin or two in my time. But I wanted to go home. My place was back home with Sal, nearly nine hundred kilometres to the south. My passage to freedom was to bust up this outlaw bunch.

I had obtained a topographic map in Roma. I paid meticulous attention to the vehicle tracks that entered various parts of the ranges. I had to drop the lorry on a remote track well away from where these men might ride. Several kilometres to the east of my camp there was an abandoned farm house marked on the map. According to the map a track still led to it.

By ten o'clock next morning the supply tank was full. It was time to leave. I anticipated a five-hour walk from the truck, lugging a heavy load. The track appeared to carry a bit of traffic and that worried me when I turned off. After three kilometres I discovered the reason. There was a bore with a pump jack on it. Beyond the bore the track all but disappeared. There were washed-out gullies and where the track passed through pine forest I had to push regrowth down with the bullbar. About eight kilometres in, the track swung to the east. It was as good a place to leave it as any other. I nosed the cabin into a thick clump of pine.

The army tent I rolled up very tightly and attached a strap to it to sling it across my shoulders. Thanks to the paralysis ticks I couldn't leave the tent behind. Carried by kangaroos and wallabies, these ticks grow to the size of a small spider and will home in from metres away. They are poisonous and if not removed may lead to paralysis.

All the food I crammed into the backpack with two billies and a plate. One change of clothes I fastened to the top of the pack. The four litres of water and my bolt-action rifle I carried. I was amazed how comfortable I felt when all loaded up. You always feel the weight for the first few minutes.

To the west of where I left the truck the range ran due north. The track in had hugged a creek that cut through this range in a deep perpendicular gorge, which I had pinpointed on the map. I now had to climb to the top of the range and walk along the crest for some kilometres to reach the paddock in which my cattle were running.

I had two options—climb diagonally to the top or face it head on and get it over with. The load anchored me like lead as soon as I commenced the upward steps and I opted for a head-on climb. I had to scramble over two bands of rock and when I reached the summit, over two hundred metres up, my clothes were wet. Mercifully the weather was mild for central Queensland in January. The range at this point was higher than the broad tablelands to the north. I found myself on a genuine plateau, dead flat on top with steep slopes rising into cliff formations. I walked into a mob of Brahmans and, startled, they bolted for a little way and stopped. They didn't see humans much. Satisfied I was not a threat, a few cheeky ones followed me for a while, but kept their distance. I saw lots of kangaroos and wallaroos. Kangaroos are not often sighted on the Maranoa any more, since the roo meat industry took off. I think using kangaroo meat is a sensible solution to population reduction. The problem appears to be sustainable reduction. In Mitchell alone there are possibly ten young men who sleep all day to shoot all night. These men are efficient and can clean out an area very quickly.

There were still three hours of daylight left when I stopped for a rest at the fence of the paddock containing my cattle. A mob of red heifers grazed nearby, fat and shiny in their short-hair coats. These were some of the heifers that had come direct from Myall Plains in November. They were only about a kilometre from the cave spring and probably watered there.

For the next hour I walked through the bluegrass. Everywhere on the plain-like landscape were little groups of cattle. The entire herd was now feeding up here. I had not seen the cows look so good for two years.

The hidden camp site I had in mind was in a steep ravine—too steep and boulder-strewn for cattle. At the top end, close to the tableland edge, a small trickle of water supplied a couple of rock holes. The only problem was where to pitch the tent. It had to be concealed and the most hidden corners were all rock. Below the waterholes, where the sandstone commenced, a huge ironbark tree towered above a thick copse of lime trees. The tent would be obscured from every direction. I went into the trees and found a patch of ground free of rock. It was only when I collected the tent and carried it down that I felt uneasy about sleeping there. I rejected the site and finally settled on a flat piece of ground above a rock fall. It was thoroughly closed in with stout little trees, which

I think were a species of wattle. I made my tent poles out of the branches and the wood was hard enough to make crude tent pegs.

The collection of firewood was a bigger job than normal. I usually light a big log. The ashes stay hot and if I want a flame I only have to throw a few twigs on. Central and eastern Queensland hold high humidity levels throughout the summer and the incidence of bush fires is much less than in the southern states. On this job fires had to be small and could only be lit at night. I had to collect armfuls of scrap wood.

That empty feeling of hunger took hold long before dark and, sitting on a rock with no fire in a gloomy gorge of boulders and cliffs, I had a moment of self-doubt. I had been driven by anger to set up an arrest. Driven too by rumour and innuendo. Like the ratbag horse on race day—if you don't know, it's okay. Calm now, I began to accept the calf killing may have been the work of a drunken driver. The cattle were inclined to use part of the road as their trail.

Self-doubt is like a parasite when confronted with solitude. There is no one to talk to. Yet good could come out of this little commando exercise. If the tank was topped up and the cattle left alone I could go home. Divide my time. When I was away I could pay the blokes in beer to kick the engine up. A boil-over of wishful thinking, but for the moment it smothered those self-doubts.

I slept well and woke before dawn. With a quick billy boil I had the fire snuffed out as the first rays of the sun landed on the tree tops. If they were going to make a move on my cattle they would start early. I needed to be up on the tableland edge, traversing the bands of rock. Sound carries early in the morning before the heat stirs the air and the millions of leaves in the forest canopy begin to whisper to one another, swallowing all but the loudest of sounds.

For two hours I trekked north, keeping below the lip of the

tablelands. I heard cows and calves calling each other, the occasional screech from an eagle, once or twice the high pitch of a whistling kite, and the passage of one vehicle. By lunchtime I was satisfied nothing would happen that day. Back at the camp I was busting for a mug of coffee with a dash of powdered milk. Very rarely in my life have I been denied coffee at mid-morning and tea every other time. Smoke, unfortunately, just a wisp of it, can be detected fifteen kilometres away. Lunch had to be a few dry biscuits and spring water. I had to think about the rest of the day.

I had foreseen a lot of sitting around and jammed *Back o' Cairns* into the backpack. Weeks before I had decided to read about situations far worse than mine and just a few chapters into this book made my weeks feel like a prolonged picnic. The heat was on the lift again too, and past noon I needed to be occupied with a book. To the north storm clouds had gathered, lightning flashed far away and gusts of wind could be heard high up, as they passed through the skyline trees.

The curlews woke me before dawn. When I was a boy there were curlews in the timbered country of New South Wales. Some called them storm birds and others scream birds. By the late fifties the foxes had killed the last one. When I arrived out here I hadn't heard one for forty years and didn't recognise their high-pitched call until I saw a pair in the headlights one night.

A great variety of birds chattered away in the gorge for the first couple of hours after sunrise and I would have given anything for a bird identification book, a pair of binoculars and someone to say this whole exercise was a crazy dream. I had woken up with a different outlook. I boiled the billy again at eight o'clock and had a mug of coffee. To the north-east, maybe two hours hike, I had heard talk of a deep black canyon. I could be back for a late lunch and still have time to check the cattle.

The mere thought injected some enthusiasm into the day. I shouldered the haversack and left the rifle in the tent.

A slight breeze from the north stemmed a rapid rise in the heat and I took little notice of the puffy white clouds. The tableland plains gave way to steep rocky ravines and the vertical drop into the canyon pulled me up suddenly, not unlike the spectacular valley plunges seen west of Sydney in the Blue Mountains. The difference here was the colour. It was like looking into an eerie abyss. The cliffs were black and at the bottom huge scree slopes swallowed the canyon floor almost all the way to the dry watercourse. I found myself looking for vegetation and animals found nowhere else, but that of course was a reflection of my mood triggered by this sombre place.

Vegetation sprouted from the gullies and the crevices. Figtrees were in abundance and I was amazed to see so many kurrajongs. There was just one waterhole in this box canyon. Looking down a few hundred metres, the water appeared black like the rock. Anywhere I touched the rock it was fragile. It was a place I think the Aborigines left alone, for I felt it welcomed not a living thing. The figtrees, the kurrajongs and the rock-clinging shrubs were there under sufferance. Yet I had no sudden desire to leave and maybe time had stood still. Whatever it was I was quite taken by surprise when I heard a thunder clap and saw a streak of lightning.

I broke into a steady jog on the way back and after twenty minutes had good reason to curse my nervousness. All the surrounding country was covered with large round black stones. Their size varied upwards from that of a cricket ball. I stumbled on one and went close to a sprain. I got away with it, but had to walk with a limp. Dark clouds were massing from the southern horizon to the north.

Back in the gorge the first thing I did was gather wood and put it in the tent. I had watched one storm envelop a range far to the west and without doubt it was wind driven.

Not a breath of air stirred and the birds were silent. I hastily lit a fire, opened a tin of lamb casserole and tipped the contents into a billy lid for fast heating. Time had run out for a cup of tea and I placed the pannikin directly onto the flame to make coffee.

There appeared to be three storms threatening to break from the west. I watched with apprehensive curiosity and within the space of a few minutes they merged into one. The approaching dark mass took on a greenish underbelly, like the inside of a carcass let to rot in the sun. Dark fingers broke away from the mass, recoiling and changing direction like a bunch of serpents suspended in the sky. Then a roaring sound filled the air and I knew it was cyclonic force wind striking the opposite spur. I sprinkled some coffee into the pannikin, grabbed the stew and headed for the tent.

In the tent I stacked the wood to the windward side and tied the fly to the tent pole in three places. The sound made me think of an oncoming train about to burst from a tunnel.

Somewhere up on the range I heard a crack and a second later another, as though a great forest tree had been split to matchwood. It was a frightening portent of the fury of the gale and when it struck I thought the tent would lift despite the weight of myself and the wood. It blew out like a balloon, every tent peg let go and it seemed a miracle the seams held. I had a vision of being sucked into the tunnel of the tornado for the greatest ride of my life; albeit the last. Everywhere around me timber cracked and snapped. The volume of the wind went beyond a roar. It was more like the passing of a jet overhead. If there was lightning I never noticed and after the tornado the hail came but no relief from danger. The hail stones hit with wind-driven fury and with the tent pegs blown out I only had the canvas for protection. A drift of ice formed and ironically anchored the tent. If it had not been for driving rain coming on top of the hail I think the tablelands, which normally bake in a hundred degree heat on the old scale in January, would have been white under a mantle of ice.

The longest part of the storm was the rain. After the rain, shafts of sunlight flooded the gorge and I emerged from the crumpled tent to a strange stillness. Water ran down the gorge and miniature waterfalls sparkled in the sunlight. The birds had started their chatter again and as I walked around more and more voices joined in. A lot of trees had snapped at the trunk and those that stood as before shed cold drips of water. Compared to tropical heat the air was bracing and it reminded me of sunlight after a snow storm. I had a spare shirt, still dry in the backpack and I put it on over the one I was wearing.

From the edge of the rock fall I looked down into the lower gorge. Most of the vegetation had been blown down. Then I saw the tree, the huge ironbark. Two metres above ground it had snapped and the piece of ground where I had briefly planned to erect the tent lay under five tonnes of timber. Had I erected the tent there and sought protection in it, I would have been killed.

I didn't dwell on it. Back in the tent I remembered the dry wood and the cold stew. But it was warmth I wanted. I wanted a blazing fire to cheer myself up as well. Most of us, at some stage in our lives, cheat death. Usually it's a narrow miss on the highway. We try to imagine not seeing, hearing or feeling and it's totally incomprehensible. We are simply left feeling cold and empty. In a matter of minutes I might have recovered from the brief shock and thought no more of it. It was the billy that sent a cold shiver down my spine. Meaning to collect some water from a fresh rock pool, I picked it up, took off the lid, and there inside was the bottle top from a XXXX stubbie. Frankie had left his calling card. He only drank XXXX.

Too late I remembered I had been told that the Wild Bunch tracked everything. Every vehicle that passed through was noted. They knew the tyre prints of the police vehicles. If it wasn't a summons the police wished to serve (and rarely ever did), they would be there to ask questions about some robbery. The most recent incident had involved a shire bulldozer and a load of fuel on a trailer. Someone had taken the lot, even drained the dozer.

I had become so obsessed with the wanton mutilation of my calves I failed to recall what I'd been told. The big wheel tracks of the lorry would have been a breeze to the Wild Bunch. They had found it hidden and knew exactly what I was up to. Finding my camp was not a fluke either. Every spring and puddle hole was known to them. In my anger I had underestimated them. These men were specialists in outlaw survival. They were free of the pimps and informers that plague the rogues of urban society and therefore kept one step ahead of everybody.

I got the rifle out of the tent and checked the magazine. It hadn't been touched. Sometimes a sense of security is something in the mind. The Wild Bunch had rifles that could strike a man down at five hundred metres. My little Magnum would be viewed as a toy, except at close range. For my purpose it was ideal. The rifle is light to carry and the speed of the bullet is greater than that of the big guns. Under seventy-five metres the Magnum rifle is deadly. Yet the grim reality was the reverse of any perception of safety. With a gun in my hand I made it easy. If I was killed or harmed, a good barrister would seek a ruling of self-defence and win. It made good sense in one respect to hide the gun, but the unknown was their tracking ability. The ground was soft from the rain and if one of them was exceptional the gun would be found. If they knew I was unarmed, they could track me down without fear of an ambush or at the truck set up an ambush themselves and have no need to watch their backs. Such tracking skill in the modern world was unlikely and I had only ever seen it twice—in the Aboriginal who taught me as a child and in an American Indian from Montana. This poor young man had got Coolangatta and Coonabarabran mixed up at Sydney airport. When he arrived at Coonabarabran, nearly five hundred kilometres into the interior, he asked where the girls and the surf were to be found. The year was 1968 and American servicemen on R and R didn't have long. He should have been sent straight back to Sydney in retrospect, but Sally and I had him for the holiday and he could track any animal through sandstone. We think he was killed on his return to Vietnam.

I had got myself into a bit of a mess. In daylight it was four hours to the truck and the moon was into the dark cycle. To attempt to reach the truck at night without knowing the gang's whereabouts would be a panic reaction. On the other hand I couldn't stay where I was. For the moment I felt safe. The storms would have forced them to take cover, and nightfall was only an hour away. I decided to light a fire with the dry wood from the tent, cook a big feed and drink a billy of tea. I never went far from the Magnum.

In Ernestine Hill's *The Territory*, I have read many accounts of stockmen leaving their camp fires at night and sleeping at least a hundred metres away. They usually packed an old blanket, already full of holes, with anything they could lay their hands on and left it on the ground as a dummy. If hostile blacks were about a dawn raid was always on the cards and sometimes the dummy would be anchored to the ground with several spears.

The practice became unwritten law for stockmen in the Territory and as late as the early 1960s, stockmen in the Limmen Bight region, between the Roper and the McArthur rivers, still felt it prudent to set up the camouflage camps. The Territory spears caused gruesome and usually fatal injuries, due to the shovel-blade shape of the point.

Getting a decent sleep must have been near impossible and as I moved out into the dark and stepped carefully over the rocks I wondered how I could get comfortable enough to sleep. I had re-erected the tent in the same spot to give the appearance of a continuing camp.

I found a soft grassy spot up on the edge of the tableland. The cattle had eaten the old grass to ground level and the fresh green shoots were like a mattress. To stop the ticks burrowing into my skin I pulled my socks over my trousers. My shirt sleeves I buttoned at the cuffs. The only access was via my neck and that depended on how heavily I slept. My rest was fitful and light. The storms had done more than drench the ground. The invisible current of electricity had breathed life into the trees, the arid shrubs and the wilting grasses, and in the animals it triggered a zest for life. All night the possums made their strange blowing sounds and the native cats let forth their high-pitched shrieks, and if you didn't know what they were you would dream of large yellow eyes of the night. The wallaroos barked a warning and their telltale hopping thumps drifted through the clear night air from every direction. Only the dingoes bothered me. A chorus of answering calls began far away and at first I thought no more of them than other night sounds. Then close by there were two long howls. I drew my knees up into my chest and I screwed my head into the backpack which was my pillow. For the first time in months I wished for a blanket. The dog had smelt me. I had a vision of it searching for the scent; nose stretched out. It would soon leave, but that howl, that most lonesome sound of all living creatures, a sound that had echoed through these mountains for four thousand years, would hang on somewhere under my eyelids until the sleepy hour of dawn.

Faces floated by and then there was Sal. She was looking at me across a crowded room. Her hair seemed darker and her long evening frock captured the light. It wasn't a bright white, more a dull white and made of some high-quality material. She looked serene and stunningly beautiful. I walked towards her and she evaporated. I looked everywhere in that crowded room.

I woke with a start and the ground felt cold and damp underneath me. Only the stars were visible and away to the north, where the black canyon carved a trench in the earth's crust, the dingoes were wailing again.

Maybe I slept again for an hour or two, for the faint yellow of dawn seemed to arrive too quickly. I was stiff and cold and my mouth was dry, almost parched. I remembered I had left the water container near the tent.

Fearful of what daylight might bring I shouldered the backpack, picked up the rifle and crept back into the gorge. The policeman's words were reverberating in my mind and I wanted to get the water and get the hell out of the place.

I was letting my instincts guide me now and not giving much attention to any set plan. The truck and the bore were the least safe options. I could make a break for a homestead, but that meant leaving the protection of the range. If they saw me they could follow on horseback and shoot me way beyond the range of my rifle. The only safe place was the sandstone escarpments. If I trod carefully and kept changing direction they would never track me. In the thick clumps of wattle they would be hard pressed to see me.

Most people live their entire lives without ever once having to thwart a deadly form of pursuit. Those who have experienced it will know the most unnerving aspect is straining to hear. Every few minutes I stopped and listened. The clatter of a stone; a disturbed bronze-wing and the whirr of its wings; the nose-clearing snort from a horse—to hear anything out of the ordinary might have been expecting too much, for the bird life responded instantaneously to the increasing light. In the half light of dawn came the shrill call of the curlew, then as the sun reached the tree tops on the high points the magpies sang their dawn songs. Slowly the sun's rays crept into the valleys, the black cockatoos let forth their guttural squawks and the first to fly were the galahs.

Amongst the heaviest timber I could find I descended the basalt escarpments and headed towards the road. To reach the sandstone I had to cross the road. Vehicle sound is very tricky. If there is a slight head-on breeze it will smother sound downwind. When I reached the road I took a quick look either direction and crossed. The dash across might have taken less than eight seconds, but it was an awful moment of exposure. I kept moving quickly and two hours after sunrise I was well into the sandstone country. I began to feel the hollow pinch of no breakfast and opened the last of the casserole tins. It seemed to disappear in a few mouthfuls and I didn't care to think about the next meal. The rice I had left behind. It had to be cooked. The pasta I could soak in water and eat. The only quick and easy tucker from the scrub was the large white grubs. Under bark in shade areas enough of them can always be found for a meal, but they have a lingering taste which makes me spit for half an hour. It is little wonder the Aborigines of the interior quickly discarded their tucker for the white man's sugar and flour.

From a sandstone bluff I could see far across the valley to the south and the bore. The tank itself was out of sight, but I could spot little groups of cattle coming in for water. Everything was normal. For a while I felt safe.

The loneliness had gone. Maybe I had not been lonely to begin with, merely used to the normal mixing from day to day. In most land areas of the planet it is hard to imagine a world devoid of people. Here it was different. Everything went on as it should and to melt into such tranquillity posed a temptation, although it would be unthinkable for all but the insane. There's a frequently uttered phrase, 'Too much time to think'. The reality is, we modern people have too little time to think. If to dwell upon the world causes pain, then you are running.

I felt dirty and a bit ridiculous. I was grateful I couldn't see myself. In fact I think the sound of gunfire came as a relief. There must have been thirty or forty shots in rapid succession. They came from the tablelands. I waited. I watched the eagles circling, high up. When they see something foreign on the landscape they glide in for a peep. There was no sign of that. Clouds began to gather again and I began to sweat from the humidity. I knew there would be no second twister. In Australia it's a freak event—maybe once every three years. An afternoon storm would wipe any tracks and I could replenish the water container without going to the bore.

The storms contracted to the north. The sun re-emerged and the heat rose. In the wattle not a breath stirred and the kangaroo ticks could smell my sweat, for they moved in every time I shifted position. Brown and orange in colour they were easy to spot by their haste to get to me, a mammal.

By late afternoon I knew I had to go in for water. I wouldn't go in at night. A spotlight will show a man up, whereas the very shadows cast by the sun offer protection to the wary. Once in a spotlight there's no escape. Blinded totally, the victim is at the mercy of the marksman.

There was good cover all the way in. The hardest part was trying to avoid leaving a track. There were a few galvanised burrs which I stepped on. Cattle step over them and a good tracker would know. The best I could do was slow him down.

I must have gone in very well concealed because none of the cattle hanging around the trough saw me. I scaled the tank on the hidden side and using a stick with a hook on it I filled the container. The tank was only a quarter full. It should have been no surprise. I was near the end of the third day. The rain after the twister I thought may have provided some paddock water and given the tank storage another day. It didn't appear Frankie was going to start the diesel.

There was no one waiting for me at the bore and the cattle would drink the tank dry by noon the next day. I decided to start the bore. The fear, whether founded or unfounded, had begun to wane. If these blokes were as bad and as dangerous as everyone said I felt I would have seen some sign. I didn't read too much into the burst from an automatic. Guns were their life. They carried them like a city businessman carries a briefcase.

Nightfall closed on an uneventful day and back in the sandstone I slept better. Before bedding down I had to scrape clean a patch to sleep on and burn the little circle of leaves that made the perimeter. It was a slight risk. The smell of smoke carries on the slightest of breezes, particularly in the evening. But if I hadn't done it the ticks would have screwed into my body. Up in the tablelands there were not so many. Here among the wallabies and the scrub they lurked underfoot. I wasn't even sure the narrow strip of burnt ground would stop them.

I woke more hungry than scared. A mile or more to the south I could hear the chug chug of old faithful. The tank I knew would be more than half full. The birds probably began the day with the same order, but I didn't take it in. Through the night I had eaten the last of the tasteless pasta and thought the grubs might have been better. I know a lot about conserving energy and I knew that morning I had to get out while I still had the energy to outwit them or outrun them. At least I had to believe that. So far they were one step ahead of me.

No ticks had come through. The ground heat from the little fire would have soon cooled. The only thing I could put it down to was the smell of burnt leaves. The smell had smothered my body odour.

To ignore hunger all I needed was a distraction and that

arrived. The first sign was a flash of red hide in the timber. Sometimes cattle trot into water. But a headlong rush means they're fleeing from something. The eagles were not up yet. Lazy big fellows, they waited for the sun to warm the air and produce the updrafts. It might be mid-morning before I had their unwitting assistance.

I didn't expect to see any signs apart from the cattle. If they came it would be to run me down. One shot at five hundred metres would be enough. It's been written you don't even hear the shot, which spooked me all the more. I had a lookout and good cover. I waited. More glimpses of cattle running. They were mustering. The bore pumping—my presence confirmed—it was the last thing I expected of them. To them I was so ineffectual they were going to take a wing of cattle and let me watch. What they didn't know was that I had been through too much to let that happen. In the past I have forsaken my dignity and self-respect to achieve a peaceful result, only to be looked upon in contempt, and I have lived with the ghosts that consume the cowardly. I made an instant decision to stop the rustlers irrespective of all consequences. Like many decisions in my life, it was one of haste.

Before I started down into the valley I had to formulate a plan. If I came up against serious confrontation I didn't wish to be dragged into court as some sort of Rambo on the attack. Disarming them was the objective. If I could surprise them I could get their guns and send them home. The guns would be the evidence, but whether I could hide the guns and get to the nearest homestead on foot was a prospect I didn't care to dwell on.

Within sight of the bore I waited and watched. Working in pairs they were bringing in little mobs at a time. I had to wait until they were all together. That meant smoko or lunch.

I lay up in a patch of sandalwood. The heavy-leafed scrub absorbed the heat and held it. The sweat trickled down every part of my body and as the minutes went by the little tree ants got busier. The ticks I squashed with my boot. I found it nearly impossible to stay still, but so intent on the cattle were the stockmen I wondered whether they ever took a casual glance to see if I was around.

Late in the morning one pair dismounted after poking a mob of about fifteen head through the gate into the trough access paddock. It was difficult to calculate with so many trees obscuring my view, but I thought a hundred head in all had been mustered.

The two riders lit a fire and sat on a log. They seemed small. From a distance I couldn't be sure and the wide-brimmed hats made it harder. Perhaps they were women. Not long after, two more riders arrived. No cattle and they dismounted as well. I only had to observe their walk to know they were men. They too sat down on the long log and there appeared to be no attempt to boil water for tea. I scanned as hard as I could for signs of a rifle. Rumour in the district claimed they carried pistols.

Maybe half an hour later the last pair of riders came in with a few head of cattle. They didn't dismount though. There seemed to be a brief discussion and the other four remounted. It looked like I wouldn't get an opportunity. I expected them to turn the cattle out the gate and head off with them. Instead they commenced drafting on horseback. One rider worked as gateman, the two smaller riders who I thought may be women took no part and the other three worked their mounts among the cattle. The speed of the work was staggering. Most of the cattle were being let out—the poll Herefords, which were mine. From a distance it seemed they were turning back horny cattle and I only had three or four in the entire herd. I had to get closer. If they were taking only strangers I intended to stay out of it. It was a good time to move. All eyes were fixed on the cattle.

Only fifty metres from the fence I took cover behind the trunk of a big ironbark. I reached it just as the drafting stopped. I could see the cattle clearly now—about twenty-five head. Six or seven of mine were among them. The two small riders were female. All of them were still too far away to recognise. To my relief they all dismounted and tethered their horses back onto stumps, trees and low branches. The quart pots were removed from the saddles and filled from the trough. Some heavy sticks were thrown onto the fire. I waited until they were all seated on the log before leaving cover.

It seemed a long walk. What I hated most was carrying a rifle, cocked, ready to use against people. I don't like guns. I feel the civilised world has outlived their use in the backyard and the paddock. Rifles are now so sophisticated that hunters are having themselves on when they say it's a sport. I am a hunter too, but I dive with a speargun. The odds are still stacked my way, yet the fish I hunt have a chance. An error of judgement and I can drown within a few minutes. And always there is the shark and the fear and the privilege of entering a wild unspoilt world on its terms. What's more, guns are only an illusion of security. If someone wants to get you badly enough they will. And as I walked towards these people, gun in hand, I was doing it because I thought they may have guns. If one reached for a pouch, and these men of the bush had pouches slung on their belts, I had to catch in my sight what came out. These were the thoughts flashing through my mind as I reached the fence. The sweat poured off me. They still hadn't seen me.

The first rider to spot me was the tall bloke. I hadn't seen him before. He said something I didn't hear and all eyes focused on me. No one moved. I stopped about fifteen metres from the log. Their facial expressions were all different. I watched their hands intently. They all knew and kept them to the front. There was another bloke I hadn't seen before. A stockman type—good stamp of a man. He was clearly alarmed. Frankie looked at me as though he were trying to hold back a smile. The tall bloke seemed unperturbed, as though he saw this sort of thing every day. It was the woman and a girl who made me feel like digging a hole and jumping in. The woman was Jenny and she was clearly very frightened. The girl, tall for her age, looked on in fascination.

'What's goin' on?' I said harshly. 'You're in my paddock handling my cattle.'

The tall bloke rose and casually walked over to me and shook hands. It was cool. I admired his guts and I felt smaller still. He said his name and went back to the log. It was a gesture of genuine friendship. Almost without a word he said it all.

'Come to get the strays, Mick,' Frankie said smiling. 'Also got your cleanskins. We reckoned you'd show up, so thought it a good opportunity to plonk your brand on. You don't want unbranded cattle walkin' around the place in this country.'

Maybe I had struck a chord with someone, or were they testing me? Whatever it was I felt immediately humbled.

'I am sorry,' I said, and never in my life had I meant it so much. I took the magazine out of the rifle, ejected the bullet from the barrel and put the magazine in my trouser pocket. The bullet I left on the ground. 'There are so many bad rumours about this place. Then someone killed a calf and maimed another.'

'Been a bloke at that for a while,' Frankie said. 'Just another bastard tryin' to give us a bad name.'

There was a tree behind me and I leaned the rifle against the trunk. Then I took off the backpack and dropped it beside the gun. Anyone watching could see it was empty.

'When did you last eat?' Jenny asked.

'Only ran out today,' I said, still feeling acutely uncomfortable.

'We bought plenty of sandwiches,' she said, relaxed and her old self again.

'I've got food in my main camp.'

'There's more than we can eat.'

'Got some grog in that camp?' Frankie asked eagerly. 'Ride back over that range'd be so much easier.'

'Got rum. I'll get it.'

'No,' Jenny said sharply. 'He can wait until tonight. We got the cattle. Let's get back with 'em.'

I would have liked a drink, but I wasn't going to argue. Neither was Frankie. The other two blokes weren't interested. The tall bloke was older than me. He began talking about the cattle and the feed as though my intrusion was no more than that of a passing motorist. It broke the tension.

The corned beef sandwiches from the saddlebags were all put near the fire on a piece of bark and when the quart pots had boiled we started on them. I could have eaten half of them in five minutes. I ate slowly and kept my eyes off the pile.

'You got yer brand in the truck?' Frankie asked.

'Yes. I can make it to the truck in three hours. Pick up the tent on the way.'

'Take us two hours to the yards. You come up in the truck, we'll brand 'em and you can load 'em in the morning.'

'In the morning?' I queried.

Frankie had that smile again. 'You've had a quiet time out there. Better throw yer bunk in, stay the night.'

'Who tracked me?'

'We call him Boon. Half black. Mother was a full blood from Muckadilla. Does a bit of ringing here and there.'

I didn't ask any more questions such as where the strangers came from and all the different brands. I wasn't going to be told and it wasn't my business. The men drained their quart pots and I finished the tea from the quart pot cup Jenny had given me. The girl looked about twelve and chatted non-stop about her horse. To me the chatting was a sign that all the tension had gone. Maybe my appearance with a gun was nothing much out of the ordinary.

Everyone went to their horses and I picked up the gun, the backpack and the water container. At the camp I left everything. I could get a drink at the spring and from there I could walk to the truck without water.

CHAPTER 11

Dwellers of the Rangelands

When I got back to the truck I found the tracks of another vehicle. They were old tracks, made about the same day I came in. They had picked my tracks coming off the main road.

I drove back to my base camp at the bore and tossed the bed-roll into the float. There was no food worth taking up to the hut. I couldn't imagine any of the men eating rice. The only thing of any value was the rum. Before I left I turned the bore off.

It was late afternoon when I arrived at the hut. The last of the sun's rays caught the dust drifting from the yards. The heat hung in the air, like the dust, and through the amber light the cattle and the horses were slightly blurred. The horses, a dozen or more, were held in a small paddock joining the yards. In the yards two hundred head of cattle circled restlessly. The little mob brought up from the bore were in a separate yard.

The old fireplace at the front of the hut had a cluster of black billies and in the middle of a small flame was a cast-iron camp oven. Nearby on a four-gallon drum was a pile of tin plates. An assortment of cutlery emerged from a dented billy.

On winter camps everyone loves a log fire. On this midsummer camp no one wanted a bar of it. They all sat well away. Seats were scarce—swags, rusty four-gallon drums and old tyres.

I parked the truck near the yards and walked over to the group. The first thing I saw was the red bandanna on Johnny.

'Here comes Wyatt Earp,' he yelled out. I expect I deserved it. The first time he met me I was Starlight. I wondered who I'd be next time.

'Only Wyatt always had a woman,' someone countered.

Johnny giggled after almost everything he said. It was infectious and everyone laughed, although I could see some didn't know why they were laughing.

'Oh, he's got one alright,' Frankie added with that cheeky smile. 'He just doesn't want to know about her.'

I felt uncomfortable again and didn't know where to sit or what to sit on. The tall bloke produced a saddlecloth.

'Better sit on this, Mick,' he said. 'With the bloody dog burr around here you can't sit on the ground.'

Johnny had stopped giggling. 'Any of us would have done the same,' he said soberly. 'All them rustlin' stories would worry any bloke sick.'

'No one out of this camp's going to touch your cattle Mick,' the tall bloke put in. 'If you stay out here long enough you'll find there's no black and white. The country's hard. The men in it are hard and unforgiving. The women who follow them are hopelessly in love or insane.'

'I beg your pardon,' Jenny said indignantly.

Everyone laughed and I felt at ease. Someone had pushed a stubbie into my hand and I eagerly screwed the top off.

Anne and Johnny sat on the same swag. Josie had her own fold-up chair. In tight riding breeches she looked sexy and I had a feeling the camp would never be dull while she was about. Ike and his horsey girlfriend, Mary, were seated on an old truck tyre. They were talking quietly and I guessed the subject was horses. Frankie was into the beer and already had that glazed look in his eyes. Not that you saw his eyes much, as he looked everywhere but at the person he was talking to.

Seated on a couple of car tyres Lenny kept to himself. Like Frankie he was probably an alcoholic.

There were two blokes missing. One was the stockman I had seen at the bore. His name was Geoff. The other was the tracker. I hadn't met Boon. He was part Aboriginal and kept to himself.

Geoff wasn't far away. I just couldn't see him through the dust. He had been with the horses and when I turned to glance back at the yards I saw him walking over. The coming darkness brought the girl in as well. She had been wandering around through the timber. There seemed to be a simple, unspoilt radiance about her. Never having had a daughter, and a sister so much younger I never knew her, I found myself stuck for words. She asked me if I had any pets. Her whole life was probably pet animals. Twelve to fourteen years old, she may have only had patchy schooling.

'Sheep dogs and horses,' I replied. How boring! 'What do you have Clara?'

'I've got a wallaby at home. Everyone calls him a stinker, but I don't think he's a stinker, except when he gets in the house and does you know what. And I've got a hen. She follows me about and clucks a lot.'

The chatter went on and on. The men got back to talking among themselves and halfway through the second stubbie Jenny called from the fireplace.

'Come and get it.'

The meal was kangaroo stew with potatoes and carrots. The lean meat is delicious and has a slightly richer flavour than beef. Out here on these wild tablelands finding a roo for dinner was probably no more than a fifteen-minute hunt.

I sat next to Jenny to eat my plate of roo stew. She sat on a saddlecloth as well and had her plate between her legs. The stubbies were passed around again and Ike drove a battered

Mike on Circus at home on Myall Plains.

Millie, veteran of the Queensland adventure, with her pup by the half-dingo Caramel.

Sal in the Snowy Mountains, October 1994, while inspecting stock routes. A brief holiday from care.

Mike on Vodka Jack (third from the front). Leg injuries mean this might have been Mike's last race.

Mike with three of his sons at Claravale stockyards. L-R: Richie, Nick, Mike and Tom.

Loading weaners at Mount Kennedy for agistment at Jerilderee.

Roadtrain bound for Myall Plains. The weaners had two weeks' rest there before continuing south.

Approaching the pass, Mount Kennedy. This gives some idea of the wilderness of the area and the isolation of droving.

Typical droving camp. Each day the truck would be driven to the next campsite to set up in readiness for the horsemen who would slowly bring the cattle along.

Scalp was a crack shot and made money from shooting dingos for the bounty.

The dingos are 'scalped' and the skins taken to town as proof of the kill.

Mustering at Muckadilla bore.

Not a Wild West posse, simply the end of a long day in the saddle.

Newly repaired water trough, Mount Kennedy. The trough was supplied from a fibreglass tank.

The black hole at Mount Kennedy where some of the cows, desperate with thirst, were trying to drink toxic mud.

Tableland camp, winter 1995. Sal, Richie, Nick and Tom all helped out on this trip.

Selling the cows from Amby Creek, Roma sale yards, January 1995.

Cranking up the old diesel engine, Mt Kennedy. Pre-World War II equipment is still to be found in the Outback.

Smokie branding at Claravale. The calf is held in the cradle while the brand is applied.

looking ute up to the side of the hut and slipped a Bruce Springsteen tape into the player.

Johnny must have decided beer was too tame and he poured himself red wine from a flagon. Just the look of the flagon sent a wave of biliousness through my stomach. Next thing Lenny emerged from the edge of the lantern light and Johnny filled his pannikin. He was never called Lenny, I soon found out, only Pig's Arse. He had probably been called that for years and saw it as part of his acceptance in the clan.

'They don't mind you Mick,' Jenny said after a mouthful of beer. 'They see you as one of them. Doesn't matter about your cattle or whatever else you got.'

It was no good saying I had inherited an estate left in a shambles, because these people had nothing. They shared that rare freedom bestowed upon the poor. There was nothing to lose. Only their lives could be taken from them.

'What did they all do before?' I asked. I began to feel the third beer relax me and whether I was one of them or not, I might as well be.

'Before everything collapsed, you mean?' Jenny said and went on without waiting for me to comment.

'Ringers, shearers, fencers and Mack, the tall bloke,' she gestured towards him, 'he followed sheds all over western Queensland. Top woolclasser. Today the survivors class their own wool.'

She must have read my mind, because I didn't like to ask.

'Money's hard to come by. Most now are on the dole. Not these blokes. They live on their wits—grab a day's wages here and there.'

One pannikin of plonk and Johnny was away. The swags, old tyres, drums and saddlecloths were carried in to make a circle around two lanterns while Johnny danced with total abandon. He pulled Anne to her feet and Josie dragged Pig's Arse by the arm into the dirt and ash-trodden floor. I didn't think a bayonet would jerk him into action, but once the fat joints loosened up he demonstrated superb rhythm and eyes that were normally half closed began to bulge with animation. Josie would have held the floor anywhere. She glided around Pig's Arse like a butterfly and loved teasing him.

'Like this every night?' I could feel the beat myself. Apart from Muckadilla, I hadn't danced for two or three years.

'Every night,' Jenny laughed. 'We girls might have a couple of nights here. Can you see Josie washing herself out of a horse trough for a week? But the men love it out here. It's freedom. The strict behavourial rules of modern society don't exist here.'

Geoff got up on his feet and coaxed the little girl to dance with him.

'Clara loves the bush,' Jenny said, delighted to see her daughter laughing. 'The simple things are missed by children in the towns. Television and the video have destroyed initiative.'

Jenny spoke two languages. Away from the bars and direct contact with these rough-speaking men she was honest and articulate.

Springsteen bawled out 'Born in the USA' and the stockman swung Clara round in an old sixties rock 'n' roll style till her black hair spun out almost level with her eyes and she began to giggle. Pig's Arse was mouthing the words, sweating profusely and stamping like a caveman. Ike and Mary had shifted beyond the lantern light. Frankie just sat on his drum, looking at Josie through heavy eyes.

'Where's Scalp?'

'Pulling scrub. Everyone wants scrub pulled. Fear of native title and God knows what else.'

'Good money?'

'An acre of wilderness is worth twelve dollars.'

The cost squeeze was having a devastating effect on Australia's last vast belt of forest—central Queensland. The profit margin per beast had become so low, survival depended on numbers. The problem with old fragile soils is vividly demonstrated once they are exposed to the wrath of the sun and relentless wind. In a good season the introduced buffel grass will provide tonnes of feed per hectare, but the ideal season may appear once in three years. More often than not the wind and the sun rapidly burn the feed off and in the winter frosts destroy any nutrient left in the old feed. There is no doubt that buffel grass increases carrying capacity, but exposure to the boom and bust cycle of the seasons is doubled. If farmers would only leave a sprinkling of trees when they clear, exposure would be minimised. I have been on a property northwest of Roma where this was done. The carrying capacity per hectare was the highest in the region and sucker growth had not been a major problem.

The tragedy for the Australian interior appears to be locked up in our inability to destroy the image of the wealthy pastoralists. For more than a hundred years the elite were those kings in grass castles. Right across society there was a feeling of envy and jealousy. The bitter shearing strikes of the 1890s aptly demonstrated the feeling in the community. Today the only wealthy pastoralists are those with off-farm investments. A farmer with an income above what middle-income earners make in any city would be exceptional. There are a handful of wheat tycoons and the cotton farmers are probably on borrowed time, considering the level of pesticide resistance now apparent in the United States. Yet if a politician were to announce a direct commodity subsidy his or her political career would cease to exist. The Australian community will never tolerate a commodity subsidy to owners of rural land. And sometime in the next century historians will be lecturing students about the great agrarian blunder in Australia's pastoral industries. Apart from those surviving in National Parks, the great belts of pine and brigalow will be gone. Wind and water erosion will have compounded to cause such massive environmental problems that legislation will have to be passed to remove all environmental power from state governments and place it in the hands of the Commonwealth.

Of course not to clear at all is as short-sighted as drastic clearing. The native pine has a short lifespan and there is nothing more useless to farmers or cattle than a thick patch of brigalow scrub. The Aborigines before us systematically burnt patches every year. The whole Australian environment of the interior had been adapted to the fire cycle for thousands of years. Australian archaeologists refer to Aborigines as the firestick farmers. Their methods were imprecise and there would have been instances of overkill, but they definitely understood the need for balanced preservation.

Geoff and Clara stopped dancing. They sat on the ground beside Jenny and Mack joined us as well. Johnny offered us his plonk and told us we had no heart for not drinking the stuff. Josie had danced Pig's Arse to a standstill and hauled Frankie to his feet. He wasn't keen on dancing, but if Josie said jump he did.

We yarned until midnight and before that hour we shifted towards the fire—at six hundred metres above sea level the nights cooled off. The stars sparkled, an owl hooted, and the possums squawked and raided the camp for titbits. At last I threw my bed-roll onto the ground and fell into a deep sleep.

I woke to the smell of camp fire smoke and the sun in my eyes. The cattle were hollering and dust drifted from the yards on a light northerly breeze. The temperature felt perfect. If it could have locked in at seventy degrees Fahrenheit for the day I might have sprung off the swag and headed for the trough.

But before smoko time it would be knocking at the old hundred.

From the yards I heard 'Whoa there, whoa there.' I raised myself on one elbow and watched Geoff catch a horse. Mack stood among the horses too, bridle in hand. A little closer I could hear water being splashed. Ike and Mary were at the trough. 'And wash under yer armpits,' I heard her say to him.

In the opposite direction smoke drifted away from the camp fire. A little figure sat near the fire, almost huddled, as though cold. It was Anne. Jenny stood over the billies. One was near the boil and I knew the tea-leaves were in her hand. Clara stood away a bit, bent over. She was feeding something. At a distance my eyes were down a bit on small objects. 'He's already eaten half the cheese,' Jenny growled. When she was irritated she had the voice of a woman whose hormones are not quite right. I still couldn't see, but I expected a possum was overdue for bed.

Away a bit to the left of the camp fire, maybe thirty metres, a crumpled heap lay under a blanket. An empty flagon lay on its side. Beyond him two figures lay entwined. Not a move from either. And where was Pig's Arse? The vehicles were scattered all over the place among the trees. I saw a pair of boots sticking out of the window of one of the utes.

I took my turn at the water trough and walked over to the camp fire looking for a mug of tea. On the way from the trough I passed by Johnny. A heavy-calibre rifle lay beside him. I strayed off course to get a closer look at Frankie's swag, which at twenty-five metres looked like a big lump under a blanket, and sure enough a rifle lay beside him as well. No one noticed me until I reached the fire.

'How did you know I just made it?' Jenny said, greeting me with a smile. She hadn't been to the trough and it would have helped.

'I saw you watching the billy. And Clara you were feeding a possum.'

'Possum in the daylight!' Clara exclaimed, as though I should know better.

'A cheeky bloody goanna,' Jenny growled. 'Feed the bastards once and they're everywhere but in yer bed.'

I said good morning to Anne and she nodded, but with no enthusiasm for the day. Johnny had bombed out and I wouldn't have liked being near his breath.

'Get some toast and jam into you Mick.'

Jenny had given Anne a mug of tea and let her be. I soon got the feeling Jenny didn't want to hang around the camp fire for long.

By the time I had eaten some toast Mack and Geoff had walked across from the yards. Their horses were saddled and tethered to the rail. Ike and Mary were in the process of catching their mounts. The plan which emerged from breakfast conversation was for the four of them to run the big mob of horses in from the ranges. They spoke of them as the brumbies, but in actual fact breeding was strictly controlled with just one stallion.

The cattle in the yards were the responsibility of Johnny and Frankie. Jenny thought they would have to be let out into a holding paddock as neither of them would swing into a saddle today. Where the cattle came from and where they were going was not my business and no one made me any the wiser.

The two stockmen were after horses. Geoff was a contract musterer and it seemed Mack was doing part-time work for him. The work was infrequent and over twelve months earnings were less than those of a stationhand, but it was a life in the saddle and freedom. I told them I knew solicitors in Sydney who earned more money in one year than they would see in a lifetime, yet would trade them places tomorrow if circumstances allowed.

I didn't feel very comfortable in the camp, even though no-one had been unfriendly. I drained my tea mug and went over to the yards where I gathered an armful of dead wood from under an ironbark and lit a fire. I waited for the red coals to form and put the brand on, which I always had with me in the truck. I wanted to brand the cleanskins, load up and get out of the place.

Most cattle yards have a long narrow race where work can be performed on the animals at close quarters. I needed a hand and it was Jenny who volunteered. I stood on top of the race, leg either side and she passed me the brand from the fire. The brand had to be returned for reheating after each beast. Cattle have exceedingly thick hides and although they jump a bit when the brand's plonked on, it doesn't hurt them much. The cleanskins were cows and had missed out on their brand when they were calves. Either they missed out in the muster or they were out-of-season calves.

With Jenny's help I loaded them onto the truck and took them down to South Bore where I jumped them off, near the trough. There was an unloading mound there.

I did a bit of camp straightening and then left for Amby Creek. There was still a big mob there and not much feed. I didn't want to sell them. Cows are a breeding man's capital, but the only country available was the north-west portion of Mt Kennedy and I had been told the bore was out of order. That could be fixed of course, but the presence of the Wild Bunch had me deeply disturbed.

The Old Boy was away and I didn't feel like driving eighty kilometres back to the camp. It was hot and I felt exhausted. I continued south and at the Muckadilla pub took one of their rooms. I had a shower and when I hit the bed I didn't wake until late afternoon.

In the bar Donna had a message for me. 'That bunch from up there,' she said and rolled her eyes. 'They dropped in for

a drink and wanted to talk to you. I told them to leave a
message with me.' She paused and handed me another beer.
'They've gone to the rodeo at Taroom and wanted you to
throw the horses some hay in the morning. Also check the
water trough.'

'They're breaking in several young ones,' I said. 'I saw the
hay in a trailer.'

'How do they know you'll be back up there?' Donna asked.

'Pump water. My cattle are drinking thirty thousand litres a
day.'

'Seems out of character to me,' she said.

'What do you mean?'

'They wouldn't give a stuff about them.'

She was wrong, I felt. The breaking might have been on the
rough side, but they wouldn't leave the horses locked up
without feed. It was their general behaviour in the hotel she
disliked so much.

'In effect you're saying someone wants me to go to those
yards.'

Donna shrugged. 'Just watch yourself.'

I was getting weary of the rumours and the innuendoes. I
had made a fool of myself the day before and the whole thing
was getting to me. I thought no more about it.

I left at daylight next morning and two hours later reached
the turnoff to the yards. There was a vehicle track—fresh.
Vehicle tracks didn't stay fresh for long, because kangaroos,
wallabies, goannas and snakes were continually on the move.
These tracks were no more than four hours old. I decided to
walk and have a peep from the protection of the forest before
I drove in.

I locked the truck and with the magnum for protection, I
went in through the pine forest. Three hundred metres from
the yards I skirted away to the side, crouched low, my head
level with the taller grasses. I reached a wide gully that ran

down the slope towards the yards before it swung away to the left. I instantly spotted the roof of a vehicle and when I moved a little closer I saw it was an old model Holden. It was an assortment of colours, as though someone had started to re-duco and abandoned the task.

The sides of the gully were thick with sandalwood and it was some minutes before I could focus on two men. They were carefully hidden in the sandalwood, frozen still, looking into the timber in the direction of the truck. They had heard the truck and were expecting me. I could surprise them from behind, risking confrontation. But one bolt-action gun against two was hopeless odds. I backed off and when I left the pro-tection of the sandalwood I got down on my elbows and knees for about two hundred metres until the forest had closed off all around me. Whoever they were, they had made the decision for me. I would sell all the cows and calves at Amby Creek. Upon reaching the truck, I headed for Roma to make the arrangements with Dalgety's.

I arrived in Roma in the late afternoon and went straight to Dalgety's before they closed. On the way in I'd had a quick look at the cattle at Amby Creek. The feed had cut out in my absence. I discussed the situation with the manager at Wes-farmer's and he agreed I had no alternative but to meet the market. There was no agistment in the district and every drover was tied up with a mob. Bleaker still, the drought looked like extending into the whole of western Queensland. He predicted that if no rain fell before the end of the month the store market in Queensland would collapse. It was the Queensland store market that had put a floor in the market for drought-stricken New South Wales cattlemen desperate to sell. The elimination of this market spelt total collapse. In fact the only feed in eastern Australia south of the tropic line was in the Augathella and Charleville districts where there had been storms. He said my cattle would go there. It seemed I was lucky to have buyers so close.

It was approaching mid-January. With the Hamilton boys— Annette the 'switchboard's' brothers—to help, I mustered up about two hundred cows on Amby Creek and sent them to Roma by roadtrain. Taking two days the Dalgety men split the cows and calves into twenty-head lots and the dry cows were drafted out for Mt Kennedy. I anticipated the market would be tough and decided not to sell them.

While the drafting was going on in the Roma saleyards I bought some Santa Gertrudis bulls and floated them out to Mt Kennedy. I still had to keep going out there to run the bore, no matter how busy I was. I wasn't needed at the yards and I decided to camp the night and return to Roma early next morning for the loading of the dry cows and about thirty weaners.

It was a Monday. It just seemed like another routine day— check the bore, cop the heat and snatch a beer whenever possible. When I got to the Roma yards there was a semitrailer waiting for the cows and the pen of weaners were waiting for me.

A very willing young man, Stephen, was the driver of the semitrailer. He and his boss loaded the semi first and I pushed the weaners into the loading yard just as Stephen bolted the semi's loading door.

The whole western end of the Roma saleyards is a raised ramp stretching for fifty metres. Several loading chutes terminate at the edge of the ramp. Roadtrains load from the side and smaller trucks are backed into these chutes. The edge of the loading ramp is plated with steel and when I put my right hand on the steel to do a little jump off the ramp I was unaware it had only minutes before been replaced and welded at the joins.

The shock of pain sent me reeling. I fell sideways and down

the side of the ramp. My right leg buckled underneath me and I thought I had broken it. The pain was swift and intense. I tried to steady myself and control my breathing. For a few seconds I didn't want to look. I expect all of us receive a shock of pain from a minor accident in almost any year, and after a minute or two it goes away. I can remember screwing my eyes shut, waiting for that pain to go away so I could get on with my work. It didn't and I made myself look down. The leg was bowed inwards. Accidents have the same effect on all of us. You cannot believe your personal situation can change so drastically in the space of two seconds.

It is more than one hundred and forty kilometres from Roma to Mt Kennedy. The driver of the semi had not the faintest idea where the cattle were to be unloaded and there was no one else to drive my truck. Furthermore, the cattle had not been fed since the previous afternoon. The owner of the trucking firm didn't think I could make it, but when I explained the situation to him they loaded my truck.

With only weaners aboard, my truck only had about six tonnes in weight and I found I was able to operate both the clutch and the brake with my left leg. The injured leg I placed on the accelerator and lifted it off when I wanted to stop. It wouldn't have worked on a busy highway!

If we could have simply jumped the cattle off on the side of the road I may have received medical attention by early afternoon. These cattle, however, were strangers to the paddock. They may have followed the other cattle to water, but in 100 degree Fahrenheit heat the risk was unthinkable. They had to be unloaded in the bore access paddock.

The track into the bore was narrow. I had no problems with my truck and unloaded the weaners near the trough. Because of the timber, the driver couldn't turn the semi directly onto the track. He had to manoeuvre the big long vehicle to get a straight entry. I checked the ground for him and thought it was okay. To my horror I saw the front cabin wheels sink in the sand, right up to the axle. I hobbled over and wondered how the hell I had directed him in there. I think he did too, but he was one of those very decent placid blokes.

There was only one thing to do. Unload sixteen cows at a time into my truck and shuttle them to the trough. My knee had become very swollen and the fluid had formed a sort of casing, allowing me to put a little weight on the leg without it giving way. I didn't know then, but the two principal ligaments had been seriously damaged. My hand felt raw and very sore, but compared to the leg it was no more than a scratch.

The next hour and a half must have been one of the worst I have ever put in. Stephen couldn't help me. He had to get in with the cows and count sixteen out each time. Standing among cranky cows that are hot, tired and thirsty can be very dangerous. Not because of bunting, but because of savage kicks.

For me the nightmare was opening the heavy sliding door to let them out on a raised mound near the trough. Normally the door is simply pushed open at ground level, using thigh and back muscles. I had to haul myself up the side of the float and kick the door open with my left leg. It only took three or four kicks, but the shot of pain from each kick can only be described as excruciating. The right leg was only hanging and I don't know why that happened.

With the cattle off, the next problem was the semi. I carried a heavy chain and when it was hooked between the rear of the semi and my truck there was sufficient length in it to allow the rear wheels of the truck to get a solid grip on the road. Not having any weight left in the semi was a great help and after a lot of tedious hand-scraping around the semi's front wheels we managed to extract it by about four o'clock. Stephen had been driving throughout the previous night and looked about as close to collapse as I have ever seen a man. When I set out for Roma hospital I felt as sick as he looked. I soon knew I couldn't make it to Roma and headed for Mitchell. At the hospital they strapped my knee and gave me a set of crutches and some painkillers. I went on to Muckadilla and I don't remember much—in fact I don't remember arriving.

Some of the pills were sleeping tablets I think. I woke in the morning with a heavy head and dull ache right through my leg. I went to sit up and saw my hand, as though for the first time. The first layer of skin was peeling off. I felt the soft breeze from a fan and there was a jug of water beside the bed. In disbelief I looked at the crutches lying on the floor by the bed. Time seemed to float and I became aware of a woman in the room.

'You'll have to have a shower,' she said quietly. 'I've brought you some plastic. When you feel up to it, tie it around your leg to keep the bandages dry.'

I don't know whether she dressed my hand or I did it, but there was a problem holding the right crutch. Eventually I got going and drove the truck to Roma where I called at the hospital to have my hand examined. Then I went to the sale.

It was the worst cattle sale I had seen since the crash of the mid-seventies. Little did I know then there was much worse to come in 1996. The auctioning went on all day to clear a massive five thousand head. It was like listening to bursts of machine-gun fire and overhead the sky rumbled and lightning flashed on the western horizon. That night it rained inches. It came too late.

12 Bore Crisis

After the sale I drove back to the Muckadilla hotel and lay on the bed for a while. Early in the evening, when it had cooled off a little, I telephoned Sal. Her immediate reaction was to fly up and be with me. Nick and Greg were ploughing up country around the clock. There had been some rain and Sal had seized upon the opportunity to fallow for wheat. I explained there was nothing she could do for me. At that stage I had hoped it would be simply a matter of rest. Reluctantly, Sal agreed to stay and look after Nick and Greg. Shift work on the tractor is tiring and incredibly boring. Good meals and a cheerful face when you come in are essential.

The only public telephone was a hundred metres down the road from the hotel. It seemed quite a way on the crutches and on the way back I had plenty of time to take the weather in. A huge bank of clouds had formed in the west, blocking the sun and casting a sombre light across the plains. The sweat poured off me. It was going to rain in tropical fashion and I was thinking about this when shots exploded from the other side of the village. Dogs yelped and there were more shots. I swung my way into the bar and bought a bottle of rum. The bloke behind the bar I hadn't seen before. In late middle age, he looked distinguished and retired from a profession quite different to running a country pub. It turned out I was right.

He was a retired man from Brisbane and just relieving.

'How did the sale go?' he asked cheerfully.

'It was okay on the day.'

He nodded gravely. 'The leg?'

'There's two sorts of painkillers. Pills or rum. The rum tastes better.'

He laughed. 'What about a good meal? Judy's getting fidgety in the kitchen.'

The hotel specialised in fish. God knows where it came from, but top quality frozen fish was brought in from the coast. With a few rums and a good meal I felt a lot better. Of all the western pubs I've had a beer in, New South Wales included, this one had a unique homely atmosphere.

Even though it was a Tuesday night, the local farmers soon filled the bar. One couple and their children took up a table next to me for dinner. The bloke had a beard flecked with grey and a straight-brimmed hat. He said his name was Gil Campbell and he owned Claravale Station, north of Mt Kennedy. I was instantly tempted to ask him about the October duffing raid the visitor to the bore had mentioned, but it was none of my business.

The crutches aroused interest, something I found I had to get used to, and Gil Campbell told me he had a steel plate in his knee. He had gone to pull a bore and when he climbed the anchor pole to attach the block and tackle, the twelve-metre pole gave way. That he survived was a miracle.

'I am not fifty yet,' he said. 'But by fifty there are not many of us left unscarred. You got past fifty before this!' He grinned. 'Then you got a bonus.'

What he said was true and I hadn't thought about it before. In Queensland the risk of serious injury on a property is high. There's isolation, rugged terrain, cattle not often handled and half wild horses, not to mention the heat which saps concentration.

I drank half the bottle of rum and I don't know how I got to my room on the crutches. The rain began about midnight and next morning the Muckadilla creek was a banker. If it had not been for the relieving manager and his wife, the next three days would have been miserable.

They had a copy of a manuscript called 'Black and White', by Blagden Chambers. In 1865 Chambers set out alone with one packhorse from what is thought to be Chesterton Station, not far to the north-west from where my cattle were. He was looking for new pastures on the upper Warrego and indeed found bluegrass tablelands, similar to those I have already mentioned. But during his ride north he saw stark evidence of atrocities committed by the Mounted Native Police which apparently had the sanction of the colonial government. A tragic but all too common story of those days, but what makes this account unique is Chambers' actions in preventing further bloodshed, and the friendship that was shown to him in return.

It was a Saturday when I left Muckadilla. If it had not been for the crutches I would have left a day earlier, but I had to be sure the roads were dry enough. To bog the truck and then swing my way to the nearest station in the heat was an endurance test that may have been beyond me. I wasn't worried about the cattle. The rain had been general across the Maranoa and I thought there would be some surface water.

When I arrived at Mt Kennedy I was surprised how quickly the puddles from the rain had dried up. I still hadn't got used to the high component of sand in all of the country here, except the high basalt tablelands. Water on the ground one day; gone the next.

At the tank there was a day's supply left. I went over to the bore and put the two crutches on the ground. Holding the compression lever I could stand on my good leg and I bent down to pick up the crank handle. It was then I saw the tracks.

Someone had come to the bore since the rain. I tried to see through the shadows of the surrounding timber and saw a dingo lurking a hundred metres away. One of the calves, still sick from the germ-infected water of the black hole, had died. The smell of the carcass invaded the whole area and as I stared at the footprints the smell grew stronger. I picked up the crank handle and started the engine.

I waited by the bore. Ten minutes and still no water. Sometimes the valve a hundred and fifty metres below got sediment trapped in it and let all the pipe water leak out. If that happened it took twenty minutes for water to appear. After twenty-five minutes I stopped the engine and sat down on one of the diesel drums. Cattle were streaming into the access paddock to drink at the trough.

It was times like this I headed for the 'switchboard'— Annette. I hadn't seen any of my friends in Mitchell for about two weeks. I went into the bakery and received the usual burst of mirth.

'I heard there was a war out there,' she said. 'Looks like you're losing.'

I never went into the bakery without having the delicious coffee Annette served. Better still, she always found time to have a cup with me. As always, she knew who to go and see. His name was Rob Carr and he lived only a block away.

'And you can't camp out there in that condition,' she added firmly. 'There's a room in our house and that's where you stay.'

Rob Carr's wife, Caroline, told me he was at a bush fire brigade conference and wouldn't be back until Sunday night. The good news was he would definitely fix the bore.

I knew the cattle would run out of water on Sunday and I knew they would be alright if they got a drink on Monday. In emergency situations it was usually possible to have water carted in with shire tankers. Following the heavy rain the dirt roads would take no weight and even if they did, a big lorry tanker would never make it through the sand-based soil to the trough.

I tried to shut my mind to it and drove out to the racecourse to see Bill Anderson.

'They got ya,' Bill said grinning.

'No, it was . . . '

'No need to explain. Lucky the bullet never went through your head.' When Bill laughed his whole chest shook. 'Now this horse. He's burnin' the track up. Wandoan's this week. We got to go there.'

I hadn't seen Vodka for two weeks. He'd gone from a daggy-looking hack in November to a muscled-up racehorse with a sleek dark brown coat. I could see he was restless. He was never quite at ease with humans and never entirely settled into a stable routine. I waited by the rails of his exercise yard and he walked up to me, just briefly. He kept looking at me with one eye, never taking it away, as though I alone might understand him.

I had seen the look before and later listened to the jockeys. Then maybe it was my mood. Bill and I went inside and we had another one of those very long tea breaks. Afterwards I went out to Annette's home, Rowallan.

The family made me feel very welcome. I have never seen a homestead in my life where so many people came and went in any given hour between midday and midnight. I settled back with a rum and found myself yarning with a bull rider, only he wouldn't be riding again for a while—his whole arm was set straight in plaster. Next minute Annette's brother Jamahl burst through the door with his electric guitar and sang his version of 'The Boys from the Bush'. I would have given anything to have heard this version sung at a conservative picnic race ball down south. Noel, who'd been minding the poddy calves, didn't say much sober, but as the rums went down his eyebrows shot up in rapid jerks and he didn't shut up. Kids wandered in and out, some of the prettiest little girls I have ever seen, and somehow Noel's wife Joan got the last word in. At some stage in the evening Annette fetched me to have dinner with her and her husband, Billy.

On Sunday the Rowallan camp remained as diverse as before. On the verandah there was guitar practice and out in the workshop two or three blokes tinkered with cars and trucks. I found a quiet spot and read. Never far from my mind were the cattle.

On Monday morning Rob Carr, Caroline and I left Mitchell very early. They followed me out to Mt Kennedy. It was to be a three-person team—Rob to disconnect the rods, Caroline in the four-wheel drive and me on the big rod spanner.

To pull the bore, a steel-cable pulley had to be secured to the top of the fifteen-metre bore pole. Steel spikes led the way to the top and Rob climbed up to assemble the gear. Then a clamp was attached to the rods and the four-wheel drive took the weight. Caroline reversed until Rob raised his hand, which indicated the join onto the next rod had risen above the level of the bore. I placed the rod spanner under the join and, obeying another signal, Caroline drove far enough forward to lower the spanner across the bore pipe. With the weight of all the rods below resting on the spanner, Rob was able to disconnect the rod above ground. Another signal and Caroline drove forward to lower the rod so Rob could lay it along the ground.

The monotonous procedure seemed to take hours. I felt the swelling increase in my leg and every time I looked for a brief escape I saw the white faces milling around the dry trough. Late in the morning we stopped to boil the billy. There were at least three hundred cattle at the trough now and they were beginning to make a bit of a din. I don't think any of us enjoyed the tea much, but with the heat rising again we had to have a short break.

By early noon we had all the rods up and inspected the

leather buckets in the pump. There appeared to be nothing wrong and this disturbed us. Reluctantly, we spent the next three hours returning the pump and rods down the bore. The last rod was the one that pushed the pumping buckets into the pump cylinder. It wouldn't go in. The buckets refused to slide into the pump.

It was very serious now. The cattle were becoming more and more vocal. There were now five hundred venting their misery. I have never seen it, but western Queensland stockmen have told me cattle will pass into a mindless panic without water and self-destruct by running and overheating.

Rob and Caroline commenced the re-pull. All the pipes would have to come up and Rob needed at least one strong man to help him. I didn't know what was going on up at the hut, but it was worth a go. When I got there the horses were in the yard and Scalp was there himself with Ike and Pig's Arse. They rallied immediately and back at the bore Rob and Caroline were more than halfway, despite being a man short.

The pulling went on through the night and into the early hours. Caroline reversed the Toyota to haul out the last pipe and the pump cylinder screwed on at the bottom.

The cylinder was full of shale. The bore had been sabotaged. No one said anything. We washed the shale out and with his newfound offsiders Rob began the massive task of lowering twenty-five lengths of pipe and the same number of rods. Caroline had been relieved from the Toyota and I had ceased to be of any use before the sun set. The men worked from the lights of my truck. The cattle intensified their din and seemed to focus their attention on us. It was as if they knew we could help them—I am sure they did.

Not long after dawn every piece had been reconnected. Scalp kicked the old diesel up and we all stood there and waited for the water.

First the air came, then the gurgles, more air . . . then that wonderful sound of water falling on the dry bottom of the tank. Minutes later there was feverish activity at the head of the long trough. For hours the poor things jostled and pushed one another and it may have been mid-afternoon when the last thirsty animal got its fill.

Everyone was exhausted. Bore pulling is not only hard work, but demands a hundred percent concentration. We didn't even boil the billy. Rob and Caroline went back to Mitchell. Scalp and his men headed back to the hut. I slept in the tent and didn't wake until late afternoon. The fluid on my knee forced me to re-adjust the elastic bandage.

I stepped outside with the crutches and had a look around. Most of the cattle had gone. Hungry after their drink, they had headed up into the tablelands. It was such a relief I didn't think much about my leg. I had a yearning for about three mugs of coffee and slowly collected some wood.

No one had uttered a word about the shale in the pump. Whatever you might do in the outback, don't be a trouble-maker. It's unwritten law in the Australian bush, and I think maybe it's a unique character trait known only in this country.

I don't know who sabotaged the bore. The stakeout was an impulsive reaction to the calf killing and maiming (the injured calf died within a week), sparked by anger. The Wild Bunch would have been very disturbed. The bore may have been to force me to muster up quickly and head for the nearest water, which was towards Mitchell. In short: get rid of me. They didn't know I was injured and I would never accept that they intended the cattle to perish.

While I sat drinking coffee and breathing in the smoke, for I am addicted to camp fire smoke, I suddenly remembered the horses. They hadn't come in for water. A feeling of dread over-took me and I felt like burning the crutches. With two good legs I could have started looking instantly and hopefully had peace of mind for the night.

I hadn't brought any fresh food out. When we left Mitchell I'd thought we'd pull the rods, charge the buckets, drop everything back and head back to town. Anyway, rice and stew out of a tin was always tasty with a heap of herbs thrown in and all washed down with rum. I made sure I slept okay.

I left the tent soon after dawn and didn't have much for breakfast. The spring in the gorge! They had to be there. The problem was covering the ground. The skin on my right hand had healed and I found I could get along at the speed of a slow walk on one crutch. The spring I could reach in about an hour and a half.

I took a bridle and some biscuits. Using the crutch I had to watch the ground most of the time and not far from the spring I began to see a lot of flake. Among the flake were the core stones, from which the Aborigines had moulded their tools. The spring had been a source of water for a tribe and somewhere in the vicinity the signs of a camp might still be traceable. It wouldn't be in the gorge. Too cold in winter and too open to attack from above.

The spring was a muddy bog hole. Desperate for water, some cattle had walked away from the bore to suck up a mouthful of soupy slime.

Good springs don't stop seeping water, so keeping to the side, where the rock gave firm footing, I got into the cave and cupped my hands under the trickle running down the side of one wall. The horses had been going to the mouth of the cave and pawing a hole in the mud for a drink. Once the trickle of water reached the muddy bottom it was converted into little more than liquid mud. There was a danger their kidneys would pack up in the hot weather.

The tracks were not hard to find. They were using the main cattle pad to walk up to the bluegrass. The sensible plan would have been to wait until they returned for water, but the gorge was heating up and if I took it slowly I could make it to the top.

Flake lay on the ground all the way up the escarpment and not far from where the cattle pad led over the final lip onto the tableland I noticed a raised point that served as a natural lookout. I have some sort of a compulsion towards lookouts and didn't have a stone age tool site in mind when I poked my way over.

What I stumbled on was an archaeologists' paradise. Stone tools lay everywhere. For the next hour I was like a boy lost in a David Jones' toy department. There were spearheads worked into shapes like the famous clovis points of the early American Indians. Backblades of a classic type were so prolific that I didn't even examine samples that would normally be declared as a trophy find. The backblade, or stone age skinning knife, can be razor sharp. A famous American archaeologist was so keen to prove a point he insisted a surgeon use a backblade on him when he was undergoing an operation.

The most exciting find was an axe head that had been hafted to wood. The wooden handle had disintegrated, perhaps a century or two ago, but the haft stains on the artefact were clearly visible. It was a battle-axe head as the shape was too broad on the cutting edge to use on timber. An archaeologist once told me that relics of this ancient weapon are so rare in the southern half of the continent that the few that had been found were probably traded from the north. It depended on the stone source. In other stone cultures throughout the world axes were popular battle weapons, but in Australia the Aborigines had invented the boomerang, which they put to deadly use in tribal warfare.

I became so absorbed with this site I forgot about the horses for a while. To a lot of people it would seem a bit loony getting around on a crutch in the heat and examining stone artefacts.

But I had studied archaeology at the University of New England and had a basic grasp of Aboriginal culture. With the people I'd had only minor contact—it had mainly been with rabbiters and trackers when I was a small boy.

There was no sign of the horses and I couldn't track through the litter of volcanic stone. The stone the Aborigines worked was chert and they had carried it in. At the foot of a tree was a large chert rock weighing about twenty kilograms. The carrier had intended to use it as a core stone and one would be inclined to think not long after this stone was placed on the ground the white pastoralists arrived.

Thirst drove me back to the spring and the cave. The horses would come in. It wasn't much of a place to wait, so I found a flat rock in the shade and fell asleep. When I woke up Yarramin was standing almost over me. The biscuits were eaten. He was still sniffing the paper. I sat up and felt the irritation immediately. A roo tick had got to me. I had forgotten to pull my socks over the trouser cuffs and the blood-sucking insect had burrowed into my groin.

I carry a small sharpening stone in a separate belt pouch and immediately put an edge on the small blade of a pocketknife. Then I scraped a few leaves up, put a match to them and scalded the blade to kill any germs. Going through the skin is the worst part. Once through, the blood flows and it doesn't hurt so much. This was a big tick and when I got it out I had to reheat the blade and hold it against the wound. Sounds gruesome, but it was all over in two or three minutes.

Yarramin had never minded a bridle going on as I think he identified it with food. It was a slow old lead back to the bore and Circus, as always, followed behind. They looked a bit tucked up and had a long drink at the trough. I got Circus's bridle and tethered them to the trough while I backed the truck up against the earthen loading ramp. Climbing up the side of the float and winding down the tailgate was just as difficult as the performance a week before, but it was a relief to have them both on board.

The diesel engine wouldn't catch up for another thirty-six hours. I filled the fuel tank and decided to let the supply tank overflow, which meant I didn't have to return for two days. The most pressing issue was to see the local doctor. There was no improvement in my knee and with the ongoing problem of supplying water for the cattle I didn't know what to do about it.

The thought of a beer was never far away when I got to town. I parked the truck and bought a case of XXXX. There are four hotels in the little town of Mitchell. One was the local bloodhouse—every town in western Queensland has one; one was where you looked for accommodation; another had the weekend bands and there was another owned by a lady. She always greeted me and asked how things were. It was nothing of course, but when you're a stranger you appreciate it. I bought all my beer and rum from her.

When I got to Rowallan there was just enough light left for the horses to wander out into their new paddock and get their bearings. The feed seemed to slide off their bellies as they walked away from the yards. Mitchell had been drenched by several storms in the past month and with me unable to ride them I wondered how fat they might get.

'At least they'll be there when you want 'em,' Noel said with his usual eyebrow jerk. He'd walked over from the house to unload them for me.

The Rowallan homestead is only a kilometre from the river and has a commanding view of the town which hugs a bend in the river on the south side. It was once headquarters for a large pioneer station, but in post-war times has been cut up into farms. Billy and Annette owned the homestead block and Noel and his wife, Joan, shared one side of the old house.

Everywhere you looked there were relics of a once gracious standard of living—stables where horses were groomed and harnessed every day; sheds built out of milled timber where a coach and two or three sulkies were parked; the original old timber yards with water troughs hewn from tree trunks. Such a place spared by time is rare in Australia's north, because if the white ants haven't eaten it the storms will have blown it down.

Beyond a spacious garden at the front of the house the form of a tennis court still had a solid netted fence around it. There was little sign of the original surface. Native grasses and shrubs had claimed it all. I wondered about the past of this place, and about those who'd lived here in those 'good old days' long since gone. But with the horses safe at last and Noel carrying twenty-four cold stubbies, I didn't have the mind of a poet that evening. If I am remembered for anything at Rowallan, they will admit I spared them my poetry. My father tried to write poetry sometimes and it was maudlin and I always feared mine would be worse.

Drinking with Noel always followed the same pattern. You had to get two or three drinks into him. Then the eyebrows would start moving and he was away. He was a very interesting man with a great deal of self-acquired knowledge. Give him a brumby and he'd break it in so that a child could ride it bareback. Show him the timber and he'd build a set of stockyards so neat a cigarette paper wouldn't fit in the joins. Such men have almost vanished and technology will not replace them.

We were sitting in the lounge room and into about the third stubbie when he told me what had happened.

'John lost his best pig dog last night. Bloody boar tusk ripped him and the bugger bled to death.'

The dogs provided basic income for the Hamilton family. They were no ordinary paddock dogs. They were bred to pull down boars weighing one hundred and fifty kilograms, revealing a combination of crosses for bull terrier, wolf-hound, ridgeback and, for sheer size, great Dane. Any one of these dogs could pull a man down and kill him almost instantly. I always followed a strict routine at Rowallan if not accompanied by a member of the family. When I arrived in a vehicle I simply got out and waited. The dogs smelt me and I spoke softly. Once acceptance seemed obvious (and that was simple enough because if you weren't accepted then Noel wouldn't have to feed them) I made my way slowly towards the house, talking quietly and saying any idiotic thing that came to mind.

A successful hunting night with the dogs could realise more than the basic weekly wage—and they do most of the work. From their perch in the back of a four-wheel-drive utility they can smell a pig a kilometre away. Depending on their training, they will growl or bark to alert the driver. Conservation of energy is vital and usually one dog is released for the job. So strong is the sense of smell of these hunting dogs that one dog can close in without sniff tracking, and by instinct it will select the largest pig in the mob. Noel's dogs will actually run past smaller pigs.

Once the selected pig is held, a single bark every few minutes helps the operator locate the position. The dog holds the pig by the ear and his master despatches it with a knife to the throat. After basic slaughtering, the carcass is ready for delivery to the local 'pig box'. The 'pig box' operator pays the hunter in cash and freezes the carcass. Most Australian game pig goes to Germany.

'It seems a hell of a life,' I said. 'Working in the dark with a high risk of snakebite for eight months of the year. Blood all through your clothes and in your hair.'

'It's hunt or work for the railway or main roads. I reared all my boys in the bush. They hate the thought of nine to five.'

I had reared my boys for the city. I didn't want to, but I

knew it was the best favour I could ever do for them. For Noel there was no choice. He'd managed stations and it was all his children knew. On one station they were one hundred and fifty kilometres from the nearest post office and the children were taught by the School of the Air.

'They're all good stockmen,' Noel went on quietly. 'No place for them anymore.'

The kitchen door opened and Noel's wife, Joan, came in. She always gave me a warm welcome.

'We thought you'd be home last night.'

I started to explain.

'God struth,' she laughed. 'Camped out there on crutches.'

Joan had done it hard all the way . She'd raised six kids and survived outback station life, yet she was always bright and full of fun. She was fond of the dogs too so we kept away from that. The youngest sons, Jamahl and John, had been booked to provide the music for one of the hotels in Roma on Saturday night.

'If they don't get their necks broken at Surat,' Joan laughed. 'Both entered for the saddle ride and Jamahl will probably have a go at the bareback.'

Musicians are usually a breed of their own, often burdened with an over-sensitive attitude to life. The Hamilton men, however, are more likely to be branded with a multiple of bruises while they strum out such contradictory tunes as 'Sweet Caroline'. Their whole approach to life was a complex one. In the film *Geronimo*, a US cavalry lieutenant asks an Apache warrior if he will join the ranks of the cavalry. The Apache looks at the ground and says he has things to do. The lieutenant asks, 'I wonder what your answer would be if I wanted you for a raid into Mexico?' When I ask the Hamilton boys to do a day's work on a fence they are always busy. But I know if I were to ask them to run a mob of scrubbers out of the mountains, they wouldn't wait for breakfast.

The romance of the Australian cattle stations has possibly gone forever. Yet you can still dream about running in the horses before dawn, men saddling up when the first fingers of sunlight appear, the smell of tobacco and the clunk of the bell on the night horse. Someone reversing the lorry towards the loading ramp and the familiar rattles of every station float in the still air. No one ever spoke much at this hour. It was the boiling of the quart pots sometime later in the morning that brought everyone together. The horses, the mates—men had a sense of belonging on stations in those days, but from my observation it was always tough going for the few women that went out there.

Today there is little work and on a purchasing power basis the wages are low. There's not much incentive to work on remote stations anymore.

The days at Rowallan were full of interest for me because I had never before witnessed the powerful web of an extended family. I had been an only child for many years and although Sal was brought up with family around her, they all lived in Sydney. The Hamiltons not only gave tremendous support to one another, but they formed a whole community within themselves. If any of them had much money I was never made aware of it, yet they were basically happy people.

Noel and I would begin the day about the same time with black tea and toast. The women had long gone to the bakery. Annette managed it and Joan helped. Annette's husband, Billy, had been in bed about three hours after baking bread and cakes all night. Noel would light a cigarette and talk about which family car he intended to repair. There were no new cars and no vehicle ever went to a garage.

After Noel left I would read for a while, but by smoko another wave of the family would emerge—the pig catchers. Out to about three in the morning their day started just before lunch. There'd be more tea and vivid accounts of those savage boars.

There was no such thing as lunchtime and I hobbled out to the truck and drove to town about this time. Night calls to Sal were much cheaper, but I didn't want to embarrass the family by leaving at night to make a phone call. There had been 100 millimetres of rain at Myall Plains; not a droughtbreaker, but the farming was going so well I suggested Sal fly up so that we could have a few days together early in February. Our wedding anniversary was on the third. Western Queensland in the height of summer was not an appealing destination, but Sal agreed.

The thought of her coming up lifted my spirits and I went back to the doctor hoping for a better report. He told me it was a ligament injury and tried to book an appointment with an orthopaedic specialist who flew in from Brisbane once a month. The surgeon was booked out until March and I couldn't leave the bore. Even staying with the Hamiltons worried me as it only took a storm to cut me off from the cattle.

With school out the old homestead became the family playground for several offshoots of the Hamilton family. A car would arrive and I would look on, open-mouthed probably, as ten or twelve kids would clamber out. I think Noel quietly loved them all, but he had the knack of showing the same indifference as a bushman with a swarm of flies on his back. Sometimes the great-grandfather, Noel's father, showed up, gave one or two a pat on the head, and with his dry humour said one day, 'If they ask this family to leave Mitchell there'll be no one left.'

Every second day I went out to the bore, a drive of nearly eighty kilometres. I ran it for forty-eight hours and I turned it off for the same period. The tank overflowed each time, but it was the only way to avoid a daily trip. I had been at the Hamiltons for about a week and was heading out to the bore when the driver of a four-wheel drive waved me down.

He said a drover who knew my brand had told him some of my cattle had been seen on a float parked outside a pub. He said a big mob of longhorns had been yarded and he had just looked through them hoping to spot his missing cattle. When I asked if he had seen any of mine he said he didn't know my brand. My cattle were poll Herefords and would have been obvious.

'Lot of pollie cattle in the yard,' he said. 'You'll have to go and look.'

This bloke had a bit of money. Well dressed, late-model vehicle. I thanked him, but I felt uneasy. Everyone knew my cattle by now as they saw them to and from town. The cows were a little on the small side and an even deep red Hereford. I felt this bloke had seen some and didn't like to say.

At the bore it was the pumping shift. I kicked the engine up and drove the extra kilometres to the hut camp and the cattle yards. The first thing that put me on guard was that there was no one at the hut. The hut was always the regular camp. Near the cattle yards a tattered green tarpaulin had been pulled over a rail suspended between two pines. Exposed to the sun, it would have been hot and breathless inside. The tarp sides had been pulled out about two metres and covered at one end with hessian.

In the yards there were about three hundred head of cattle. Without getting out of the truck I couldn't see much except pale yellow hides and a sea of horns. They weren't cattle I had seen before. But there were tens of thousands of hectares I had never been anywhere near.

I sat in the truck and carefully scanned the surrounding timber. Smoke from the coals of an old fire drifted towards me. There was no vehicle to be seen and I thought maybe the campers had gone to town. No horses were saddled. The cattle looked full enough, which suggested they had been yarded that morning. In fact I had no good reason not to get out of the truck and have a walk around the yards. Yet something stopped me hopping out, and as a further precaution I placed the rifle on the front seat beside me, cocked.

I had my eyes on the cattle, trying to see some sign of a dark poll Hereford. The dust rose, the fine decay of old manure, and I strained to see through it, not wanting to leave the truck on a crutch. I heard nothing and saw nothing. The door suddenly opened and this bloke had me half out of the truck with one jerk. It was the crutch that saved me. I kept it on my right-hand side and used it to steady myself. When this big bloke grabbed me and pulled, my waist was jammed against the crutch and he couldn't budge me. I swung my left hand back and reached the rifle. He didn't see it for a second and that gave me long enough to swing the barrel towards him so that the gun lay across my thighs.

'Back off.'

'Need money,' he growled and let go.

I had never seen him before. He had a week's growth over his face, looked very dirty and I think was half drunk.

He turned and walked slowly back to the dark space under the tarpaulin. Before he reached it an empty XXXX bottle fell softly to the ground, tossed from within. There was at least one other person inside.

I turned the truck around and had it facing towards the track leading out. Then I got out, locked it and carried my rifle in my left hand. The crutch I had in my right hand. I didn't think there were any of my cattle, but I had to make a point of looking. Also I didn't expect any trouble. Whoever they were, grog was all they wanted. They had probably run out and had no money left. Still, I didn't intend to be caught unarmed. Once I got among the cattle I began to wonder who posed the greatest threat. Some of those longhorn cows, especially those with black tips, lowered their heads and eyed me off with scared glances.

I had a thorough look and left. No one emerged. The place spooked me and listening to the purr of the engine as it took me away was better than hearing the crowd cheer after a winner.

Returning to Mitchell I telephoned Ken Bennett, an old family friend in Coonamble who was a semi-retired agent. Sal had told me the Coonamble district had received up to two hundred millimetre of rain and I thought there might be some agistment becoming available. The cattle were in great order and it was a pity to move them, especially at the height of summer, but I'd had enough.

I explained the situation to Ken and he told me to ring back the following night. After the call I went back out to Rowallan where I received the usual ribbing.

'We'd nicknamed you Geronimo,' Noel laughed. 'But you haven't fired a shot yet. We'll have to change your name.'

The next evening I telephoned Ken and he had found a property that could take the lot. I immediately began to organise transport. The weather was still humid and stormy and roads were often closed for a day or two, so I deferred the move for a week hoping for fine clear weather. In retrospect I think I probably didn't want to stop Sal flying up. I knew after the cattle left I would have to stay behind until all the stragglers were mustered and that might be another week.

The bore routine had become very dull and Vodka Jack's race start had never eventuated—he'd gone lame. We'd had a vet look at his hoof and it seemed like a stone bruise, but the Mitchell racetrack is the softest sand track I have ever seen. During his previous preparation at Dubbo there had been problems with Vodka. I began to conclude he was unsound.

Far more worrying was Bill Anderson's health. In a matter of days I noticed the trainer deteriorate and he told me confidentially he'd had a bleak report from the local doctor. While we had a cup of tea I noted his pill bottles and packets on the table. Some of them were the same as my father had taken in his final illness. Bill was such a cheerful bloke. Vodka would come right, he said. There was a race at Charleville made to order for him! I left the house feeling neither would ever recover.

The day before Sal was due to arrive I went out to start the bore. Each day the weather seemed more humid and the scattered storms more frequent. I left early. A storm before ten o'clock was unlikely and I could be back in Mitchell by then. But as fate would have it I got a puncture on the return trip, only eight kilometres from the bore. I had two dreads in the rangelands—coming under gunfire and a truck puncture. For a few grim seconds I thought the bang was a shot, but the tyre had burst and the truck lurched to one side. From experience I knew the lurch meant both dual tyres had gone.

I got out and found both tyres in shreds. I had never had a double blow-out like this in thirty years of driving trucks. On those rough roads full of potholes and corrugations, punctures and blowouts were normal. My imagination needed considerable containment these days. Yet I couldn't help thinking of that straight eye that had made Frankie a legend. A dingo's head at five hundred metres suggested he could hit a truck tyre at seven hundred metres. If he'd fired from the top of a ridge into a head-on breeze, I wouldn't hear the report.

A double tyre change is a good excuse for a burst of foul language under the best circumstances. With one leg held together by a tight elastic bandage I just leant on my crutch and looked at the damage. Towering to my left was an ancient volcanic rock formation. The cliffs were as dark as black ink and with heavy cloud forming above, the whole landscape sent a shiver down my neck.

To describe in detail how I performed this job would not only be boring, but would appear to be inviting sympathy. I was very well equipped. I carried a large block which is essential when a double lift of the jack is necessary to provide sufficient clearance for the spare. For undoing the big bolts I had a long piece of pipe. It wasn't that bad, just a lot of heat and dust mixed up with sweat. I kept looking skyward and scanning the cliff lines. Eagles hovered above for brief periods, then continued their hunt for prey. On the ground nothing moved.

The wheel hubs couldn't be left by the road. One I lifted with the spare tyre ratchet and the other I bolted on beside the spare. The spare would run hot and the only way to minimise the heat was slow driving.

During that two hours it took to change the tyres the cloud cover dropped, dark and menacing like a tropical monsoon. I had ninety kilometres ahead. The racetrack teaches you to weigh probabilities. I should go back to my camp and dig in. But Sal was already in Sydney. I wanted to be at the Roma airport.

Thirty kilometres down the track I had to pull up and consult a district map. A storm had broken to the south. Streak lightning struck the ground to a sound like cannon fire and the very darkness of the cloud foretold raging torrents down every creek enveloped by the storm. My only hope was the east. The map showed a track running east for about seventy kilometres. It formed a junction with a road running north to Injune and south to Roma.

I had been on a short section of the road before, as it was the back road to Roma. The track passed through heavy black basalt soil—five millimetres of rain and any conventional-drive vehicle would clog up with mud. I had to take the back road to Injune. It kept close to the ranges and hopefully away from the black soil.

I struck a big storm at the top of the low divide. The soil was grey with a high component of sand. It was a matter of keeping the pace up. Sometimes I hit sheets of water so hard the lateral spray reminded me of that from a speedboat. Down one slope a car was bogged right in the middle of the road. There was nothing I could do for the occupants, and if I stopped I too would be bogged. I dropped a gear and gave the engine full bore. The last glimpse I had of the car was the occupants diving over into the back seat. In the rear-vision mirror I saw a wave of mud engulf the car. I wanted to say Roma airport at all costs, but knew I would never see those horrified faces again.

I reached the junction and there was so much mud over the windscreen I couldn't read the road sign. If I slowed down I'd stop. Taking the turn was risky. If the map was accurate Roma was to the right, some eighty kilometres to the south-east. I spun the wheel to the right, went into a broadside, wiped out the sign and somehow straightened. Another twenty minutes of wild driving and the road was suddenly dry and dusty. I drove on and only thirty-five kilometres from Roma recognised Sandra (my cousin) and her husband's property, Kooyong, on the right. I had never come to their place from the north and didn't realise this was their road. It had been nearly a month since I had bought two bulls from them. I pulled in through the gate.

'Why didn't you come to us?' Sandra cried, after I briefly explained the crutch.

'Mitchell was far enough,' I said. 'The bore still has to be run and no one else will do it.'

'Is it that bad?'

'No, it's not that bad,' I said seriously. 'The worst that's happened to me so far is a drunk trying to pull me out of the truck. It's the rumours that are scary. They reckon Frankie got so drunk one day he started to see things and fired bullets into tree trunks, gateposts and any lump of rubbish with a bit of size. Someone came into town and said he was shooting at anybody he could find. That's how it starts. Starlight never fired a shot in his life, but by the time the storytellers had done with him he'd held up more coaches and banks than Billy the Kid.'

We went inside and they wouldn't hear of me going straight to Roma. If there was a storm they would make sure I got to the airport. In fact I was to take their car.

Sandra cooked one of her delicious meals and was genuinely upset I hadn't gone out to them after the accident. The truth was, of course, I didn't know it was going to rain and provide three or four days of surface water.

The storms kept away from the Roma area and next morning I took the truck in for tyre replacements after I had met Sal. I arrived at the airport half an hour early.

I couldn't have looked worse. A badly bloodshot eye, hair that hadn't been cut for three months and a crutch under one arm. It was hot outside the waiting room, but I chose to wait under a tree and listen for the aircraft. I felt agitated and almost cursed aloud when a private plane broke the silence for a warm-up. The pilot taxied out onto the main runway and I wondered whether he knew the big one was about to come in. The baggage collector had arrived and he didn't know either. I had everyone worried for nothing and then enormous head-lights appeared low on the northern horizon.

Clearly, the Flight West pilots were taking no chances with the little plane on the runway. The pilot of the private plane taxied to the side and I found myself trembling. I wondered what the hell had gone wrong with my nerves.

The plane landed and the engines were shut down. The door opened, up went the staircase and I waited. She would be the last off! I couldn't remember when I had been more pleased to see her.

'Heavens, look at you,' Sal said, shocked. She hadn't even made it off the tarmac.

'Welcome to Rome.'

The lame joke didn't go over. Sal had voiced second

thoughts about the trip during one of our telephone conversations. It was the heat that worried her. She said that if I swapped the 'a' on the end of Roma for an 'e' she would come.

'Rome's a hot place too,' I had told her, but she knew I had never been there.

'Oh, it's beautiful. Full of history and culture.'

'There's a distinct culture here,' I countered.

'I'm sure.'

Now Sal gave me a kiss; a quick one as though I were some distant relative. I could see she was instantly troubled by my injury. I realised too, for the first time, how disturbed she had become by the prolonged nature of my Queensland campaign. Everyone had desperate problems directly related to the drought, but no one else that she knew of had been forced into a six-month separation.

'I don't know what I expected,' Sal said, while we waited for her suitcase and the hot wind blew her hair everywhere. 'It's as flat as Coonamble and probably twice as hot.'

'Come on,' I said. 'I'll take you to a coffee shop that Double Bay couldn't beat.'

The coffee place was part of a plant nursery so it was surrounded by hundreds of pot plants. The green and lush atmosphere of this little corner softened Sal's mood and we began to discuss the future.

I have presented an austere image of Sal on this occasion, but she had every justification to be thoroughly fed up with the Queensland campaign. She had nursed my father in the final six weeks of his life, organised the feeding of the whole herd for two months, overseen the trucking arrangements and when the last truck had departed she still had one hundred and fifty cows to feed. In addition were the constant needs of three boys at university. I had it tough in a different way. It was mostly interesting up here and sometimes a bit of fun. Sal's end of the bargain had been boring and lonely.

There was lots to talk about and the proprietor of the nursery–coffee shop must have been wondering whether we intended to sleep there as well by the time we left. I telephoned the owner at Southlands Station, right near Mt Kennedy, and he said the roads would be passable next day. For the moment the weather had cleared and it looked like the mustering and the loading would go ahead as planned.

By the time the truck was ready for collection from the tyre place, we were both feeling the humidity. In February southern Queensland's as hot as anywhere in Australia and for a brief period the northern Wet moves as far south as Moree in New South Wales. The only escape from the discomfort of this weather was Sandra's garden. By planting native trees Sandra had created a green oasis and with the garden straddling one of the highest ridges in the district a breeze always found its way there. Sal was immediately inspired by this thirty-year effort and after walking through the garden all trace of resentment towards this vast country evaporated. In addition, Sandra and Bill gave Sal a warm welcome and they will never know how grateful I was. When we set off next day Sal was eagerly looking forward to seeing the cattle and the country. Bill offered me a vehicle, but I explained quietly that I felt safer in the truck.

On the two-hour trip out to Mt Kennedy only one station homestead could be seen from the road.

'It's so isolated,' Sal exclaimed. Yet Sal has a quick eye for beauty and when we crossed the dingo fence and entered the rangelands she instantly fell in love. I tend to see landforms and trees, but not much else. Sal gets exasperated sometimes and says I don't even see a flower if it's thrust in my face. At least I'd noticed that in the sand-based soils of the Carnarvon outcrops there's a wide variety of plantlife. When we arrived at the bore I started the engine and we walked up one of the sandstone escarpments.

There had been a storm across Mt Kennedy, but once again

not enough to fill any of the billabongs. The main effect of the storm was a brief drop in temperature up in the range, which is about three hundred metres higher than Roma.

At the old base camp we boiled the billy and ate the sandwiches Sandra had cut for us. I never said it to Sal, but I hadn't wanted to take her there. I knew when she left I wouldn't be able to camp there again—her memory and presence would be too strong. I took little comfort from the arrangements in place for moving the cattle. It was the Wet now. Deep down I knew I needed a degree of luck to get out.

We took the long road back to Bill and Sandra's via Mitchell. First stop was Bill Anderson's place. We sat down for the long cup of tea, but the horsetrainer was quiet. He wasn't well and his face had an ashen look. Vodka hadn't improved either and the younger horse looked sour and fed up with his yard. We knew his family was deeply concerned about Bill and we didn't discuss the horses much.

The next stop was the 'switchboard'. Annette's days were long and very busy, but she took fifteen minutes off and had coffee with us. If Sal hadn't realised it before, she certainly knew now that Mitchell had become a second home for me. I had developed a strong attachment to this area and I think this may have been disquieting for her. The truth was I wanted to get home and I simply made the best of a difficult situation.

Any woman would have felt the same anxiety that Sal had experienced. Living with agisted cattle—like I was—was unheard of. The situation at Mt Kennedy was more than abnormal—it was bizarre and belonged in the nineteenth century. The vital role I played in the survival of the cattle was slammed home to Sal, on her third day. We had to go back out to turn the bore off. It was a stinking hot day and a beast had broken a trough rail and the broken piece had fallen onto the float. The trough itself sat like an island in a flood of water. I had to cut another rail and leave the engine running. The next day

Sal was to catch the plane home, so we couldn't stay at the camp.

'When will you come back out?' Sal asked as we drove away.

'Tomorrow. Only enough diesel to run the big engine until tomorrow evening.'

Sal was silent for a long while. The heat had sucked in the storm clouds again from the north. Tomorrow looked ominous.

'What if it rains? Big rains?'

'I can't hold the agistment at Coonamble. Even if I can't get the cattle out,' I paused and took her hand, 'I'll be home soon.'

Next day there seemed to be no sunrise, as though time stood still and that period of light soon after dawn never developed. A darkness filled the whole northern sky. Word came through that Longreach and beyond were cut off. We left early for the airport.

'I'm so glad I came,' Sal said, looking miserable. 'You're hopelessly stuck here and no one would believe it unless they saw it all.'

The flight from Charleville landed on time and the engines were only turned off long enough for the extra passengers to board. Sal was fighting back tears and I felt a sense of loneliness so deep I had never before experienced it. I waited to watch the plane, but within seconds it soared through the cloud ceiling.

CHAPTER

13 Stampede

For the next five days no one moved on country roads unless the highway ran past their front gate. I made it back to Sandra and Bill's, but only just. The rain came in cyclic squalls—sheets of water followed by brief periods of rumbling heavy cloud cover and no rain.

I had no choice with the Coonamble agistment. If I held it I had to pay for it. Most of New South Wales remained in drought and plenty of graziers were looking for feed, especially in the central west. Reluctantly, I made a phone call and released it. I had no idea when I would get the cattle out. Of particular concern to me now were the weaners or the big calves. The cows had survived a terrible twelve months and needed relief from their young ones in order to recover before the next round of calving.

With nothing much to do but read, write letters—sometimes to people long forgotten—and gain unwanted weight with Sandra's fine cooking, I telephoned all the local agents about a paddock for the weaners. Within forty-eight hours I had a paddock at Surat to inspect. It sounded so good I didn't think two hundred weaners would mark it and when a Mitchell agent told me about a small mob of cows and calves he had for private sale I agreed to inspect them as well.

Staying at Bill and Sandra's was like an interval at a cinema screening a long-winded western movie. The only difference was I didn't want to go back in as the second halves of western movies are always the bloodiest. Sandra kept reminding me it was good for my nerves to rest. She did, however, spare me by not saying, 'Good for your nerves to be rested before you return to hell.'

Despite being as comfortable as I could be anywhere else in the world other than home, I began for the first time to feel totally cut off. For the moment the cattle represented the engine of the whole family estate business. Failure in Queensland spelt bankruptcy in New South Wales. I had been down that road once and now had an overwhelming fear of it. I'd never understood why English gentlemen shot themselves if left destitute by the wheels of fortune until I went close to the brink myself. It is a living death and perhaps worse than death to know that you have failed and the world turns its back on you. I would stay in Queensland as long as it took to secure our future, but I wanted to go home.

By the time the road out to Mt Kennedy was dry enough for a truck it was mid-February 1995. This time the big Wet had arrived. A billabong near the base of the plateau was full and the black hole had overflowed. The foul stinking water had been flushed out and replaced with fresh run-off. With slightly cooler weather entrenched since the big rain, I estimated the surface water would last about six weeks.

I bled the old diesel and started it. Despite the surface water a lot of cattle were still watering from the trough, but I expected them to gradually drop off as more and more of them became aware of the billabong and the black hole.

Enough surface water for at least six weeks gave me an opportunity to rethink my position. I could go home for a little while. If autumn rains fell in the south I could move the cattle back home. The problem was leaving them unattended. Two months ago I would have considered it unthinkable; now I felt a certain acceptance from those who appeared to live on the edge of the law. It was also time to get things into perspective. There was an opportunity to put a large area of Myall Plains under wheat at minimum cost and I couldn't achieve that sitting around a central Queensland bore. And more important was the family. Sal had been left alone long enough and the boys would begin to wonder whether their father had left home for good.

Before I left Mt Kennedy it would be essential to take the older weaners off. I expected to draft off a hundred and fifty of these, in addition to about fifty older steers. It meant another week of waiting and watching the weather. The road out from Mitchell was still too wet and cut up for heavy transport.

I used Rowallan as a base again. The road was in such a bad state, ten millimetres of rain would cut me off and I had got sick of the camp. With time to spare I went down to Echo Hills near Surat to inspect the agistment. On the way I called in to see the owner of the Surat Hotel. Agents had advised me he had two properties and grass available. What I didn't know was that he was so sick with cancer he had only a couple of weeks to live. Like most dying people he desperately wanted to live and how he found the courage to prop himself up in bed and discuss my problems is beyond me. In cities the plight of others often never even reaches next door. The bush culture embraces everyone. He had heard about my story and wanted to help. I don't think money was an issue, although naturally I would have paid him the standard rate. I thanked him and left. If Echo Hills didn't suit I was to contact him.

South of Surat the open downs give way to sandhill country. Low red escarpments, no more than thirty metres in height, form a barrier to the vast plains of box and mulga in southern central Queensland. It looked to be good sheep country, but for cattle I had reservations until I saw the paddocks.

The red base soils of this terrain were the most fragile I had ever seen, principally because it had been undisturbed for millions of years. The earth's rich soils manifest from volcanic activity and the advance and retreat of ice sheets over the ages. Here there had been nothing, except wind, sun and the leaching effect of rain. Bad farming practices in these areas can decimate an environment within twenty years. The owner of Echo Hills, Ken Slaughter, had assessed this country from the start and put in place contour banks and large dams for water storage. Reducing the flow of dry creeks in floodtime is essential or they spill over and carve out scores of extra gullies. In every paddock, belts of trees had been left for shade.

Ken was one of those quiet achievers we sadly don't hear enough about. Typical of this stamp of man, he had few words; almost all his energy went into creative activities. He had two paddocks available for agistment. The summer feed was halfway up the door of Ken's four-wheel drive and lush. It would not only carry the weaners and steers for a couple of months, but possibly fatten them. I still had an offer of forty cows and calves at Augathella and I told Ken. Like most western graziers he was conservative and thought I would have to move the cattle in May. I was keen to make up losses from the Roma sale.

The cows and calves were on a property about one hundred and ninety kilometres north-west of Mitchell. I had heard just about every family was doing it tough in this area and this place was no exception. The husband was away working with the wife at home alone. The cattle themselves were evidence of hardship, as only the very oldest of the calves had been marked and they were nearly as big as their mothers. Most of the calves were bulls and at least eight months old. They were three-quarter-bred Santa Gertrudis and marking them was going to be no picnic. Over the years I had marked a lot of overgrown bull calves and using penicillin I never lost one. These young bulls had weight. The market was strong and this mob looked like a quick turn-over. The Santa-cross cows were unjoined, but I had two bulls spelling at Amby Creek.

The paddock price per head was too high. I made an offer to the agent and we set off across the paddock to the little cottage. I waited in the car while he talked privately to the woman. I think he knew she would accept. The agent had probably set the price and a much lower offer than mine may have been accepted. It's the sort of buying I hate as the human aspect has to be considered. They were doing it tough. How far should you cut the price and feel okay inside when you leave?

As it turned out they got a wonderful price and probably remember my arrival as one of the few good days in 1995.

The cattle were loaded about two days later and I had to find someone to help me mark the young bulls. I wanted to get someone from Roma. It was two hundred kilometres from Mitchell to Echo Hills and if I took a man with me I had to get back the same day.

Mick Bourke had already done some mustering for me. He was an Aboriginal stockman in his late fifties. From far south-west Queensland he had at one time or another faced every conceivable nightmare relating to cattle, from stampedes to wild scrub bulls. With Mick alongside me I knew we'd get these mickeys done.

Mick belonged to a generation of Aborigines who by the turn of the century will have disappeared. He was trained on an outback station and probably knew more than most white men when it came to horses and cattle. Mick and others like him had the edge on us white blokes in the real outback, because he could melt back into the bush with the same ease as a scrub wallaby. If tucker ran out a goanna was thrown on the fire and he never seemed to be physically uncomfortable, whether there was a heatwave, a gale blowing or torrential rain.

The first time I took Mick on board I had to turn around about ninety kilometres out of town in the face of heavy rain. There were no stations for miles and I had no food in the truck. The thought of getting stuck had me deeply troubled, but when I glanced at Mick with a cigarette protruding from the side of his mouth I knew he couldn't care less.

'I'll get a lift to the pub,' he said now, as I turned to get back into the truck. I had found him on the edge of town in a rented house. We had agreed to leave at five o'clock next morning for Echo Hills. A lift to the pub was the last thing I wanted to give him, but I couldn't refuse.

Mick was a nuggety man, no taller than me and in the modern world of centimetres neither of us knew what height we were. He had that craggy, full of character Aboriginal face and when he laughed it was a burst of spontaneous mirth. He had a bit of white in him, of course. Away from Cape York and the Torres Strait Islands there would be few fullbloods left in Queensland. In his sombre moments I caught glimpses of a harsh existence in the early days, somewhere west of the Warrego. He had gone a flecked grey which was normal enough, but for all his joviality I didn't see him as a man who was in good health.

When Mick also drew on his wages I knew he was heading for a big night and worse still the Commonwealth Hotel on a Thursday was the brightest place in town. If I wanted a man for the morning I had to stick with him, which wasn't hard. I have never seen a man of his age throw so much zest onto the dance floor. Women didn't have much say about whether they danced with him or not and none of the blokes looking on got upset as they got too much fun from watching him. I kept saying or probably shouting that I couldn't dance but towards the end of the evening I know I did attempt some sort of comical stomp.

It was about one o'clock in the morning when I pushed Mick

into a taxi. I wasn't game to drive him home. I went upstairs
to my room and felt I had only been on the bed for five
minutes when one of the kitchen girls knocked on my door. I
had arranged for an early morning call and I felt lousy. Mick
I thought wouldn't even make it.

The hotel had a tea and coffee room. I boiled up the jug
and before I made the tea in walked Mick. He looked a bit
pale, but otherwise no different.

'How did you get here?'

'Me nephew drove me. You said five.'

'Like a cuppa?'

'Let's boil up out there. Might feel like somethin' then.'

After that wet return to Roma I'd had with Mick, I'd made
a policy of carrying a box with a billy, mugs and biscuits.

'You're right,' I said. 'I don't feel like it either.'

Ken Slaughter had agreed to muster the cattle the evening
before. When marking calves in the heat the one thing you
don't want is rapidly running pulses fresh from a morning
muster.

It was still quite cool when Mick and I arrived after about an
hour and a half on the road. We both agreed to get stuck into
it and boil the billy afterwards. There were thirty-three mickeys
to mark and with a headstall and adjustable crush we reckoned
we'd do fifteen to the hour. The marking was enough at this
age and size, so I left the brand in the truck and used the ear
punch for identification.

The drafting took about fifteen minutes and we ran about
ten calves up the race leading to the crush. The operating gear
I placed on the top of a forty-four gallon drum. It consisted of
a scalpel, spare blades, Dettol, ear pliers, hypodermic needle
and penicillin, which had been stored in the hotel kitchen
fridge.

The first calf into the crush was one of the biggest. Mick
locked the headstall and I pushed the gate-like side of the

crush firmly against the bull to restrict movement. I took hold of the purse with my right hand and was looking for the correct spot to make the first incision when the kick came. The bull couldn't see and from his point of view it was a kick of extraordinary luck. His hoof caught the tip of the scalpel handle and drove the blade just about through my right hand. It didn't hurt very much and the cut wasn't very wide. The problem was the blood. The blade must have severed a principal vein in the hand. It bubbled like a fountain and I couldn't stop it.

'I'll see if there's some cat gut at the homestead,' I said to Mick, frustrated and unable to accept the obvious consequences.

When I got out of the truck at the homestead the blood was running down my arm, my side and even my leg. I still had the silly notion of sewing it up with cat gut and going back to the job. Ken was working in a shed near the house and I walked over to him.

The sight of blood affects everyone differently. Bleeding doesn't bother me, but blood drawn by a syringe nearly causes me to faint. Ken's reaction was total inability to speak or act, so I went over to the house to try my luck with his wife, Rosie. I opened my mouth about cat gut.

'It's off to hospital,' she said aghast.

Rosie wrapped my hand in a towel and we left immediately for Surat. She telephoned ahead on the car phone.

It's moments like these you realise that hospital closures in remote rural centres are life-threatening. A good nurse is quicker on the uptake than most doctors and when we arrived the sister had everything ready. One nurse fainted, but the sister had me sewn up and dressed within minutes. One of the most ridiculous aspects of modern medicine is the legal restrictions placed on nurses to act in the interests of a patient's welfare if there's no doctor available. At the time of writing this chapter, for example, the Coonabarabran District Hospital had no doctor and under law no nurse is permitted to administer anti-venom. I have been bitten by the eastern brown snake which has the second most deadly venom in the world, and the time lapse from bite to coma can be less than two hours. Luckily for me, the hospital had been staffed by a doctor at that time.

I may have been kept at the hospital for a while. I don't recall anything more but when I finally returned to the yards Mick had put the cattle into the paddock.

'We'll come back another day,' I said to Mick.

'What for?'

'Do the bulls.'

'I've done 'em.'

I couldn't believe it. This aged Aborigine, whom I knew was taking pills for God knows what ailments, had single-handedly marked all the bulls.

Any stockman in Australia would recognise what Mick did as an extraordinary example of animal husbandry. Even more impressive was his willingness. Mick had every excuse in the world to simply turn the cattle out for another day, but he appreciated the urgency of the job.

'I finally boiled that billy, Mike,' he said with a grin, a cigarette stuck between his lips once again.

'Next drink better be a beer.'

He nodded vigorously.

Mick drove the truck back to Roma and by about four-thirty we were back in the bar of the Commonwealth. It didn't take us long to drop a few beers. Mick had dried out from sweat and I needed to top up my blood. There was no chance of making it back to Mitchell so I telephoned Joan Hamilton at Rowallan to tell her where I was. She nearly dropped the phone when I told her my crutch arm was now bandaged up. I was about to hang up when she said a Fiona had asked to speak to me from Sydney. She was flying up to visit a friend at

Injune and planned to do a feature article on the drought. Joan gave me her telephone number.

I went back to the bar and some of Mick's family had turned up. He introduced me to his two daughters and a son-in-law. One daughter said very firmly that Mick wasn't going to drink until midnight again. I very much doubted whether he would last until sunset.

'When do you reckon we can muster the cattle at Mt Kennedy, Mick?' I asked him.

'Any day you like boss. Tomorra even.'

'Better make it Sunday,' I said. 'I've got to line up the Hamilton boys. They'll be chasing a rodeo somewhere tomorrow.'

'What about horses?'

'Bring your own. We'll leave daylight Sunday morning and pick up the horses at Rowallan on the way out.'

Provided at least one of the Hamilton boys was available we were set. All I had to do was provide the food and help a bit with the mustering. What was really bothering me was the phonecall. I hadn't seen Fiona, a freelance journalist, for twenty years. All I could recall was her voice, which had a melancholy cadence that made you listen whether you wanted to or not. If she wanted to do a story on the drought and take photographs I guessed there was no harm in it. Mustering camps can be dour affairs and I thought she might brighten it up a bit. I telephoned her and agreed to meet the evening flight from Brisbane on Saturday.

I couldn't use the crutch with my hand bandaged up and I soon found I had become too dependent on it anyway. Provided I had my leg tightly strapped I could walk on it without too much discomfort. I enjoyed shopping for the mustering camp and put a lot of thought into it. Including myself I expected to be cooking for five. Joan Hamilton said one of the boys would be available with a horse, provided their legs or their arms were not broken at the rodeo. The third man might be Mick's nephew, but he had to find out if he had a horse. If Fiona came she was going to be the camera lady. The thought of a sophisticated woman from Melbourne's exclusive South Yarra on a rough mustering camp in the Blank Space amused me a little. I was down to one useful leg and arm, so I felt like a bit of amusement.

'How did you find me?' I asked, when I met Fiona at the airport.

'The post office. The man there said everyone in town knew who you were.'

'But Queensland?'

'Close friend.'

I knew by the look in her eye she didn't want me to ask. She had aged quite a lot. Once a beautiful young woman, it distracted me for a few moments. I had aged too and she may have been thinking the same.

Neither of us said much to begin with. I really couldn't believe she was actually here, under my care. At first it seemed like a bit of fun. I knew from old that Fiona loved the company of men and would keep the camp on its toes. Mustering camps can be dull—long hours in the saddle and no grog at the end of the day. To take grog into a mustering camp can undo the whole job.

I don't know what she thought of the transition from an air-conditioned aeroplane to a dirty old truck, but we went straight to the Commonwealth and after I had showed her the room I had booked for her we went to the hotel dining room.

'I can't wait to see the looks on their faces in the morning.' I shook my head, laughing softly. 'Lady photographer in the Blank Space.'

'Blank Space!'

'The Carnarvon territory is a semi-wilderness. No towns, not even a village. An area almost as large as Tasmania. There's pockets of good country, but most of the cattle stations hack out a hard, lean living.'

'It sounds exciting to me,' she said brightly. Under direct light I could see every line in her face. She was always a determined woman. Too much so. It was her eyes that had stayed the same—always clear and lively, but I expected they could be blistering if it suited her.

'It's rough,' I said flatly. 'You'll have your own little tent. When you want to wash it's the stock trough.'

'Don't you worry,' she said smiling, 'I've roughed it. On overseas trips I've lived on a shoestring.'

I bought a bottle of wine and we ordered.

'Alright if I bring some wine?' she asked. 'It's the only luxury I want.'

'Keep it in your tea mug. Mick's okay if he thinks there's no grog about.'

'Who's Mick?'

'He's one of the most dinkum old stockmen you'll ever run into.'

'Sounds like a photographer's dream,' she said wistfully.

'You just want photographs, or a story as well?'

'Both.'

'Everyone knows the drought story. You really think it's got a market?'

'Depends on the person. Everyone in the business has the same options. You chose an option different to most.' She paused and drank a little wine. 'That's what makes the story.'

Her blonde hair had been long when I'd known her. I wanted to tell her to grow her hair long again. The terrible thing about middle age is that we have to accept our older image whether we like it or not. With Sal I have always been spoilt—she never looks any older.

'What's wrong?' Fiona asked suddenly, quite serious.

I couldn't tell her it was her hair.

'A drought story about me. I'm sure the dull and comfortable world of Australia in the 1990s wouldn't believe it.'

'That's a bit cynical isn't it?'

'Not meant to be. It's just a fact of ordinary life. Ask me what I did in 1992 and 1993 and I would have to think about it. Ask me what I did in the last six months and I can relate every day.'

'Then you've enjoyed all this business in Queensland?'

'No, very little of it. It just hasn't been dull.'

I began to explain how she might get the best shots, that the cattle should be heading for the bore access late in the afternoon when the light was at its best for photography.

'Oh, I'll go on the muster and carry the camera on the horse,' Fiona exclaimed with growing enthusiasm.

'Well, that's the way to get the best shots,' I agreed, not wanting to say anything that might dampen her excitement. Heat, scrub and mile upon mile of riding: it won't work I thought to myself.

Fiona left for bed soon afterwards and I walked into the bar for a nightcap. Mick was seated on a stool and as jovial as ever. He was drinking with two blokes—one an Aborigine in his thirties and the other one of the most weathered, scrub-beaten men I had ever seen. He was on the dark side and I couldn't tell whether his skin had been darkened by years in the sun or was simply genetic. I shook hands with him and when he smiled he had one tooth left, on the lower jaw.

'His name's Boon,' Mick said.

My blood ran cold and I looked at the man more closely. He knew what I was thinking. He was the tracker working for the Mt Kennedy gang. He had tracked me down.

'I've left,' he said soberly. 'Been a showdown out there. Real bad one. Just a miracle no one was killed.'

'Don't tell him,' Mick laughed and drained his glass which was nearly full to begin with. 'He'll call the muster off.'

'This bloke turned up,' Boon continued. 'Ike and I were handling horses in the stockyard and we hear him yellin' at Frankie. Frankie was over in the camp with Jenny. Next thing Frankie grabs his gun, takes aim and nothin' happens. This bloke grabs the gun off him and belts Frankie over the head with the butt. Then Jenny produces a shotgun. The bloke takes no notice. Just keeps laying into Frankie with the gun butt. She fires a shot in the air and the bloke jumps back. She shoves another shell up the spout and fires again. This time the bugger drops the gun and Jenny yells for us to come over. Just as we get there Frankie's got to his feet and he's screamin' mad, "Who unloaded me gun? Who unloaded me gun?"'

'With blood streamin' from his face he races in and grabs his gun lying at the feet of this bloke. Jenny yells at us—grab Frankie before he gets the bullets. We grab him and Frankie puts up a helluva fight and we got his blood all over us. We hold him and this bloke pisses off into the bush.'

'Who was he?' I asked.

'Jenny never said. She just said he'd been released from the slammer. Had some score to settle with Frankie.'

'Jenny was pretty smart unloading that gun,' I said.

'She and Frankie had a big blue over it. Jenny reckons Frankie cleaned his gun when full of plonk and forgot to load it. Anyway Frankie's gone lookin' for this bloke on horseback. He wanted me to track for him and Jenny tell me to go. She tell me Frankie and Ike will die from a policeman's bullet and if not from that, then from their enemies.'

The next day was little more than picking up horses and getting out to Mt Kennedy. Fiona was up early and looked very smart in her tight-fitting jodhpurs. After an early breakfast at a roadhouse we collected Mick and his horse. When I introduced Mick to Fiona he was speechless. He apologised for his mate not being available and when I said Fiona would ride in his place the whites of his eyes seemed to undergo extraordinary expansion.

Nearly two hours later we arrived at Rowallan. A very subdued John Hamilton was waiting. He had Circus, Yarramin and his own horse ready in a yard, each with a bridle on. John had escaped injury at the rodeo, but Noel told me quietly that victory had eluded him. I told both John and Noel that Fiona was a hired hand.

'I wondered why that old fat tub was to be loaded,' Noel said with a smile.

'Yarramin's had it pretty easy,' I said.

'New one on me,' John said dryly. 'Mounted nurse. With only one leg and arm workin' I reckon you need her.'

'I'm not his nurse,' Fiona giggled from the truck. 'I am a photographer.'

'Well the way he's goin',' John said, still dry and serious, 'you'll need more bandage rolls than film.'

It was a tight fit in the truck cabin for the four of us. Mick drove and I got John to sit Fiona on his knee. It was a long trip and John remained expressionless throughout. Sometimes Mick would hit a bump and Fiona would shoot up in the air and land heavily on John's stomach. I asked him if he was comfortable and he said it was just part of the job.

We had a late lunch and probably some of the cattle could have been mustered before dark. The heat of the day was a bad time to start and the holding paddock around the bore needed some repairs. Mick and John cut rails and strained wires and Fiona walked through the surrounding timber testing the light and taking photographs of the men working and cattle gathering around the long trough.

I got my camp kitchen organised and lay in the tent for the rest of the afternoon. To get through the muster I knew I had to rest at every opportunity. As long as I didn't bump my hand it was okay. In fact on light work I had very little restriction. The prospect of the bloke Frankie was looking for showing up without warning bothered me. I kept my rifle within reach and told Fiona not to leave sight of the camp. The danger was tens of thousands of hectares of forest, I told her. I never mentioned anything else.

An hour before sunset there was nothing left to do. Without Fiona it might have been steak and potatoes and a long night, although I don't think Mick would have minded a long sleep. While I cooked, Fiona induced these two taciturn men to relate their life stories. They were both sitting on their rolled up swags, and every time I looked at them I had to turn away so they wouldn't see me laugh. It wasn't that Fiona was behaving abnormally by being curious about these two men. It was that her two subjects were typical of the Australian outback stockman. They don't weigh the value of their lives or dwell on the past. They don't see themselves as being interesting. I once heard a young man from the city ask a veteran stockman a very common question.

'What's the most important thing in life?'

The answer left the young man gaping, unable to comprehend.

'Right now! That's the most important thing in life,' the veteran immediately replied. Then he added, 'But you may have to live out most of your life before you understand.'

Next morning the mustering plan was simple enough. Mick and John would head off into the high country and turn the cattle into the valleys that sloped towards the bore. Fiona and I would ride the heavily timbered valleys to the north. I didn't expect many cattle in that area, but it still had to be ridden. I hadn't ridden for several weeks, since my fall at the Roma saleyards. Apart from the swelling and the pain I thought riding a horse would cause, I couldn't get on without being legged up like a jockey. But Fiona's presence prompted me to try myself out in the saddle.

Fiona said she had only ridden several times before. Thinking people always say that. Sometimes I wonder whether I ever thought much. Thirty years before I had arrived on a station and said I could ride. Boy, was I sorry. Anyway, Fiona could ride. I once operated a packhorse tourist operation and I learnt to spot the good riders at a glance.

It was great to be aboard Circus again and I felt a wave of confidence almost immediately. Mick and John had quite a start on us. They had left at daylight. Fiona and I didn't get away until about seven o'clock.

The tropical lows in February had given way to very calm, hot weather. The forests baked in a brooding silence. March was the beginning of the dry season. The only rain before next spring would be unseasonable bands of moisture whipped up from the great southern bight.

The heat came in quickly and we saw only a few wallabies. It was easy riding, along a well-used cattle pad and the fragrance of pine remained heavy in the air. Circus was keen to stride out. I think horses can become very frustrated in small paddocks and love to see new territory. He was too keen. I frequently had to rein in and wait for Yarramin. I had a fleeting memory of a little girl in pigtails who always held me up when I rode out to bring the milking cows in. She was the overseer's daughter on Myall Plains. She loved helping me and to my annoyance followed me everywhere. Reflecting back now over forty years I think she must have been a lonely little girl, because I didn't like female company in those days and I wasn't very nice to her, yet she kept it up. You can get too used to being alone and I realised while waiting for Yarramin I had to be careful not to drift back to the solitude of my childhood. It must have been in the early fifties. She took some verbal abuse from me and I'd love to see her again to say sorry.

The first beast we sighted was a Santa Gertrudis bull. He was on his way to the bore. Not long after his elephant-shaped backside disappeared into the green, we rode onto a mob which had been driven off the top by Mick and John. We had left the pine forests behind and ascended onto the hard grey basalt and stunted box. This mob skidded down the slopes above us and their hooves dislodged round volcanic stones which clattered down ahead of them and narrowly missed the two horses.

A group of four stopped in a cluster of box suckers. Scrub cattle learn all sorts of tricks, such as holding up in scrub patches, hoping the horsemen will ride past.

I turned Circus towards them, but Yarramin was already on the way and we followed them down a gully, one horse either side. I had a gut feeling about this mob. Commonsense said they would walk to the bore, but one of the cows kept stopping and looking back. One heifer kept sidling away to my left.

All went well until we reached a belt of brigalow. It was as though the big whiteface baldy had been heading for it, for she turned and galloped into a maze of twisted black tree trunks. She rushed heedlessly through it and several others broke away to follow her.

Circus was gallant in the chase as always. He cleared logs and bullocked his way through the thickest of it. The ground began to rise and suddenly we were out of the brigalow and into the pine. The cow with her band of followers had switched course and I thought we were beaten. What the cow didn't realise was the big mob ahead was under Mick's control—she blundered straight into them and there was no escape.

Both Circus and I had become very unfit. We both laboured for breath and when I heard the crashing behind I realised I had forgotten about Fiona. When old Yarramin burst clear of the pines I didn't expect to see Fiona aboard—but she was. She alone had loved every second of it.

Mick had about two hundred head in hand and he said John

had picked up a big mob about a kilometre to the south. By midday we had about three hundred and fifty locked up in the bore paddock.

I had some sliced ham and several lettuces in the Esky, which I had half filled with ice before leaving Roma. We all hoed into it with heaps of multi-grain bread washed down with about four mugs of tea. I suggested Mick and John have a couple of hours rest before riding again, but they had set themselves a goal— get the lot in one day. Every paddock in the Blank Space has a rating, based on the number of days usually required for a clean muster. This paddock had a three-day rating. A hundred and sixty kilometres north in the Carnarvon Massif there were paddocks rated seven days. Of course helicopters speeded things up if anyone could afford them. This wasn't the Northern Territory where immense belts of good grazing country and huge herds allow modern technology to be viable.

Lame was hardly the word when I dismounted for lunch. The stiffness was mainly in the knee area and I thought if I lay down for a while after lunch I could take Fiona down to the gorge later and give her the opportunity to take a few action shots as Mick and John drove the cattle down. I thought I'd maybe rest for about twenty minutes but when I put my head down I had that feeling you get when talking to the surgeon on the operating table. You seem to be cut off in mid-sentence and when you wake it takes some minutes to remember where you are. When I opened my eyes the shadows were long and it felt much cooler. I crawled out of the tent and could see the cattle in the bore paddock, restless and wanting to feed out. Circus was still tied up under a shady tree. He had been asleep too and looked at me with enquiring eyes. There was no sign of Yarramin.

I no longer had any concern for our safety. The ex-jailbird would have got back to town somehow and Frankie would have got too dry to keep looking for him. If there was to be any drama it would have been on the first night. I had come to the conclusion it was very easy to become paranoid about these anti-social characters.

The fire needed a bit of stoking and I was short of wood. The exercise was good for my leg, although painful. I had a slight nagging worry that Fiona might have ridden away with the camera and got lost. It was unfounded, of course, because Yarramin would always bring her back.

Not long before sunset the leaders of the final mob began to drift through the timber. Then I saw Mick on his chestnut thoroughbred. He had placed himself near the lead in case they broke. After a few minutes I saw John on the other side on his roan gelding. At least a hundred head of cattle were in view now. Yarramin was not there and my anxiety flared again. Mick was too far away to call to. I just had to wait until they put the cattle in the bore paddock. The last of the cattle ambled into view and now I felt very concerned. It never occurred to me Fiona might ride ahead, way out on the flank, then ride towards the bore to photograph the cattle head on. I finally caught sight of her and relaxed.

You can take hundreds of photographs of a droving unit on a stock route, but it is very difficult to capture that half wild look when cattle are first driven away from their favourite haunts. Fiona worked hard at it and she must have got some outstanding shots.

After the mob had been turned in with the others Mick rode through them for a count. I don't know how he counted them like that, but later he was to give me a figure of thirty to forty short. Meanwhile Fiona went on photographing and Yarramin decided she had had a fair go. He suddenly went down on his knees and commenced a gentle roll. Fiona vehemently protested, but to my alarm made no effort to get away. Fortunately Yarramin regained his feet and when I asked why she hadn't scrambled to safety, she said it was because of her telescopic lens. She had strapped the case to a saddle dee and to abandon that would have been an expensive loss. Minutes later all horses were unsaddled and fed with hay from the truck.

The thought of cooking a bush dinner weighed heavily on me that evening and when Fiona pushed a mug into my hand I knew it had better work. I sat on the big log by the camp and let the red wine spread through my veins. Fortunately I had boiled the billy and made tea. Poor old Mick would have loved a mug of wine, but I needed his expertise so badly I had to keep him dry.

'Didn't quite get 'em,' Mick said, a little subdued. 'Others might take a day or two to find.'

'I'll feed the big mob out.'

'Reckon you can hold 'em,' Mick said, not very convincingly as he poured himself a second mug of tea.

'Going to be a bit of a spread. Six hundred head need access to at least three hundred acres.'

It was going to be hard to hold them.

'We better ride in later in the mornin' and check how it's goin',' John suggested. He already had his swag rolled out and didn't look like staying awake for long.

'Reckon we'll get you started before we go,' Mick added. 'Push 'em down into the box country where there's a bit of feed. They won't look to walk for a while.'

While we were talking Fiona got to work with the food. Under the lantern light I couldn't see exactly what she was cooking, but I was so grateful I could have hugged her on the spot. Mick pretended she wasn't there. Educated in the old school, he may never have seen a woman in a mustering camp before. John was more responsive and when dinner was served he suggested I be sacked as cook. I don't recall what Fiona cooked but I remember agreeing whole-heartedly with John.

From memory the men fell asleep where they ate dinner, exhausted. Fiona was fiddling around with her camera when I headed for my tent and I remember telling her not to go far from the camp fire. I noticed she had gone to a lot of trouble to groom herself and for the first time she had changed into a skirt. She wanted to change my bandage. I told her it was alright and I would soon take the old one off and throw it away.

I lay on the thin mattress, uneasy and tense, listening to the night birds. Sleep should have been almost instant, but I still lay awake after midnight and listened for the sounds that would make my skin tingle. The dingoes howling near the camp didn't bother me. The cattle were used to them by now. It was those indistinguishable sounds most likely to spark a stampede that I worried about.

I don't know what hour I drifted off. When I woke it was with a start. The silence was total, a stillness out of character in a wilderness of nocturnal animals and birds. I pulled my boots on and stood outside the tent. It was so quiet I could hear Fiona breathing nearby. I walked over to the glowing coals of the fire and threw a small log on. A mug of weak tea often did the job of soothing my nerves and when I lay down again I usually went back to sleep.

The billy boiled quickly with only a little water. The cattle I imagined to be all lying down. I thought no more about them and contemplated taking the bandage off and washing my hand. The sudden rumble was a sound I had never heard before. It slightly resembled thunder, but remained distinctly animal. It only lasted a few seconds. The whole herd had moved as one and stopped. I expect the fence held them on the lower side of the little paddock.

I glanced at my watch and saw it was three-thirty. The first crack of dawn was still an hour and a half away. A stampede across the camp seemed extremely remote and I knew if I woke Mick and John they wouldn't get back to sleep. I thought of the Mitchell stampede a century before and wondered how six hundred large animals could be so silent. There was not so much as a cough or belch. The horses were in with the cattle and they must have been bewildered.

Back in the tent I felt envious of the others. They had slept through the night. With the knowledge of dawn approaching I relaxed and finally fell asleep. When I woke again it was still dark, but not pitch black. Something had woken me, and very drowsily, as though my head were under weights, I strained to listen. When it came again it was a wail. It wasn't a dingo. I tried to raise myself on an elbow. I knew I was very weak and wondered whether I was hallucinating. The minutes went by and I put my head down again. The next wail seemed human and I forced myself to sit up and pull on my boots. I staggered out of the tent and called quietly to Fiona. The fire had gone out and I could just see the dark form of Mick sitting up in his bed-roll.

'It's the missus.'

'Not my missus.'

'She go for a pee and get lost. Them cattle too quiet. Don't call to her.'

'I'll go to her.'

'You go slow. Very quiet.'

I had only my underpants on. The tent was untidy and I fumbled around for my trousers. When the dingo howled it was high-pitched and blood-curdling. It was the same dog that had come to smell me up on the escarpment. It howled again and the cattle broke. First that strange thunder of hooves, followed by several sharp cracks as the fence posts snapped. They were heading our way and I bolted from the tent shouting, 'Get down, get down.' Mick was roaring obscenities, jumping up and down and flicking his lighter. He had the presence of mind to realise dropping to the ground was futile. Our bodies would be spread like butter. I watched as though mesmerised. But I couldn't see them. The ground trembled and the timber erupted in a stick-splitting roar. I could just see Mick jumping wildly and the fire spark of his lighter. The rush came at us and enveloped the camp. Yet we were still standing, unharmed. Everywhere I could hear the snapping of small trees and the sharp cracks of dead wood. The cattle had split and gone around us. It probably all took less than twenty seconds. In horror I swung around to listen to the roar of destruction heading in the direction the original wailing had come from. I began to walk aimlessly, numb with fear at what I might find. The silence returned quickly and the only sound was Mick moving around, searching too.

'What the fuck's happened?' I heard John yell out. He had just woken.

'That missus is out here,' Mick called.

The light seemed to be gathering by the second. The adrenaline flowed and I felt wide awake and fit. When I found Fiona she was huddled by a tree. The cattle had missed her. As the light grew I saw that it was only by metres.

'Why didn't you come?' she whispered reproachfully.

'I didn't realise until it was too late.'

She rose stiffly and her arms fell around me. She was shaking to begin with, then sobbing. I held her as strongly as I could, as though strength alone might smother her fear.

In silence the three of us walked slowly back to the camp. John had the fire going and a couple of billies in place.

'Think I can see the horses in the far corner,' he said calmly. 'They'll do that when spooked. Get close to one another and stay put.'

Mick pulled an old jumper out of his swag. It wasn't cold. He was never going to say it, but my guess is he'd thought sudden death was almost certain.

'They'll stop when they strike decent feed,' he said, standing over the fire. 'We'll soon get 'em.'

'Think they'll be any better tonight?' I asked.

Mick didn't answer for a while. He stared into the blaze and drew his arms tightly across his chest. Fiona had gone to her tent. I sat on the ground near the fire. I didn't feel cold, just weak. John got some hay from the truck and headed towards the horses. Whatever decision we made, John knew it was going to be a big day for the horses.

'Ya hear the howl?' Mick said at last. 'Just before the rush?'

'I've heard that dog before. High-pitched and long—scary sort of howl.'

There was something on Mick's mind, but as deeply troubled as he was nothing would be said. I'd seen it often as a boy. The men from two skins and two worlds were torn and confused. Sometimes I saw a level of acceptance and a depth of wisdom profoundly beyond my experience of civilisation.

'Cut ya losses and walk straight for them high yards,' Mick said quickly, still staring into the fire. 'Might miss a few weaners. Get the buggers next muster.'

'What if we don't make it before dark?' I asked. It was a fifteen-kilometre walk from the bore and the cattle had stampeded in the opposite direction.

'We'll be followin' a fence won't we?'

'Heavily timbered though.'

'Don't matter,' Mick said. 'If the night come too quick we'll hold up in a valley and night-ride 'em.'

It was decided upon without further discussion. I broke a stick off one of the pines, smoothed out a patch on the bare ground and drew a map of the terrain as I knew it.

'You're going to need three horsemen, Mick.' I glanced towards the tent and I thought Mick looked a bit dismayed. 'Yarramin's not a bad old cob and she'll stick. She's got to come anyway.'

'Hard enough findin' them cattle without watchin' out for a horse all the time.'

'Put her in between you both.' I didn't wait for any further argument. 'I'll ride ahead, open the gate up on the pass and wait out on the north side in case the lead misses the gate.'

We had breakfast while the horses ate the hay. The meal was simply toast and tea, but we ate all we could knowing the next billy boil was unplanned and uncatered for. Fiona had lost that ashen colour in her cheeks and when she sat down on the camp log I noticed the camera bag.

'We'll lock your camera in the truck,' I said.

'I'm taking it.'

Mick and John saddled the horses and I packed my backpack with the basics—billies, tea, coffee, bread and biscuits.

'There's one bottle of red wine left,' Fiona said seriously as I began to close the backpack. 'I know it's too heavy to carry. Perhaps one of those saddlebags, the canvas ones, could go onto my saddle.'

'The top will stick out.' I paused and took the bread and biscuits out of my backpack. 'You put these in those dual bags and I'll take the wine. If we don't make it tonight our camp's a fire and backs to a tree. The wine might put us to sleep.'

'You're sending me with the men,' Fiona said, in a tone which told me at once she wasn't happy. 'But you've forgotten. You can't get back onto Circus by yourself.'

She looked away when I spoke. 'If there's a rider behind the mob Mick and John can flank either side,' I said gently. 'You're not just being cared for. We need you out there.'

'Mick doesn't think so.'

'Communicate with John. He doesn't say much, but if you're not riding in the correct spot he'll quietly put you right.'

Mick tossed me aboard with a hefty thrust and I headed north for the pass.

Circus strode along in his usual way and I reached the gate in less than an hour. The clip was okay, but the gate dragged a little on the ground and Circus had a bit of a hang-up about pushing gates open. On every attempt I moved the gate a little more and eventually it was fully open.

Only two hundred metres from the pass a high ridge overlooked the narrow defile leading up to the watershed crest. To the north the water flowed all the way to the Fitzroy and emptied into the sea east of Rockhampton. To the south the passage was much longer. If water from a storm ever made it, and apart from flood waves it probably never did, the precious water flowed thousands of kilometres to empty into the Murray and finally the sea in South Australia.

I had to dismount. Even if the cattle hadn't gone far I knew the wait would still be two hours. I expected the lead to pass through the gate without hesitation, but if something spooked them they might swing to the east and walk into the mountains.

I tied Circus to a shady tree with a bit of grass in reach. It was a chance for a short nap. After the drama of the stampede it was delightfully peaceful. A cool breeze drifted across the sandstone escarpments which continued towards the southwest until they were a distant fading blue. Small birds chattered overhead and as always the eagles soared.

When I woke the coolness had gone and it was quite hot. I walked to the edge of the steep slope and looked down. Cattle were filing through the gate. Looking north I could see them disappearing into the timber, suggesting the lead may have passed by an hour before. The cattle were strung out and there was no sign of any riders. I had to go for the lead immediately and steady them.

I had never in my life had difficulty getting on a horse. Sometimes I have had difficulty staying on. I tossed the reins over Circus's head and lifted my left leg to the stirrup. The pain struck with such force I gasped and fell back. Within seconds I was sweating. After the pain eased I tried pulling myself towards the saddle, but my hand, already swollen, refused to grip. It was hopeless. I couldn't get on. Walking in the rocky terrain was very difficult, but I just had to lead Circus and hope the lead cattle had stopped to feed.

I didn't reach the lead. Two hundred metres off the fence I walked as straight a line as possible to avoid pushing cattle ahead of me. I walked for more than two hours before I saw the gate and road leading to the yards and the hut camp.

To my surprise Scalp was at the camp working on a bull-dozer. Johnny was working on a saddle. When I looked closely I saw he was mounting a rifle scabbard to the pummel.

'Well I'll be damned!' Johnny exclaimed.

'No, I'm the one damned,' I said.

'I don't think that horse needs a rest,' Scalp said cheerfully.

'Can't get back on. We're mustering and the lead's bolted.'

'You goin' to move 'em?' Scalp asked.

'Just the weaners. Cows're going back.'

'He wants us to chase the lead,' Johnny said with animation.

'Right up my line.'

'Run the horses, Johnny,' Scalp ordered.

'They mightn't be far ahead,' I said.

'Don't matter if they are,' Johnny said, as he straddled a bike near the bulldozer. 'I might get a dingo scalp.'

'There's beer in the Esky.' Scalp pointed to the back of his ute. 'You look as if you need one.'

'One stubbie and I'd be drunk. I'll settle for water.'

'How's it been goin'?'

'Had a rush last night from the bore paddock.'

'Cattle don't hold well there. That bloody sandstone bluff nearby is popular with the dogs.'

'It was a dingo.'

'Johnny and I have a competition between us. A hundred bucks on it.' Scalp smiled. 'Small stakes, but we might knock out fifty dingoes or more.'

'How's the work?'

'It's like strippin' wheat all year round.'

Stripping the planet of its vegetation is what he was really saying. There was no point in saying what I thought. Men out here still had a frontier psyche: the concept or indeed the very urgent necessity of preserving the environment was not something they had ever given any thought.

We weren't talking for very long when the horses galloped into sight with Johnny behind them on the bike. They shot into one of the yards. Johnny closed the gate and gave the bike full throttle again as he came over. Scalp grabbed a saddle from the back of his ute and Johnny took the one he was working on. They caught and saddled their horses within minutes and led them over to the bulldozer. Then the rifles came out from the front of the ute. Johnny strapped his to the saddle scabbard. It was open-sighted and looked like a Hornet 222. Scalp had a much heavier rifle mounted with a scope. It had a sling and he carried it on his back.

'You look more like a raiding party than a couple of blokes riding for the lead,' I said, a bit bewildered.

'The dingo pups are weaned now,' Scalp said. 'They're everywhere.'

Johnny legged me up on Circus and I rode out with them. While they were saddling up, I'd found a couple of empty bottles and filled them at the trough. I had missed the water-hole coming in and I didn't feel confident of finding it on the way back.

We parted at the gate. Cattle were walking past and I had a sinking feeling the lead might be kilometres to the north.

Scalp and Johnny made an odd sight for the 1990s. It was the wrong time of the day for dingoes. I felt sure dingoes had nothing to do with those long-barrelled rifles.

I rode south, back over the same ground. All the way cattle were walking towards me and about an hour later I reached the tail and the musterers. They were in thick pine.

'You got water?' Mick's voice was hoarse.

'I think it should be boiled,' I said. 'I'll boil the billy and make tea.'

'Bugger the boilin'.'

I began to take the backpack off.

'Missus first,' Mick whispered gallantly. 'She don't say anything, but that little woman must be dry.'

'She doesn't drink gallons of beer like you either.'

I handed Mick one bottle and rode over to Fiona. She was about a hundred metres away, riding along with John. I had the other bottle in my hand before I got to her. To my surprise she didn't look affected by either heat or lack of water.

'Mick insists you drink first,' I said.

'Sounds like I've really made it.' Her voice was a bit croaky. She drank a quarter of the bottle and handed it to John.

'John says we've lost the cattle. He says the lead's miles ahead.'

'Scalp's gone for the lead,' I said. 'If they don't pull up he'll probably shoot one or two.'

'Who?' she exclaimed.

'Oh, it's a long story. Scalp's a bounty hunter.'

John passed the bottle back to Fiona and rode off. I caught a smile on his lips.

'I should have realised,' Fiona said quietly, almost to herself. 'Your sense of humour!'

'I don't have one. At least, what's supposed to make me laugh doesn't.'

'There are three tiers of humour,' Fiona said seriously. 'The contrived, the real and the outrageous. It's the last one you enjoy.'

We rode on in the heat. It was four o'clock. I had been looking forward to a breeze off the ranges that usually picked up about this hour, but it may have been fortunate it stayed hot as the bolters had overheated and stopped. When we arrived at the gate it was open and most of the cattle had gone through. Scalp and Johnny had dismounted and waited in the shade.

I knew Fiona had a horror of guns and was not surprised she hung back. Johnny, of course, couldn't contain what was in his mind. From a distance Fiona looked very young. Her clothes were youthful and she kept her figure in excellent shape.

'Blonde and all,' he said loudly. 'To leg ya on, I suppose.'

Only for the ache in my leg I would have taken Fiona with me and ridden back to the bore. There was a heap of grog in the ute and it looked like being a rough camp.

There was nowhere to run the horses. Scalp had thirty in his horse paddock and to let ours loose among them was unthinkable. After the cattle were yarded Mick and John gave them a long drink at the trough and led them to a patch of feed where they held them. They did this for an hour and then put them in a spare yard.

The only food we had was the bread and biscuits in the canvas saddle packs carried by Yarramin. We all drank so much water I don't think anyone was hungry. I placed my back against an ironbark near the trough and that was where I intended to stay. I didn't argue when Fiona took off the bandage that was now charcoal-coloured and put my hand in a bucket of warm water.

'Give me your pocket knife,' she said. 'I'll have to try and work these stitches out. Your hand's swollen too.'

'Did Mick think he got them all?'

'He thinks a few got away.'

'Drafting won't take long. I'll have to ask Scalp if he'll drive to Southlands and ring the transport people.'

'Why have they got guns?'

'Been a bit of trouble out here. I'm too tired to explain.'

'Well I'm here now and you're not fit enough to protect me.'

'No one will bother you.'

'One looks wild. He's got a red thing tied around his dirty hair.'

'They're just misfits. Among men of the world they're close to innocence.'

'Look like cattle duffers to me.'

'They're not. One's a contractor and one's a rodeo rider.'

'I don't feel safe just the same.'

'Out here you'll find desperate men.' I looked over towards Scalp and Johnny. They had let their horses go in the paddock. Johnny had a fire going and Scalp had some tinned food and saucepans on a big cardboard box. 'But you'll be hard pressed to find a bad man. Most of *them* go to work in a hundred dollar shirt and a hundred and twenty dollar tie.'

'You'll be asleep in a minute.'

'And you'll be entertained. They're bushmen. Plenty of good yarns and I can see a meal being put together.'

Fiona was right. I soon fell asleep and didn't wake again until sunrise. The men had an early breakfast and put the mob through the pound. In Queensland a few cattle at a time are run into a small forcing yard. The next little yard is known as the pound and has four gate outlets. The poundman has a long drafting stick and cuts one beast off at a time. As the beast trots into the pound the poundman yells out the yard it's to be placed in—'steer', 'weaner', 'cull', or 'cow'. The man at the appropriate gate (and sometimes one man operates two gates) jerks the gate open and the beast darts through. The drafting procedure is very fast and this mob of nearly seven hundred were put through in under three hours. I'd had the easiest job. I sat on a tall post and when a possible cull ran into the pound I gave the nod.

In the end Fiona took Scalp's ute and drove down to South-lands to telephone for the trucks. They were on standby in

Roma and left immediately. When she came back her camera ran hot again.

'Barely had a photograph taken in me whole life,' Mick grumbled.

'She's made up for it then,' I said, looking for a bite.

'About bloody five hundred of me in the last two days.'

We would have liked to have camped through the heat and taken the cows back in the cool, but they were thirsty and we had to keep moving. John caught the horses and we saddled up. The cows knew the bore was their next drink and strode along. By mid-afternoon we had the billy on at the base camp and we began to think about packing up. Scalp and Johnny had turned back after the last of the cows trotted through the gate at the pass. Scalp offered to help load the two semis when they arrived from Roma. The young cattle and the steers were headed for Echo Hills, Ken Slaughter's place near Surat.

'They were okay last night?' I asked Fiona as they rode away, with their rifles strangely prominent.

'Scalp made a rice pudding. It was really delicious and Johnny told me all about bull riding. I want to go to a bucking bull rodeo now.'

'And Johnny would have told you Injune's on next week.'

'Oh yes.'

I took Fiona to her friend's place in the Arcadia Valley and dropped the truck at Rowallan. Next day I caught the bus from Mitchell. I was heading home.

CHAPTER

14 An Autumn of Reflection

I arrived home to a community that had not been so hard hit since the Depression. Everybody had aged. More striking still was that tired, despairing profile that I had never seen before in the country. It was as though we had fought a war and lost. Eighty percent of properties in the district were unofficially on the market. Families whose forebears had owned the land since the last century were ready to sell. No one had a trace of optimism.

In 1994 forty decks of cattle were sent to central Queensland from one New South Wales property. There were many stations in New South Wales carrying more than a thousand cows. The 'big lift' reflected the folly of running large numbers without adequate fodder reserves.

Yet the 1965 drought had been more savage than the drought of 1994. It had begun in December 1964 and the next fall of rain across western New South Wales was not until the following November. By the end of March no one had any feed and we went into a winter of brown dirt. A dust haze emerged from any breeze and in July we endured a freak fall of snow. Where snow had never before fallen it lay ankle deep. On the Warrumbungles a foot of snow caused heavy sheep losses and roads were blocked. Seven hundred kilometres to the north the Carnarvons were also under a mantle of snow—a sight not previously witnessed by white man.

On Myall Plains the crunch came in July 1965. The old AML & F Co, a pastoral agency, was very strong in those days. The Sydney office got busy with its Victorian branches and they found us agistment just outside Melbourne at Dandenong. We booked a train. The cattle were loaded at Binnaway and were unloaded at Wodonga where they had twenty-four hours rest and a feed of hay. The second leg of the journey took us through the centre of Melbourne. I can remember surprised peak-hour commuters staring into the cattle wagons. For some reason we had to stop and wait at Melbourne's central railway station. Compared to Queensland twenty-nine years later the trip was a breeze. We lost only three cows and two calves. The bureaucracy was much more flexible in those days. At Junee they stood the Melbourne to Sydney express on a side line while we went through. The cows and calves were given priority over people.

The train drovers travelled in the guard's van at the rear of the train. Old Jack had been at it all his life. In his early days the steam trains accounted for almost all stock movements. Roads that are highways today were little more than sulky tracks in his youth. Property owners walked their stock on horseback to the railheads and a train drover took over. The first thing impressed on me was the value of a good engine driver. At Dubbo we got a bad one. When he stopped it was a chain reaction jerk. The cattle were thrown forward and weak ones fell. At any stop of more than five minutes we got into the wagons and helped them up. To avoid kicks I was taught to stand against their rumps and the worst cattle to be in with, old Jack said, were Angus. 'Kick like mules,' he said.

The other professional train drover was Roy—a small thin man who spent most of his time rolling tobacco. When he started to talk it lasted forever, but he didn't bore me. I sat there spellbound at his tales of the war against the Japanese in New Guinea. He had been a sniper. It must have been a lonely and spine-chilling task. On one occasion he waited in a tree for five days near a Japanese company camp. He waited for that one shot at an officer—the best way to demoralise the troops. 'I was almost out of range,' he said. 'When I got him he was taking a drink from a pannikin. He tilted his head back to drink the last of the fluid and I fired. The bullet went through the bottom of the pannikin and into his mouth.'

Rolling another cigarette as though he were telling me about a hole in one, he recalled the next few hours. Soldiers ran around like ants, spraying trees with bullets and he knew if he were discovered a bullet through the heart was the best he could hope for.

Roy was still younger in 1965 than I am now. He had fought for freedom and virtually given up four years of his life. Addicted to heavy smoking I doubt he would be alive today and that might be a blessing, for Australian farmers have lost their freedom without a shot being fired. Foreign companies have taken over the vital components of the beef export industry. They can manipulate the prices. Grain growers are not only vulnerable to world supply and the weather, but now must bow before a new element—massive trading on futures. The market can be manipulated to inspire heavy planting and then sent into a spin at harvest time. At home, banks charge farmers exorbitant interest rates and the government scavenges on what's left. Farming in Australia is possibly the most exposed industry in the western world. Modest subsidies would lead to better protection of the environment and pump lifeblood into inland towns. The denial of this assistance has led to the destruction of the Australian inland culture. Farmers have lost out to subsidised commodities and the corporate takeover has already begun.

During my six months away, the banks in all the small towns

had closed. At Binnaway the post office had closed and the business transferred to the newsagent. The race club looked like folding and if it were not for the enthusiasm of a handful of people the annual show would have folded as well. Sal was show secretary that year and show day must have been the only bright day that little town had seen in twelve months.

For the next three months Sal and I went back and forth to Queensland from home to inspect the cattle and the water situation. With the cooler weather the waterhole hung on and Scalp kept the water up to the supply tank. He was pulling timber close by in the months of April, May and June.

On one of our brief autumn trips we had met Gil Campbell's wife, Eunice, at the Mitchell hospital. She was a sister there. I'd had to go to the hospital to enquire about x-rays taken in January. I had already met Eunice briefly at Muckadilla with Gil and her young family. She had asked Sal and me to call in at their home, Claravale Station, the next time we went to inspect the cattle, which happened to be the following day. Instead of taking the Maranoa road we took the old Injune road. It was about morning tea time when we arrived and we were lucky to strike Gil looking for a half-hour break. Gil was one of those typical western Queensland stockmen—lean and hard with direct blue eyes. He rarely ever took his hat off and he finished off every sentence with an 'ay', which has been a form of dialogue in Queensland's outback ever since I can remember.

I didn't waste much time in raising the subject of the October raid. Gil was reticent to begin with. Eunice became pale and momentarily silent, and I began to realise it was more than stolen cattle that bothered them. In reality they were as vulnerable as the white farmers in Kenya in the 1950s, only it was not the indigenous people terrorising them, but outlaws from another time. They feared for their home, their bores and even their children. The fear I knew had gone. It had been unfounded, or at least I had convinced myself of that, but for these people there was always the possibility of the unthinkable. They were too remote for conventional two-way radio which would enable them to call for help. Their satellite linkup could be tampered with and their road out could be closed in five minutes with a powersaw. The odds of such an incident were indeed remote, but like a ghost that never leaves, the fear hung on and I saw it in their eyes and their pensive expressions.

Meanwhile, there were lots of cookies and scones—and even cream for the scones. Gil milked cows at daylight and Eunice cooked on a wood stove. Their hot water came from an old donkey furnace outside. It was a home in the bush. A breeze stirred from the north that morning and I caught the sweet scent of the cattle yards. The Campbell children were taught by the Charleville School of the Air and by the way they gazed at Sal and me I knew they didn't see people often. Having reared four boys Sal has a natural leaning to children and she soon broke through that shy barrier. There were two boys, and a girl at the toddling stage.

We had been chatting for a while at the kitchen table when an old gaunt man appeared on the front verandah. Anything sweet was hurriedly removed from the table.

'Gil's dad,' whispered Eunice. 'Got a serious sugar problem.'

Stuart Campbell entered the kitchen and in the old-fashioned way he shook hands with Sal as well as me. Without asking, Eunice put a large mug of tea in front of him and some scones. I got the impression he sat in the same chair about the same time every morning and ate Eunice's scones. He was a delightful old character and asked a lot of questions.

'You got horses?'

'A racehorse in Mitchell,' I said. 'Quiet, but useless when the pressure's on with cattle. A very old one at Echo Hills and one lame.'

'That's no good,' he said. He thought for a while and nodded to himself. 'We've got plenty.'

I began to feel uncomfortable. I knew this bloke wasn't running the station anymore.

'Naturally we can't guarantee their behaviour,' Gil added. 'But if you're stuck for two or three don't hesitate.'

I hate borrowing anything from anyone. Only for the financial position I would have offered to buy three stockhorses.

'That could happen,' I replied reluctantly. 'The second lot of weaners will have to come off soon and I can't pay independent stockmen anymore.'

Gil brushed away my protestations and Stuart yarned on. The Campbells had taken up Claravale Station in the 1880s, he told us. They were one of the few families in Australia to still occupy their original lease. I took quite a liking to old Stuart and on one of our visits there he showed me where the Aboriginal camp had been. He said his father could speak the local Aboriginal language and in the 1890s had hunted with the black children. He said there was never any trouble between the family and the Aborigines.

'They slowly dispersed after the turn of the century. Bush tucker and their own ways was best for them, but try and tell them that! Be like asking a townie to go and shoot a fowl for dinner when he can walk into a store and buy it.'

Stuart said the bush skills and crafts from the early days had been handed down through the Campbells. They had all been carpenters and harness makers. Their independence from civilisation survived to the present day, he told me. Stuart himself had not sighted a town until he was twelve.

'The tracks were so rough. It was a long day in the sulky to Mitchell. Bloody boring.'

Sitting on a wooden bench on Gil and Eunice's front verandah I sometimes tried to imagine those very early days. The frontier I'd seen as a child had been so different. The men and women were rough, the half-castes sullen—lost and belonging nowhere. The trapping days of the rabbit plague were often ugly. It was a world wounded by the war. The real frontier was something else and when Stuart passes on there may only be a handful left who really know what went on in the early settlement of outback Queensland. Two tribes had once lived in peace here. Black and white children had played happily with one another. There were no flags of the British, no dreaded native police. The white people spoke the Aboriginal language and loved the corroborees as much as their dark friends. I believe the Campbells learnt from these Aboriginal people, although perhaps subconsciously. For a hundred years they have lived on what nature has provided and until just recently the environment had never been altered. But the pressure of encroaching civilisation, exorbitant annual lease rates and the fear of native title (which clearly doesn't exist in the Carnarvon region) had forced this family to enter the modern world.

Central and western New South Wales remained in the grip of drought and with the slide towards winter there could be no relief until next spring. Nick and Greg had ploughed up a big area for wheat. The bed was rough, cloddy and dry. The prospects for a crop were not good. When I arrived home Nick had left for Lismore to resume his business/tourism course at Southern Cross University.

The happy occasion during this period was a wedding. James, our eldest son, married Kari. The wedding was in Sydney and with the dancing and laughter at the reception, our preoccupation with the drought was smothered for that night and for two or three days afterwards.

There was sadness too when Bill Anderson, the horse trainer, died. I didn't know until he had been buried. On our first trip back to Queensland we called on Mary Anderson and found her very distressed. We moved the horses. The three-year-old was known around town as the buckjumper and I dropped him at Echo Hills. Vodka I moved to Mudgee and a local, Sally Rowe, took over the training. She soon ran into the same problems as Bill had and suggested I give him one final run at the picnic races in May. I was lame, but the temptation was too much. I strapped up my leg and Sally legged me aboard in the Collaroy Cup. Vodka flew out of the machine and led the field under a tight hold until the turn. Then he drifted off the track and we came down the outside rail to finish third. I learnt two things from that ride. Vodka was injured deep in the off shoulder and would probably never race again. The other thing concerned my knee. I could barely walk afterwards and immediately arranged to visit an orthopaedic surgeon. He operated in early June.

The depth of gloom weighed heavily enough with the continuing drought, the gradual loss of my horses and the death of a mate. I had only known Bill Anderson for about three months, but I'd seen a lot of him in that time. I used to go and visit him in hospital. You never forget the people who welcome you when times are tough.

To add kilos to an already bursting leadbag there was the estate. The family accountant wanted a settlement or a selling up of the whole property. He was genuine in his concern for all involved, but it was a time when rural properties placed under auction received one bid—a dummy from the rear of the room. Any form of immediate financial settlement was out of the question with the cattle away in Queensland and the prospects of a crop bleak.

The week following my operation James and Kari took a few days off work and drove up from Sydney to help Sal take the weaners off the cows left at Myall Plains. I had been discharged from hospital a couple of days when James came into the bedroom.

'Reckon you'll ride again?' he asked, in jest of course. He knew the answer.

'Might have to be my own horse,' I remember saying. 'At my age you have to ride a winner every time you leave the enclosure.' I couldn't take the edge off the disappointment I felt, but that was life, irrespective of the sport.

'You'll get back,' he said cheerfully. 'You've come back from far worse.'

'I was younger then,' I said simply.

We talked about the world of the racetrack for a while. Ever since James turned four it was his life—his dad in the jockey's room and his grandfather drinking with old friends at the racecourse bar and passing pink lemonades to James, and at home his mother shackled with babies, complaining her eldest son was being exposed to a level of racetrack indoctrination never before known. On Sundays he raided my suitcase and dressed up, silks, cap and even the whip. When his brothers grew up he made a racetrack and every afternoon they raced on bikes, held enquiries for interference and if there was a fall someone would be suspended for the afternoon. To the chagrin of them all, they grew to be big men or, in James's case, just a shade too heavy to be a jockey. At different times each one would come to me and say, 'You're lucky Dad, gee you're lucky.'

'To be a little thin guy?' I used to answer, mockingly. 'The birds don't even see me sometimes.'

'Racehorses I mean. I'll never ride in a race.'

My answer was always the same. 'You're lucky that you won't. It must be something to do with the speed of a live animal, because everything afterwards is an anticlimax.'

James and I were still talking when Sal came in with the mail.

'The bank has refused to renew the overdraft,' she said with anguish. I could see the alarm in her eyes. 'What are we going to do?'

'Looks like another manager's going to have to leave town,' James said impulsively, with a widening smirk.

With the bank it was not a question of security. I was sole executor of the estate and some months before had appointed a new company director to fill the vacancy left by my father's death. The new director, when called upon, refused to sign security papers for the bank. The big lift to Queensland had been seen by some as an extreme and dangerous move. They were frightened about the future and I think the bank was onside with them.

'The crutches,' I said, feeling suddenly very restless. 'Sometimes they're like vultures, the banks. They circle and watch and when the kill's been done they move in.'

'It'll haemorrhage,' Sal said. 'It has once already. It's too early for long walks on crutches.'

'He'll be right, Mum,' James piped in. 'It's all a bit of a shock. Do him good to hobble about for a while.'

James went to fetch the crutches and while he was gone Sal repeated her alarm again, her voice low and a trace of anger barely concealed.

'We're no more than an entry in the computer today,' I remember saying quietly. 'In the cattle crash of '74 the banks provided sensible packages so that we could trade our way out.'

'I know what they did then. This is rotten. It's bullying—call it what you like.'

'I was just stalling to find the right words,' I said, forcing a smile. 'In the world of high finance I should parade myself in a thousand dollar suit and perhaps sneak a little make-up under my eyes, and then, using those impressive words— rationalise, restructure, formula and negotiate—I'm sure I would walk away with a solution.'

'You do need the crutches.' Sal smiled at last and I swung my feet to the floor.

'Where are you going?' James asked, holding the crutches while I eased myself onto them.

'Nowhere in particular. I think better when I'm walking.' I hesitated, gripping tightly. 'Or crutch swinging!'

There was a pause and James said, 'Where are the horses?'

'Didn't I tell you?'

'No.'

'I took them to Queensland. All of them.'

I could see he was very disappointed. He had done nothing but feed cattle the last few days and he was looking forward to a ride.

'And the horses too are gone,' he murmured. 'What a drought.'

Slowly I went over to the old cottage where my parents and I had lived when I was a child. It was about two hundred metres from the homestead on the edge of a little forest of pines. At the rear of the cottage was a huge ironbark and underneath it was the old fowl house. The little yard was still intact, almost smothered in plains grass. Nearly a half century before I had been attacked by a wild cat in that yard. If I concentrated hard enough I could almost smell the purple stuff, probably gentian violet, that my mother painted all over my body and face.

The wild cats were still about, but it all seemed so eerily dead. Not far from the fowl house was the bachelors' hut. I don't think anybody had been through its door for twenty years. Whatever paint that little structure had seen had long washed off and it stood grey and forlorn among old pines that no longer dropped seeds. People had long gone from here. I closed my eyes and after a while I could hear hooves pounding the red earth and the squeak of sulkies. I heard the voices of the bushmen, the fall of an axe on dry box timber and I thought I could smell the smoke from the evening fires. In my imagination I saw the wan light of the lanterns; the lanterns of the trappers.

My world at that time was the creatures of the bush: the husky outbursts of possums at dusk, the sharp bark of the wallaroo, the rasping call of the curlew (known locally as the scream bird), and always the wind in my face, for on the high plains the wind forever stirred the foxtail tops of the plains grass and the thousands of leaves in every kurrajong whispered. Above me was another world—the adult world—I simply looked upon, like any other creature half wild. It was the mornings I remembered best. Dogs barking as horses were rounded up; the crack of a stockwhip; and the familiar clink of milk buckets.

Now it was so quiet. It was as silent as the grave would one day be. The men and women from this period had all gone. Long before them their horses and dogs had gone. Their anguish, their passions, frustrations and elations had gone with them. They had all passed through without so much as a ripple left behind. Gone too were the animals I knew. The foxes had claimed the possums, the curlews and even the poor old goanna is scarcely seen nowadays.

I started back for the homestead. To the south-west, beyond the green belt of kurrajong trees, I could hear the drone of the tractor. We had received enough rain to start sowing and Greg was pushing the hours. At my feet as always were the three dogs. Millie looked at me with her soft brown button eyes, as though to say, 'What are those sticks you're leaning on? When's the saddle coming out of the harness room so that we can fan out and run the cattle?' I know she had such thoughts, because when we passed the harness room on the way back she stood by the door and wagged her tail. The old dingo was too old to care. He just walked and panted. Ellie, on the other hand, was forever on the lookout. A hare to chase would have been her equivalent of winning Lotto.

To return to the shelter of the house again was a relief. The winter wind had arrived after the rain in late May. In the kitchen Sal had the oil heater going and when I came through the door she pressed the start button on the electric jug.

'You were a while,' she said. 'I nearly came looking for you.'

'You know me. The old dreamer. I feel good and reckon I'll be walking in three days.'

'I'm not letting you go to town,' Sal said firmly.

'Boy, I'd give anything for Butch and Sundance's horses and the canyons of Utah. I'd give 'em hell.'

'Oh, you're a mad romantic and stop teasing me. You know I hate such thoughts.' I had plonked myself on a seat at the kitchen table and Sal brought over a cup of tea. 'You can be a writer and a dreamer any day, but right now I am a boring mum who wants to sleep peacefully tonight.'

'There's a few sheep left to sell. Two or three items of machinery we never use. Some scrap iron.'

'That won't pay the bills coming in here. You never go near the mail.'

Sal was right. I looked upon the mail as out of sight, out of mind.

'I promise we won't have to cut firewood again,' I said, trying to be convincing. In the wool crash I'd split wood for firewood and Sal had loaded it onto the truck. For a woman it was back-breaking work.

Sal said nothing for a while. She drank her tea and focused her attention on the window. Clouds from the south had gathered and the light faded into the bleakness of early winter.

'I'll light the fire,' she said at last.

CHAPTER 15

Tableland Camp

I gave myself ten days to get rid of the crutches following my knee operation which was no more than repair and trimming of two damaged ligaments. For the first time in months I could straighten my leg and if it had not been for the gloomy long-term prognosis I would have expected to be able to sprint and catch a calf once again—which I had done only three days before the accident. The calf had lost direction, gone through a fence and was a good six kilometres from his mother when I caught him and strapped his legs. He was the last calf I will ever run down and catch.

I used much of this time visiting my mother in the nursing home at Coonabarabran. The cancer had her bedridden and the only thing left in her life was visits from family and friends. She loved my accounts of the Queensland bush and I did my best to make her laugh, as she'd always had a keen sense of humour.

From the crutches I went to a knee brace and I could walk quite well. The second lot of weaners were long overdue to be taken off their mothers. There was little feed for them back home at Myall Plains—just enough to get them over the long haul from Queensland before they headed into the deep south. Sally and I had taken another trip to the Murray in search of feed and had met Geoff White, manager for

Wesfarmers Dalgety in Albury. He'd found agistment for me at Jerilderie. The paddock was a lovely mixture of clover and natural grasses. After the inspection we'd gone into the little town and visited the original post office. The famous bush-ranger Ned Kelly had closed Jerilderie down for a couple of days in the late 1870s. He and his brothers and a couple of extras had enjoyed quite a blow-out, something a few of my mates and I would have loved to have done in the days of wild youth. In fairness to Ned it's recorded he paid for his drinks and whatever else he may have needed that was not available across the border and back up in the mountains.

It was about the twentieth of June 1995 when Sal and I left for Queensland with the boys.

The winter trip to Queensland necessitated some additional equipment; namely, a four-wheel-drive bike. I couldn't ride a horse but felt I would be of some use on a bike.

Nick and Richard had come home at the end of the first semester and were looking forward to a few days riding. Tom had a late exam and would fly to Roma.

It was one and a half day's drive to the camp I had in mind. I decided to break the trip at Mungindi on the border. Before the introduction of cotton no one would have thought much about this little isolated town. And if it were not for a sculpture in the hotel none of us may have thought of Mungindi again. The wooden sculpture is a giant penis perfect in proportion and detail. It seems to say, 'You may think this town is a little dot on a thousand-mile river, but you will never forget it.'

Next morning we went on to Echo Hills at Surat. The saddles were stored in a cottage there. Sal and I had returned briefly in April to draft off a wing of steers and sell them in Roma. On this occasion there was no one around. Ken and Rosie were away or had gone to town. We collected the saddles and drove out to where the horses were running. Circus was lame and in light condition. They had ample feed, so this worried me. Yarramin seemed in good form and the buckjumper had his head over the fence for a smooch. He was the most deceptive horse! You would have thought a child could be legged aboard bareback. Just the weight in the stirrup, Peter Anderson had told me, was enough to set him off. 'He's into it before you reach the saddle.'

The horses were all we had left at Echo Hills. The few cows and calves I had transported home. The heifers and unsold steers I had to truck back to Mt Kennedy, as the feed at Echo Hills had cut out and there was not enough feed at home for them. There was nowhere else to go.

At Roma we bought a week's supplies and headed out. After six weeks absence what struck me most was the dryness. The autumn green had long gone. The tall grasses were finished and even the Mitchell grass had been frosted. It wasn't a good sign for the higher tableland country.

Picking the camp site was good fun. Clear skies heralded frosts at night and I discarded the old camp site near the bore, down in the valley. I selected a site on the tablelands, about a hundred metres off the road. We had to make a track in by throwing a few logs aside. The forest had been pulled at one time and the regrowth was about six metres high. The spot itself was a scalded piece of ground that had not recovered. To the west a tree barrier blocked any view, but to the east the ground fell away to form a low depression and beyond that a sandstone escarpment walled in the new emerging forest. The rock of the escarpment was cracked in a thousand places from a sun that had baked this land for millions of years.

We only had about an hour and a half of daylight left, which is not much time when tents have to be erected, camp set up and a pile of wood gathered. To begin with the boys and I unpacked and Sal commenced the preparation of her 'kitchen'. Nature threw in the basics—a big dead log wide and high enough to be a bench and a wilga tree with wide lateral branches. Among the branches of the wilga Sal hung the food safe, the cooking tongs, a ladle and the tea towels. Underneath, in the deep shade of the branches, she placed the Esky full of meat and the dry food boxes. Three or four metres away from the tree we set the fireplace simply by scraping the ground.

With everything unloaded from the trailer and the four-wheel drive, the boys and I started on the tents. Choosing sites took longer than the actual erection. Nick named Sal's and my tent the 'presidential suite'. I'd had it made to specifications as I don't like the modern camping tents. It was the same basic design as my old French tents, but much larger. When the boys were small I used to tell them they were sleeping in the tents of the Foreign Legion and that it was a great privilege. Now the tents were old and tattered and I had a feeling that if I said anything about the French Foreign Legion the boys might have tied me up in one of them.

Richard chose a spot close to the kitchen for his tent. It was the fire he had in mind. Nick put his up half under another wilga. He loves sleeping in and I wondered whether he thought I might miss his tent on the dawn wake-up. Tom's tent they put up near the presidential suite.

'It's no honeymoon for us,' Nick said with that wicked grin of his. 'Nor will it be for you and Mum.'

Richard was in his element with the firewood. He struggled with huge logs and wandered a long way to find the ones he wanted. He loved the bush and we had done the odd rock climb together. At the early age of twelve, he'd come with me on a roped ascent of Timor Rock which is a one hundred and fifty metre climb. Looking back I don't know how he did it. I am a little older and hopefully wiser than I was in those days. The most memorable climb we did together was the twelve hundred metre peak of Mt Lindsay on the Queensland border when Richard was about twenty. The afternoon before our planned ascent we couldn't find the track leading to the base cliffs. We split up and Richard found it. The only clues were tiny patches of bare ground and rock worn from the odd boot. Under the tangle of lantana and overhead jungle the ill-defined trail lay in heavy gloom. Unable to restrain his excitement Richard climbed three hundred metres to the first cliff. It was when he decided to return the trouble began. The gloom had deepened with the sun only an hour above the horizon and looking down the jungle yielded no sign of a trail. As dusk gathered I waited by the four-wheel drive, very concerned and periodically calling out to him. When Richard emerged from the gathering dark he was covered in ticks and had been laced across his bare arms by stinging trees. He still wore the cool that saved his life, but I could see he had been through a dreadful experience. He'd made several attempts to find the trail down and each time met an impenetrable barrier. Finally he decided to crawl so that he would be able to see even a disturbed pebble. He tracked himself down. We both knew the implications of a night up there were serious, with burns from the stinging trees triggering panic combined with the slow toxic release of the ticks. It wasn't until we sank a couple of beers in the local Woodenbong pub that we learnt how serious. Only months before, a German tourist had died on the mountain. Lost like Richard, he panicked and, half crazed from the stinging tree burns, he fell down a cliff. When they found him a fortnight later the dingoes had picked his bones clean.

We camped in the bush that night and at dawn headed for the base cliffs of the mountain. Richard had no fear of the trail now. It was very steep and we seemed to be halfway up the mountain when we reached the cliffs. Our order of ascent had been reversed over the years. Richard led the way now and I belayed out the rope. There were five full lengths of the fifty-metre rope to the summit plateau. There were pitches that pushed me close to my middle-aged limit and sometimes I wasn't thrilled to glance between my legs and see the forest canopy more than a hundred metres below.

Morning mist hugged the ancient cliffs of the summit and we pushed through ferns under stunted eucalyptus in search of the highest point. Out of the mist loomed a band of rock, not more than five metres high. It was a smooth wall and a lightning-sprung fire the summer before had blackened most of it. The fire must have had great heat because the few holds we touched crumbled. It was exasperating. Unless we scaled this wall we would fail in our bid to climb the mountain. Richard's a strong man and I tried climbing on his shoulders, but I still couldn't reach a handhold. For a few minutes we felt defeated, then I thought of a lasso. It was a long shot. A very long shot. I made it out of one end of the climbing rope and began throwing it up over the rock. On the fifth or sixth attempt the rope took hold. The problem was, 'on what!' A protruding boulder would be safe, but a shallow-rooted shrub was not. We both pulled on the rope and it held.

At this point a gust of chilly wind parted the cliff-clinging mist and we saw that the ledge we were standing on was exposed to a drop of more than three hundred metres. There was nowhere to belay the rope. I hadn't brought any pegs as I hadn't planned such a serious climb.

'I'll go,' Richard said firmly. 'I am the strongest.'

'And I am lighter by at least twenty kilos.'

Richie couldn't argue against that logic. The lighter the person, the more likely the rope would hold.

I showed him a break belay. I had gone to a climbing school once and been taught some useful tricks. In snow and ice climbing the belay man uses his ice-axe to break the speed of the rope. The idea is to let the rope travel, but to steady it and finally stop it. In this situation we would use Richard's knee.

He would push himself hard against the wall and hold the rope just above his knee.

Hauling myself up the rope was desperately difficult. If I'd had confidence in the anchor I would have planted my feet against the wall and walked up. Instead, I had to do a direct hand-over-hand pull. Near the top a hand hold presented itself and I moved away from total reliance on the rope. I put my head over the lip and looked for the anchor—a tussock of grass. I couldn't go back without taking the strain on the rope once again and the edge, now level with my face, was crumbly. Gingerly, and anything but happy about it, I had to take hold of the rope again and ease myself over the lip. Richard I belayed, anchoring myself to one of the trees. The whole summit plateau was covered with stunted eucalypts.

After this obstacle Richie and I walked to the summit and examined the entry book, which is kept in a little steel box. The previous climber was Tim McCartney-Snape, some nine months before.

'Too easy!' That's all he wrote, apart from his name and the date.

We weren't impressed. For Richie and me it had been bloody hard, but we hadn't climbed Everest solo either!

We took our time on the descent and it must have been late afternoon when we walked into the pub. Apart from wanting a drink or two, we had some ticks to be removed. A bloke at the pub was an expert. Somehow he pinched the skin and virtually popped them out. We had to strip to our underpants, but the Woodenbong pub would be the most laid-back place I have ever been in. A couple of beers led to a game of pool, then dinner, and later in the evening Richie and I were fascinated by all the characters. Two drunks were watching a blue video.

'I've seen your wife in those black panties,' one said to his mate.

'Yeah, well you think you're smart,' the other said.

'Smarter than you.'

'Yeah, well ya not as smart as ya think, because just about every bloke in Beaudesert's seen her panties.'

By nightfall we had everything in order. Each of us had a log seat and the boys had taken a XXXX from the Esky. For Sal and me it was red wine. The fire was ablaze and with a glass of cabernet sauvignon the chill of the June evening was held at bay. Just half a glass made the fire seem warmer and brighter.

The darkness crept in and we were discussing plans for the next day when a little dark form appeared at the edge of the lantern light. She was later to be called Nug Nug, for a possum so keen to join us was deserving of a name. Each morning we would wake to a bit of a mess in the 'kitchen', and the only place for the biscuits was in the food safe. We learnt the hard way. She could actually open a plastic container with her tiny paws. She had no fear of us and one night when I was reading by a lantern she crept onto a log only two metres away. She sat there for some time and stared at me. I didn't move and pretended not to notice, when all at once she startled me with that extraordinary husky sound possums make. She had something to say to me alright.

That first night Sal made a casserole in the camp oven. It consisted of round steak sliced into small pieces, potato, carrot and broccoli. She tossed in herbs and spices and with red wine to chase it with we could have been dining at a luxury restaurant.

Only among the great forests are the stars sharp and clear in Australia. After rain the desert stars may be sharper still, but usually there's a high level of thin dust and in the settled areas smog and dust forever mingle.

A dingo howled from the escarpment, a curlew's scream

pierced the night air, and carrying on a light breeze from the south-west I heard a scrub bull vent his lungs to claim his territory. Tired and well-fed, we all slept soundly.

I had been in contact with Gil and he had told me to just turn up when we wanted the horses. Scalp I had written to. It was hit and miss whether he ever got the letter. There was no telephone. The only hint he was about were the dead dingoes. His favourite spots for hanging carcasses were the cattle grids.

Before any mustering could be attempted we had to repair the holding paddock where the cattle had knocked the fence down in the stampede. I had to do the same exercise again, but the odds were in my favour, I felt. The cattle had had another four months watering at the trough and would be generally more settled. Also I felt camping right away from them might help.

All the fence posts were wooden. Twelve of them were snapped at ground level, some with ugly sharp spikes protruding from the ground. The boys had to dig them out and cut new posts with an axe. At least I felt it would be axe work. Nicholas had brought up an old power saw that hadn't run for years and he was very optimistic when I left them. The only work I could do was strain the wires and that wouldn't be for four or five hours. I had the opportunity to do a thorough inspection of the feed from the back of the four-wheeler bike.

It was slow going up on the basalt plateaus. At the pass I left the road and weaved my way through an intricate network of boulders. Sometimes there was no stone or rock for half a kilometre and this is where the bluegrass grew like mature stands of lucerne, but now it was gone. The cattle had left the high country and were feeding on the tall scrub grasses, which had little nutriment. I had to move them, which meant I had to find Scalp if he didn't find me. There was other country. He had offered it before, but there was a problem with water.

I got back to the bore about midday. Nicholas had a look

on his face as though he'd been posted a distinction for every subject. The posts were cut and in the ground. Waiting for me they had begun replacing broken rails at the trough. It was my turn to work and I got busy with the wire strainers.

'If only Nick would apply the same enthusiasm to his course as he did to that power saw,' Sal laughed.

Sal's not one to sit around and watch, but she had to that morning. She'd brought with her *S'pose I Die* by Hector Holthouse. It was an intriguing story about the adventures of the first white woman into the pastoral leases of western Cape York.

'Compared to what they endured our little mustering camp's pretty tame,' Sal said over a billy-made mug of coffee.

'Let's hope it stays that way,' I replied.

There was nothing left to do that afternoon and we all went into Mitchell to meet Tommy. He had flown to Roma and then met the Charleville bus. When we got back out to the camp I caught him having a few pensive moments while he sat on the 'kitchen' log.

'Double Bay to here,' he said soberly. 'Gee Dad, it's a bit of a shock, all in one day.'

I knew exactly what Tom meant. Even after long flights, people in Europe or America basically alight to physical conditions similar to those they left behind. Modern airports, coffee shops, taxis, traffic-filled streets and the smell of tarmac. Out here we were ninety kilometres from the nearest village in dry scrub that in midwinter produced not the slightest vestige of the softness and freshness of suburban gardens.

Tommy, however, loved a bit of adventure and often asked me when the next outback trip was planned. Following the wool crash there had not been one for some years. We had gone to the Gulf together in 1984. Tom was only eight then and too young to join his brothers for a week on the ski slopes. When we all regrouped at home about ten days later it was Tommy who had all the adventure stories and his brothers were very quiet, for canoeing in crocodile-infested rivers and exploring wild remote gorges in the Territory made skiing on overcrowded trails seem almost boring.

Next morning we headed for Claravale soon after dawn. I had telephoned Gil from Mitchell and he said the horses would be in the yard waiting for us. It was about fifteen kilometres to Claravale over a rough track and when we arrived Gil offered to float the horses over in his truck. It was a major inconvenience for him, I thought, and I hesitated for a few moments. He insisted and said if the boys rode over the days were too short for any hope of a muster. I knew he was right and it had been worrying me. Also we had to take what we got in one day. The country within a kilometre of the bore was eaten out. There was nowhere to feed the cattle out while we mustered for stragglers.

Gil had three horses picked out. One was a big bay gelding that nearly snorted the place down. I thought it was all bluff, but even so when Richard got on I was very relieved to see the tail lift and the gelding walk calmly around the yard. The next horse was a black gelding of about fifteen hands, named Black Cotton, which Gil told us had been foaled about the same time as the notorious Fine Cotton ring-in case had come to light. Nick was given Black Cotton and if straws had been used I felt Nick had drawn the longest, for the third horse I didn't like.

Most horses have soft, expectant eyes. This dark bay had what we horsemen call bad eye. Such horses watch you, but never directly. They watch out of the side of the eye. They don't like humans and want nothing to do with us. You never see their ears pricked forward.

Tom and I strapped him and upon tightening the girth he ran backwards. I got Tom to lead him for a while, first just walking, then trotting. All eyes were on us now. I am sure Gil and his man were quite amused, but they were too polite to show it. Before finally coming home and sinking his roots in the family station, Gil had worked in the Territory cattle camps and managed stations in the Carnarvons. When I first saw these men ride I felt greatly humbled. I had ridden in about two thousand races on the track, but when I watched these men gallop heedlessly through heavy scrub I felt as much a horse veteran as a city yuppie would have.

On one occasion I saw Gil chasing a steer along a steep-banked creek. The steer jumped two metres, landed in deep water and he must have thought freedom was on the other side. But Gil followed. He and the horse nearly disappeared from sight in the water, so enormous was the jump. I think the stockmen of the Carnarvons are the most fearless riders on earth and they think nothing of it, because they are reared to it.

Tom wasn't nervous and I made sure what was in my mind stayed there. Horses that run backwards on mounting will rear over backwards if the mouth bit is given a sudden pull. Tom got on and I held the near rein, but only gently. The gelding took two steps back. Gently I coaxed him forward and told Tommy to walk him on a loose rein.

The dark bay did nothing and for the rest of the mustering camp did nothing wrong. Richie's big bay shied on the first day, but compensated by bounding up mountain sides like an overgrown goat. Nick's Black Cotton was a delight for him.

Gil and the boys loaded the horses and we set off for the paddock. With washouts and gutters along the track the trip took an hour. They dropped the tail board at the unloading mound near the bore and the boys swung into the saddle, eager to start.

My immediate concern was to get the boys out and back with no one lost. I drew a map of the paddock on the ground with a long stick. Richard was to ride the northern scrub valleys and Nick and Tom the plateau, which took in about a thousand hectares. In the cool winter sun I expected the cattle to move along without much pushing and converge on the bore.

I began to give basic instructions about using the sun as a compass. They let me go on for a couple of minutes, then they explained to me how to correlate the sun with the hour hand on a watch. Their cadet camps hadn't been a waste of time after all! For a moment I felt like daddy bear taking the bear scouts on a picnic. When they were little, I must have read that story to each one of them a hundred times.

The boys had their lunches in saddlebags and I didn't expect to see cattle or a rider for hours. I muttered something to Sal about looking for feed.

'Do you think we should?' Sal had that worried mum look. 'The cows can't come back in here.'

Reluctantly Sal got into the four-wheel drive and we left. If she had any doubts then, she had none by the time we had reached the pass. We saw a little mob coming in for water and stopped. To stay on track they had to cross the road. Their coats were dry and on their briskets I saw rubbed hair—the winter lice had arrived early for these parts, hastening a rapid drop in condition.

We drove on beyond the pass. The soil was sandy and the pine forest hugged the road for some kilometres. Then we dropped into a low valley, hemmed in from the west by sandstone escarpments. The pine gave way to brigalow, and there was a good coverage of dry grass grazed on by some longhorns camped just off the road. They rose quickly to their feet as we approached and I stopped to have a good look at them. Their condition was quite good and they didn't seem to be affected by lice, which flourish on cattle losing condition.

Only three kilometres further on we crossed a cattle grid and entered a paddock that appeared not to have been stocked for years. There were no telltale walking pads and the scrub grasses were tall and brittle-dry. I saw an old vehicle track disappear into the brigalow and decided to follow it. It led to a trough. It was dry. No water for years, but it was in good order. I juggled the float valve and could see no reason why it wouldn't shut off. The connecting polythene pipe had been simply laid on top of the ground. Sal felt like a walk too, so I grabbed the rifle and we followed it. The brigalow was thick and we didn't see the galvanised tank until we reached the foot of a little flat-topped hill. An old vehicle track, which had been used to bring in the materials, led to the tank. Another pipe came from the south to the tank. That was the supply line. Somewhere there was a bore. The tank itself was huge, I thought about thirty thousand gallons. It hadn't been used for a long time and the rust had eaten holes through the iron. But the structure was solid and could be fibreglassed.

'If the bore still works we can get water.'

Sal looked at the rust holes and the supply line that seemed to emerge from the scrub like a long black snake. 'No water here for years means a broken-down bore,' she said gloomily.

We walked back not feeling very confident.

'Not much good worrying about the water if there's only brigalow scrub.' I said 'We'll go back to the road and see if there's another track.'

'Please don't take any risks,' Sal pleaded. 'The boys will need us. They've never been in anything like this.'

I had to drive another five kilometres before I found another track. It ran due west and was partly overgrown.

'Scratch the car,' Sal said hopefully, wishing I'd stop.

The car lurched and rocked and the sucker growth on the track went under the bullbar. 'I didn't borrow the money to buy this thing to be a yuppie you know.'

Sal remained quiet. She was being very brave. As the depth of the forest closed behind us I noticed a little fear tighten the skin on her cheekbones. It's ironic, but it takes a little fear to heighten the beauty of a woman. Unless endowed with extraordinary beauty, a bored woman will become plain.

I pushed on for about twenty minutes and a little voice from my subconscious began to murmur something about irrational obstinacy when suddenly we burst into open country. A kilometre to the west I could see the forest line and to the south a range rose one hundred and fifty metres above the plain. I couldn't believe it and got out of the car. The buffel grass had gone wild and was up to my thighs. It was winter dry, but each tussock was like a big armful of hay. Everywhere lay charcoal and as my eyes adjusted to the new scene I noted the black burnt-out stumps.

'There was a bush fire,' I exclaimed excitedly. 'Maybe three or four years ago and someone dropped some buffel grass seed.'

'Oh, it's magnificent.' Sal was out of the car and walking among it too. We were like excited children.

There was no need to drive any further, but I couldn't resist it. It was a winter oasis and teemed with wildlife. Mobs of kangaroos, now largely shot-out in the Maranoa, hopped a few lazy bounds and went on feeding. Pairs of plains turkeys flapped their enormous wings and glided just far enough to feel safe, and under the sparse regrowth—a mere metre high—it wasn't difficult to spot the shy rat kangaroos.

The gloom we had both felt evaporated and left us fresh and positive. It reminded me of oppressive heat triggering a rain squall and afterwards leaving the air cool and crystal clear.

The lurching and the bumps didn't seem so bad on the way back to the road. Near where the longhorns were lying up I had seen the sign of a track. We headed down it and held our breath. The track was washed out and badly gutted and the scene we drove into wasn't surprising. It was a mini environmental disaster. A few days before a southerly change had brought a little rain and with the ground so compact and hard around the tanks and the bore, the water still lay everywhere in a hundred small puddles. With years of oil spillage the ground was dark grey and the oily water resisted evaporation.

It was impossible to guess when the bore was last operated. The tanks looked okay and about a hundred metres away I could see huge mounds of dirt. A dam had been sunk within the last three or four years, which was strange near a bore. Either the bore had been abandoned or no one had time to check water troughs and had opted for surface water.

The first things I inspected were the fuel tanks. People often let petrol engines run out, but not diesels. They have to be bled and sometimes air pockets form in the fuel lines. No one wants this bother and luckily both these engines had been turned off before they ran out.

The engine on the bore was a monster and larger than that on the south bore. I guessed it was a 1930s model Southern Cross. There can be nothing half-hearted about starting these antique diesels, even if they run every week. In this case, it would be essential to drive through the first kick on the engine gummed up by residues formed in a long cold stand. It's not knowing what that kick will be that creates fear. In Queensland there are horrendous stories about the old diesels. Unlike the southern states, Queensland has always been big cattle country. Big mobs of cattle demand big volumes of water and in the old days only these big monsters could do the job. Men have been found dead, struck in the head by a flying crank handle. Cast iron tops have exploded like grenades.

Having oiled the compression chamber, I drove the crank down fast, released the compression and heaved into the stroke. It was an anti-climax. So heavy were the old rods, she didn't kick back. There was a gentle throb and the handle fell away in my hand. The first few belches of smoke were black and heavy, like smoke from burning tyres, then the revs rapidly picked up.

The grin was soon wiped from my face. Diesel sprayed over me like a shower. I scrambled around the other side and jammed the fuel line back into the little overhead tank. Sal had been watching and ran to my assistance. I got her to hold the fuel line while I got some tie wire. After a lot of fiddling and poor Sal also getting covered in diesel, we had the line secure. Fifteen minutes later we heard the water gushing into the tank. It was brown, full of rust from the bore pipes.

With the engine that pumped water along the supply line I was not so lucky. It looked in terrible shape. I knew a mechanic in Mitchell and would have to bring him out. The main thing was the bore. I had water and the problem now was the cost of getting it out to the feed and getting it there in a hurry.

To wash the diesel off ourselves I filled a plastic bucket with the bore water. The tank had a leak at the base and there was no point in running the engine for long. I just wanted it to have a good warm-up and to blow out the old carbon. With Sal's help again I also had to fill the cooling tank with water, which we tediously gathered from the tank leak. The cooling tank had a capacity of about one hundred litres. I stood on an old drum and Sal carried the water. We must have looked like something out of Jolliffe's Outback working beside the two-metre-high engine and all the mess and debris.

Sal needed to spend a bit more time on diesel cleaning than me, so I walked over to the dam. There was some muddy water at the bottom. A fresh cattle pad led to it. This was where the longhorns drank. In a pinch our cattle could get one drink here. That gave me two days to get the water on. It was almost absurdly optimistic and I left the dam feeling dry in the mouth.

Back at the south bore the mustering was proceeding well. The cattle were filing through the gate into the holding paddock and the early arrivals were making no effort to leave.

I am sure the old cows know when they are going to be moved to fresh feed. When the feed runs out and the stockmen arrive, they know. I've been certain of it for years.

Richard was the first in. He looked tired and the big bay had dry brown sweat stuck to the saddlecloth. He'd been over the high plateau country and zigzagged back through the two principal valleys. An hour or more later Nick and Tommy came in with about sixty head. Glancing over the mob I thought they'd got them all. If not, then only a few stragglers would be left. The boys said they had run well and for once everything had gone without a hitch.

There wasn't much daylight left when we finally turned the horses loose after a feed of hay. The cattle looked hungry and with the long walk ahead the next day I felt very worried as I drove back to the camp. The boys would have to go it alone again. The cattle were far less robust than last time, but if the lead bolted we'd be in trouble. While they were doing the drive I had to go to Roma and see if I could find someone to urgently fibreglass the rusty tank.

Back at the camp Richie got a blazing fire going within minutes. There's something about flames shooting tongues of red at the moment of sunset. It's as primeval as the beginning of time. A mug of red wine goes back a few hundred years too, and Tommy must have thought I needed it. He poured his mother a mug as well and Nick thought he would carry the mood even further by playing 'The Last of the Mohicans' from the four-wheel-drive. By dark the nagging fear of no water and no feed had evaporated.

Sucking the draught from a short piece of hollow log, the fire smothered any sound from outside the camp and the headlights caught us all quite unprepared. The lights went out and I could see it was a typical hunting truck with a spotlight mounted above the cabin.

'How yer goin',' growled our sudden guest. It was Johnny. The cheekiest face in the world.

'Johnny!' My mouth must have fallen open. The rumour was he had been given six months in jail since I had seen him in March. Trying to break up a fight, he had fired a harmless shot in the air. Anywhere but in a town, it may have had the desired effect and been forgotten.

'It was reduced to six weeks,' he said, suddenly serious. 'Stupid drunken spree. Fired a shot skyward to try and shock two blokes out of a dirty fight. It was near the pub and the cops were already on the way.'

Johnny had a case of beer in his arms, which he put on the ground and gently brought his girlfriend into the lantern light.

'This is Tina,' he said. Tina had clear features and long fair hair. She was in her early twenties. In a different place, she would have been pretty. When she spoke there was a southern accent.

I introduced them both to Sal and the boys. 'Welcome to the Blank Space,' Johnny responded, with that wild look in his eye. Looking at Sal he said, 'Reckon you'd have to show up to keep him in line.'

Johnny pulled some stubbies from the case and passed them around. Sal and I declined as we had half a mug of wine each. I noticed Johnny screwed the top off for Tina.

'Roo shooting?' I asked.

'Chiller's payin' ten bucks a carcass. If you get among 'em it's not hard to drop four hundred bucks worth in a night.'

'I don't see many,' I commented. The lack of kangaroos had bothered me for some months. In 1958 I'd flown to Blackall on the downs further west and I would have sighted two thousand kangaroos on the way to Maryvale Station.

'Got to get onto a station not shot out. Not many left.'

The steak was sizzling and releasing delicious aromas when the lights of a car appeared on the road. For a few moments the car didn't move. The driver didn't know who we were. I walked to the edge of the camp and yelled out.

The vehicle turned in and moments later Scalp emerged into the lantern light.

'How youse all goin'?' he asked. He seemed genuinely pleased to see us all.

I introduced him to Sal and the boys. He was nervous, as though unsure of himself. I thrust one of Johnny's stubbies into his hand. Johnny had split the case open end to end with a knife.

'Youse takin' off a draft of weaners?' Scalp asked. He had a good pull on the stubbie.

'Got to move too,' I said. 'Be alright if I reconnect the water to the brigalow paddock?'

'Hell yes!' Scalp exclaimed and tilted his wide-brimmed hat so that the lantern light reached his face. 'Good feed on the burnt country. Them cattle'll do well.'

'Far fence looks like a boundary,' I said.

'Fence stops at the cliffs. Off that strainer another fence runs west and it's a boundary too, but I ain't involved there. Them escarpments are the boundary. But north of that fence . . .' He started to laugh and Johnny giggled.

'The stirrup fighters,' Johnny cut in, and giggled louder.

'Heavens!' Sal straightened from her cooking over the fire. 'What on earth do you mean?'

'When they're musterin' and there's a heated blue they fight with the stirrup irons on horseback.'

'They couldn't,' Sal uttered in dismay.

'You bet they do,' Johnny said, taking a swig.

'They must just about brain each other,' Nick said incredulously.

'They got none,' Johnny exclaimed and went off in another giggle.

'How do we keep clear of them?' Tommy asked, more than a little disturbed.

'Oh, they'll boil the billy and wave you over,' Scalp said, and then laughed. 'Just don't take any of their cattle, because they don't call the stock squad.'

'A bloke caught duffin' gets taken to the nearest trough,' Johnny added.

He saw the sober look on the boys' faces and I could see he was going to paint a vivid picture. 'From one to the other, they run him up and down the full length with his face to the bottom. The poor bastard kicks and splutters and for a whole five minutes they make him fight for his life. Then they throw him out and thump the water out of him.'

'I couldn't imagine they'd have a duffing problem,' Richard said quietly.

The comment took Johnny by surprise. I had heard of the trough treatment.

'They don't, no.' Johnny drained his stubbie.

'But don't worry,' Richard said. 'I won't ride in there. In fact if I am asked to join them for billy tea I'll go on foot.'

There was a lull then and I asked them if they had seen Frankie.

'Have a beer with him occasionally,' Scalp said, gazing into the fire.

'I heard he's been burnin' again,' Johnny giggled. 'Givin' the Dawson Bar a bad time. They lost so many cattle last year they hired a troubleshooter.'

'It's not the cattle,' Scalp said. 'This bloke's a bit of a pro. He's hangin' around Josie and she's a butterfly—lappin' it right up. He's aimin' to get Frankie mad with jealousy.'

'Frankie might make the big mistake too,' Johnny confirmed. 'But the cock-sparrow will be the mistake. Bet he don't know Frankie can drop a dingo at five hundred yards.'

'I hear this bloke's good too,' Scalp said soberly. 'If he's a pro he's only gotta catch Frankie holdin' a gun. It's one-sided.'

'Don't follow you, Scalp,' Johnny said forcefully.

'The grog's got Frankie. He runs the cleanskins sober. Carries a gun to scare anyone, but would never use it. Before his mother died he copped a lot of that bible stuff.' Scalp paused and looked evenly at us. Sal had removed herself to the dark side of the lantern and was busy with some kitchenware.

'Frankie won't shoot sober,' he went on. 'Drunk he'll do anything and it don't affect his accuracy.'

'Frankie's alright,' Johnny muttered.

No one spoke for a few moments. I sensed a loyalty among rogues. They knew each other's weaknesses and accepted them.

It was a conversation not many women would like. I started it, but I was keen to know how Frankie had been. Women like to feel secure. They don't like to have to think about a lonely man in the bush who's okay if he's sober and dangerous when drunk. Tina had gone back to the hunting truck and I think had been making up a bed in the back. Sal busied herself with the cooking. At the first opportunity I swung the conversation around to tree pulling.

'I'm booked up for months,' Scalp said. 'They're gettin' the permits while they can. Some tribe up north's goin' to claim half the Cape they reckon. If they get it the shit'll hit the fan. I don't know nothin' about it. I just push the throttle and pull 'em down a chain at a time. But that's what them blokes are sayin' up there and everyone down here's worried.'

'But why pull it if you can't develop it?' Tommy asked. Young people everywhere were worried about the forests.

'Cattle and politics, I reckon,' Scalp answered. 'Get the cattle on the country and ya halfway to winnin'.'

Scalp was right. In Queensland the rate of clearing had increased, pushed by a shift in purpose. It appeared some leaseholders were pulling to beat the fallout of Mabo. The High Court in 1993 stated native title was extinguished where indigenous people no longer had an ongoing relationship with the land. What appears to be not understood is that under Aboriginal culture an ongoing relationship need not be pragmatic. Their culture is a complexity of beliefs intrinsic to the land itself and therefore transcends physical presence. They may have vacated the land a hundred years ago, but their ancestors are buried there. The confusion may persist for decades as the finding has sparked a clash between two diverse cultures with entirely different interpretations of the fundamentals of existence.

A few beers and the sizzling of steak had stirred everyone's appetite and not much was said while we all ate, balancing the plates on our knees. Scalp and Johnny put away several stubbies in the next couple of hours and Scalp laughed a lot. Johnny got sick of the beer and carried a flagon of red wine from his vehicle.

Scalp left first. He said he'd saddle up at daylight and meet us at the south bore. The boys were short-handed for the drive and I was very grateful. Johnny couldn't come. He was anxious to get to the station and claim his shooting territory before another shooter arrived.

The wine didn't do Johnny much good and he looked like sleeping by the fire. Sal and Tina had a chat over coffee, washed up in the bucket and left for bed. Before Johnny slipped into a heavy sleep he managed to unload something on his mind.

'Scalp's got to find a fair bit of money.'

'Who for?'

Johnny stared at me through glazed eyes. 'The bank.'

'Won't the pulling help a bit?'

Johnny nodded. He had his head on an old blanket Tina had given him. 'But he won't be here. Neither will I. Yer goin to be on your own Mick.'

CHAPTER 16

The Shadows of Anxiety

Next morning a light film of frost clung to the tents, lay along logs in fine powder, formed little crusts of ice on the plates left out to dry, and in the washing bucket a dirty block of ice was stuck to the bottom.

Johnny had woken at some stage and all I could see was a crumpled quilt in the back of the truck. I didn't expect him for breakfast and when I woke the boys I whispered to them to be quiet. I was worried Johnny might decide to come and delay us.

I suggested Sal wait for me at the camp, giving her an opportunity to cleanup after breakfast. I thought Johnny and Tina would sleep in. Sal and I had made a rule that no one apart from myself was to be left alone in the camp.

Carrying a last piece of toast to the four-wheel drive, the boys piled in and we set off for the bore. We chatted about horses until the final kilometre. Would we just see trees and black dirt, or a cluster of red hides as we neared the bore? With enormous relief I saw Scalp on a grey horse and he had about thirty head of cattle pushed up against the gate. Another swerve of the four-wheel drive and there were all the cattle— a patch of red against the green backdrop of the forest. It may have only been a small thing in the broad spectrum of events, but seeing those cattle still yarded that morning was another victory over the odds. I had a roadtrain already on the way from Dubbo and I had enough horsemen to drive them to the yards.

'Where'd you find them?' I asked Scalp.

'They were here. Come in for a drink and blocked by the gate. Rogues though—night drinkers. When they saw me they tried to break.'

I opened the gate and we put the little mob through. The boys caught and saddled their horses and together we discussed how six hundred head of very hungry cattle might be held together during the initial stages of the drive.

Richard and the big bay got the worst position—holding the lead away from the steep country running to the plateau. Nick and Black Cotton were posted at the lead on the south side. Scalp was to turn them as they came out and Tommy was to run them out of the small paddock. In fact Tommy didn't have to do much as the cattle charged through the gate and everybody was instantly galloping. If the gate at the pass was left open again the lead might bolt and take days to track down. I drove quickly back to the camp and collected Sal. I had a feeling Johnny might leave immediately he woke and I was right. Sal was happy and not the slightest bit nervous. She had the camera bag out.

'There's no time for photos,' I said anxiously.

'Oh yes there is. Even if the cattle stampede there's time for photos.'

I began to think of at least ten reasons she was wrong, but the topic of photography rubbed a raw nerve and I had as much chance as a jockey trying to tell the steward he didn't push the favourite over the rails. Minutes later we arrived at the pass.

'Mum told me one day,' Sal said as she attached the telescopic lens, 'to cherish the few years you have your children. They'll be grown up and gone so quickly. There'll be days when it all seems like a vivid dream.'

'Did we ever get photos of them on their ponies?' I thought maybe I'd taken a camera on one ride.

'I was so busy I never knew where that old camera was.'

Sal set out for the craggy cliffs that overlooked the road leading to the pass. I couldn't leave. When the tail was in sight my job was to open the gate and let the bunched-up cattle go. Richard and Nick couldn't risk riding in to open the gate. On Richie's side a bolt for freedom would take the mob to the high plateaus and a canyon beyond. On Nick's side a deep scrubby ravine dropped away to the west, just beyond the little hump that formed the actual pass.

Sal didn't have much time up her sleeve. The cattle had walked quickly and I saw the dust a few minutes before I heard the mooing. Some cows and calves constantly communicate with one another and others amble along in silence. Before the lead poked their white faces over the pass I saw Richard high up. He was taking no chances. I couldn't see Nick and it was then I heard the scramble. There was the distinct thud of rocks bouncing down a steep slope and I could hear the snapping of brittle undergrowth. There'd been a break and I felt helpless. If I walked over to have a look I would spook the lead. It must have been three minutes, then there was a surge through the herd. They were coming over the pass at the trot and I flung open the gate, hopped into the four-wheel drive and sped away. If the lead couldn't pass through the gate, Richie alone had to hold them.

Weeks later the photos Sal snapped told the little story of the break. All hell had broken loose and Nick, Tommy and Scalp had to gallop to the summit of a sandstone escarpment to turn back fifty breakaways. With some spectacular riding, they got them all back, while Richie managed alone to hold the rest of the mob. Maybe we did miss those early photographs, but Sal certainly made up for it that day.

The mob went through the gate quickly and Richard and

Nick galloped forward to take up their positions. Tommy's bad-eye mount was behaving, but I never saw his ears forward. Scalp rode over to me.

'We're makin' such good time I know a patch where we can hold up for dinner. Bit of good grass. Give 'em about three hours.'

'Track in there?' I asked. 'I could drop the water and lunch.'

I was going to take the lunch to the yards before I left, but I knew the boys would be ravenous hours before they got there.

Scalp said there was and dismounted to draw a dirt map. We left immediately, picked up the overgrown track and found the burnt stump Scalp had mentioned. By the time Sal and I left for Mitchell I could feel the tightening in my stomach. Time was the enemy and I was lagging behind.

At Mitchell I went to see a mechanic who had helped me out on a number of occasions and he agreed to work on the supply line engine provided I took him out. We went on to Roma and called at a business which specialised in fibreglassing. The manager thought he could fit me in some time in about a week. I hammered the urgency hard and when I explained exactly where I was with the cattle his attitude softened.

'That's bad country to be in,' he said, shaking his head. He was in his sixties with snow white hair and the lines in his face suggested a lifetime of toil. 'It's never been any different in my time.' He paused and glanced through the door into his large shed where several men were working. 'How many gallons did you say?'

'Thirty thousand.'

'I'll do it. We'll leave at three o'clock in the morning.'

Everything was set for the deadline. Scalp said he could spare one drink for my cattle from his horse paddock dam. He thought he had only a few weeks left for his horses, then the lot would have to be bushed into his mountain country. After the horse paddock, I was relying on water from the old bore.

Before leaving Roma Sal and I both had a shower at the Commonwealth Hotel. The simple things we take for granted sometimes become monumental when they are denied. A quick coffee at 'Double Bay' also helped fortify us for the trip back to the rangelands.

The boys hadn't long started the drafting when we arrived at the yards. The roadtrain was due at five o'clock and by six o'clock it would be dark. The horses were still saddled.

'We'll have to break the rule,' I said to Sal. 'Be seven o'clock before we're finished here.'

'I'll be right,' she said cheerfully. 'I'll get the fire going and prepare dinner.'

I took Sal to the camp which was only five kilometres away and when I left I didn't think I'd be long. I wanted to see the roadtrain driver, explain the permit conditions and give him his border crossing papers. The boys could do the rest and come back to the camp with Scalp. It didn't occur to me the roadtrain driver might get lost. Fortunately he didn't panic and after a closer examination of his map he found the correct road. I tied a bit of old sheet to a steel post to mark the track he was to turn into. It was about six-thirty when he arrived. Loading young cattle in the dark is usually difficult and the driver looked exhausted. He had covered the nine hundred kilometres from Dubbo without a sleep, and not used to ten hours in the saddle the boys were very tired. I decided to stay.

Roadtrains are loaded from the side and with older cattle it works well. Weaners, however, baulk when they get to the door. They see the confined space and don't like it. We had to work hard to load that hundred and seventy-three weaners. Fortunately, the bulls walked on as though they were frequent travellers. They were poor and destined for hand feeding. As the train eased away from the loading ramp I contemplated the superhuman effort the driver would have to demand of himself to steer forty metres of vehicle, loaded with a hundred and eighty head of cattle, across the vast plains for another nine hundred kilometres. He didn't expect to reach the border until 4.00 a.m., when he planned to snatch three hours sleep before the border inspector opened his office at seven o'clock.

We all watched the train leave. It was an awesome sight; enough lights for a city arcade creeping along a track too rough for a pedal bike in a forest already enveloped in darkness. The driver wasn't young. He was grey and balding and the last we saw of him was a tiny head through the cabin window.

The horses were the next job. The boys and Scalp led them to the horse paddock dam for a drink and then let them loose in a yard with some hay. It must have been about eight o'clock when we headed for the camp. Scalp declined my invitation for dinner. He said he had to go to Injune.

About a kilometre past the turn-off to the yards we saw the four-wheeler bike on the side of the road. There was someone on it and as we got closer we saw it was a woman with hair across her face. It was Sal. She was wiping tears from her eyes and looked very distressed. Obviously she had been trying to find us, but didn't know how to turn the bike lights on.

'A man arrived in a car.' Her voice was weak and frightened. 'I jumped on the bike. He followed me. He had the lights on me and I didn't know what he was going to do.'

I led her to the four-wheel drive. 'What did he look like?'

'Cowboy hat and beard.'

'Something he did must have frightened you.' I felt very concerned.

'He just looked like a wild man,' Sal said miserably. 'He didn't do anything wrong. He had a carton of beer under his arm.'

It was a reflex reaction. Any lone woman would have reacted the same way in this territory. It was my mistake. I should have briefed Richard on the paperwork and left it to him. It's often hard to admit the truth to yourself, but I knew I'd wanted to be where the action was.

Obviously Frankie had found the camp during the day and thought if he contributed a case of beer he would be welcome. It was most unfortunate.

The incident dampened the spirit of the camp that night. It was a good example of the effect of rumour and innuendo. Fear seemed to stalk every valley and range.

'You're quiet tonight Dad,' Tommy said, soon after his mother had gone to bed. 'It doesn't really matter, does it?'

'It's a sledgehammer dose of rejection for Frankie. When society rejects a man, most crumble. Others harbour the hurt and wait. Frankie is one of those who wait.'

'But if he'd come back we'd have made him welcome.'

'I know. Problem is he doesn't know it.'

Next morning we all left the camp together and I dropped the boys at the yards. Their job was to water the cows in the horse paddock and walk them towards any feed they could find, but not in Scalp's horse paddock. That had to be saved for his horses.

Sal had recovered completely. We had a huge day ahead of us and before driving eighty kilometres into Mitchell to meet the mechanic I drove to the tank to see if the fibreglassing had started. It had more than started. The base was already done and they were working fast, upwards from the bottom. The fibreglass is applied in liquid form and an intricate meshing system holds the liquid in place while it dries. The powerful chemical smell made me feel lucky as I walked away. Ideally the tank needed two or three days to thoroughly dry, but the old bloke knew I couldn't wait and instructed me to pump just enough for the cattle to drink.

In Mitchell the mechanic, Clayton, was waiting for me and we drove out again. While he set to work with his spanners I started on the plumbing. The polythene pipe between the bore and the supply line engine had been trampled by cattle long ago. I had no illusions about the supply line. Once the water began to push up after being absent for two or three years I expected a lot of repair work.

About two hours later I saw Clayton packing up his tools. Sal was sitting on a log, reading. She closed her book and we both converged on the engine. This was the last serious hurdle.

'Valve's in bad shape,' Clayton said grimly. He picked up the crank handle and tried it. He was strong and surprisingly fit for a mechanic. It wouldn't start.

'You can't order parts for this thing,' he said despairingly, for he understood what it meant to us. 'They can be engineered. There's a place in Toowoomba.'

There was no time for a salvage job. We had to go to Roma again—three hundred kilometres there and back. We dropped Clayton on the way and arrived in Roma about midday. The boys had no lunch with them as we had arranged to have it together. It was an awful feeling, but we had entered the desperate stage now. Worse still, when we didn't turn up they would be worried and anxiety would increase as the shadows lengthened.

There was no shortage of pumps in Roma and I selected one within a few minutes. I would have to pump directly out of the supply tank at the bore and it leaked. There was no quick alternative.

A box of sandwiches, a hundred litres of diesel for the big engine on the bore, petrol for the new pump and we set out again for the rangelands. We were both exhausted more from worry than the actual hours on the road or bent over machinery.

The boys were moving the cattle towards the yards when we arrived and they were famished.

'We began to think the worst,' Nick joked. 'Shoot-out at Nug Nug camp.'

I boiled the billy and gave everyone coffee. I laced mine liberally with rum. It was four-thirty and I knew most of my work would be by lantern and torch light.

It would be boring to relate the next eight hours. Sometime after midnight I had water flowing into the fibreglass tank. There were five ruptures in the supply line which stretched for nearly three kilometres. With only a torch the line was still quite easy to follow as the original ripper had left a narrow mound of dirt covered by dry grass. It was a very private victory. I crawled into the tent beside Sal, put my arm around her and fell into a deep sleep.

We all woke a little more relaxed. My sole job for the day was to turn off a stopcock at the bore. The pumping in the early hours of the morning would have provided enough for the first drink, but I didn't want to stop the big diesel. I intended to fill the supply tank and use a piece of rag to stem the leak.

The boys were up early, keen to see the cows with their heads buried in virgin grass. The heifers and steers transported back from Echo Hills had not done at all well, because they were still growing. There wasn't enough of them to fill a roadtrain and even if there was I would have had to hand feed them at Myall Plains. I had a lucerne paddock there for the weaners. It was dry and touched with frost, but they would recover from the separation stress which lasts about a fortnight. Then they were bound for Jerilderie.

The morning wasn't quite as uneventful as I had hoped. The cattle were so thirsty that when they ran onto the trough they broke a rail protecting the ballcock, which in turn pressed the float into the water, and by the time I saw it half the water I pumped during the night had been wasted. However, the fibreglass showed no sign of deterioration under premature filling, so the broken rail was nothing more than an irritation.

I thought the boys would ride back to the yards after watering the cattle and over the next three hours I began to realise the days of my youth were a long while ago. They had a snack at the camp and headed north-west into escarpment country none of us had been in. When they came back they spoke of a deep gorge with perpendicular cliffs and an imposing flat-topped mountain which they thought may be the mesa named by Leichhardt in honour of his accompanying surveyor, Edmund Kennedy.

'There's a track through the gorge,' Richard said. 'Some years ago it was graded.'

'Great camping site,' Nick added. 'Be in the shade for at least half the day.'

'We'll climb that peak tomorrow,' Tommy cut in. 'Reckon you can manage it Dad?'

'If you're willing to wait long enough.'

The scene I wanted to see was the cattle in the burnt country. I'd measured the paddock from the four-wheel drive as about three thousand hectares. The burnt country itself may have been five hundred or more hectares and between five and six kilometres from the trough. It was tempting to push the cattle out onto the feed the second day, but milk would be inflaming their udders now that the weaners had been removed and for the next three days about half the cows would hang around the gate. Already a few had eaten their fill and were mooing their heads off. Their big babies should have been taken off weeks ago. When man doesn't intervene the big calf is chased away when the new one arrives. I'd just have to wait to see the cattle shoulder-high in buffel grass.

Richard had a heart-warming fire going before sundown and the one good thing about our frequent trips to Roma was the ice. We could all have a cold beer and another steak on the barbecue. The whole operation was doing the boys a lot of good. That sickly, pallid colour so common among students studying into the early hours had given way to a tan. It was beginning to seem like the past ten years had been wiped aside. They were boys again, free of the unquenchable pressure of modern society. Sal, too, I thought looked much younger. She was revelling in having the boys virtually by her side, twenty-four hours a day. Tableland camp may not have been a home-maker's dream, but it was a mother's dream. We had one away—James, our eldest. The city had claimed him years ago. An auctioneer, he lived in a tough world. A whinging farmer, sick of everything—work, droughts, bad prices—need only have one day beside my eldest boy and he would kneel by his bed every evening and be thankful he still had a farm.

Boys chat endlessly to their mothers. There's an instinctive bond that lasts forever. The dad, I feel, just needs to be around. All the boys had undertaken studies at university that I couldn't talk about with them. I admired them immensely, for I felt about as educated as the fringe dwellers of the rangelands. I could pluck a few words out of the air, maybe, but that was the end of it.

We were into the second beer, just on dusk, when Scalp arrived with more beer.

'Now don't you go runnin' off into the bush, Sal,' he shouted jokingly from his ute.

The boys and I smiled, but Sal was embarrassed. Scalp had got out quickly and closed the door. I didn't see the other two figures in the fading light until they also got out.

'I hope you don't mind,' Jenny said to me, coming forward with Clara. 'Scalp doesn't ring me very often. When he did I said I was sick of the place. Wanted to get out in the bush.'

I introduced everyone and said to Scalp, 'You've seen Frankie then.'

Scalp looked uncomfortable and Jenny answered for him.

'I would have run too, don't worry. There was a woman held

out here. When she got away she had bruises down her neck from the point of a gun barrel.'

'They got him though. He's gone.' Scalp kept his eyes averted and I had an instant gut feeling the offender hadn't gone too far.

'It was very bad luck with Frankie,' I said. 'In fifteen minutes we'd have all been here. We'd have given him dinner and drunk with him.'

'Yeah, well Frankie ought to have realised that too,' Scalp replied. 'He's at war with the world at the moment. Ike's comin' back. Gonna go trackin' cleanskins.'

'More like men,' Jenny butted in with her husky voice.

'He's spoilin' for a gunfight with that bloke who's had Josie stay with him.'

It seemed a shocking conversation in front of the little girl, but when I looked at her I could see she was taking no notice. She was as used to it as other children are to playground games. I think she was much more interested in the boys.

Jenny and Sal got talking with a glass of red wine and I mixed a soft drink for Clara, who sat close by her mother. She was naturally shy, and far too young for the boys to even look at twice.

'You've got the water on,' Scalp said, with a grin. 'Been wantin' to get it on myself. No money.'

'The whole thing cost about four and a half.'

'Put it down to agistment,' he said.

There was an awkward silence. Richard was intrigued by the old graded track.

'There's a deep gorge out the back,' he said. 'The road through was once graded.'

'It was an access road at one time,' Scalp confirmed. 'The station was burnt out.'

'Bush fires?' Richie asked.

There was a pause and Scalp knew what we were all thinking.

'That bloke got what he deserved. Nothing to do with me, but can't say no more.'

It seemed close to the heart and I erected the griller over the fire.

'You goin' to stay with the cattle, Mick?' Scalp asked suddenly.

'My mother's very ill. Soon as they're settled we've got to go back.'

'I start weanin' next week. I can watch the water that week. Week after that I am gone—scrub pullin'.'

'Will you ring me the day you go?' I asked.

'Yep.'

After dinner Sal suggested a card game and a circle was formed on an old rug. Everyone knew five hundred except me, so I used my knee as an excuse and went to bed. They played until midnight and Scalp and Jenny retired to the ute. Clara fell asleep by the fire and later Sal placed a quilt over her. It was a relaxed few hours, but deep down there was disquiet and at the end of the day Scalp's problems weren't so far removed from mine.

I pumped water through the night and then stopped the big diesel to check the oil. It had used a couple of litres and I had to drive down to the south bore and pick up a drum that had four or five litres left. The oil was going to be a problem, I thought. When I arrived at the south bore there were nearly twenty cows watering at the trough. I'd been worried about the cattle grid on the road, but I'd thought it too wide for the cattle to cross. They had jumped it alright and gone all the way back looking for their calves. I looked in the supply tank and there was enough water for some weeks. A small lot would probably find a bit of feed, so I decided on the spot to leave them be. I think I was getting very stale about the whole exercise. I went back, topped up the oil and kicked the engine up for another two days of pumping.

Back at the camp the boys were ready for a mountain day. It took me back to those adventure hikes we'd done so often in the Warrumbungles when they were young.

'Kennedy put his initials on that peak,' Scalp said, before he, Jenny and Clara left. 'On a slab of rock right at the top.'

That was all we needed. We were all going to climb it. I wasn't sure how I'd go, but if it came down to elbows and hands I intended to keep going.

The track in wasn't too bad. The boys knew where it turned off and it soon became apparent a conventional-wheeled vehicle had used it several times since the last heavy rain in February. The gorge had nothing like the grandeur we were used to in the Warrumbungles. It was wild though and the thought of camping in it as a bushwalking base had great appeal.

Beyond the gorge towered the mesa. From top to bottom it was no more than one hundred and fifty metres and the upper cliff line was more a jumble of eroded crags. If I went slowly I knew I could do it. Sal stayed back with me and the boys surged ahead. By the time Sal and I made the summit they had been looking for Kennedy's initials for more than half an hour. We couldn't find them. I am sure the explorer's initials are somewhere on one of the escarpments. They may be on that mesa too.

The following day we walked the cows to the burnt country. The boys spread out on horseback and Sal and I did as much pushing as possible from the four-wheel drive. When they hit the feed (and I use that word because that's the effect it had) it was like gazing across four hundred statues. It was a wonderful sight and when we got back to camp later that afternoon Sal popped a big beef roast in the camp oven and I opened a bottle of red wine. The ice had melted, but the stubbies were still cold and the boys were soon thinking and talking 'south'. We had done all we could. It was time to go.

The boys rode the horses back to Claravale and we all left for Roma. I believe pleasure in life is totally tied up with where fate lands you. One hundred and sixty kilometres from Roma with the four-wheel drive churning the dust like a tank, the ultimate pleasure for the five of us was the prospect of a hot shower at the Commonwealth Hotel.

We didn't stay more than a day in Roma. Nick caught up with a few mates he'd first met nine months before and Richie and Tom had their first insight into western Queensland culture. On a Friday night at least two live bands strum their way into the early hours of the morning. Young stockmen from as far west as Charleville and as far north as Tambo come to Roma for a fun weekend, their theme song 'The Boys from the Bush are Back in Town'. A woman once said to me in a southern city, 'There's no men my age left here.' I told her to pack her bags and head for western Queensland. Apart from basic clothes, I told her to take only a shotgun for the over-keen and a hat for the sun. Over a cocktail she gave me that sceptical look. Sal didn't believe me either until one night I took her into the bar at Muckadilla. There were station managers, ringers, drovers, shooters and bums. It is a bar where everyone mingles and by midnight everyone's drunk. In the space of three hours Sal had one direct proposal and I was asked by another man if I would loan her for $500. I would be the first to agree that a lady from the city would have to smooth off her suitors' rough edges out here, and no one would envy her the task.

To paint Roma as a bawdy frontier town, however, would be inaccurate and offensive to most of the population. It is a small town by provincial standards, yet the extent of the services provided is extraordinary. The standard of living is as high as anywhere in Australia. Cinema entertainment is equal to the best in Brisbane or Sydney. The supermarkets stock everything a sophisticated housekeeper could think of. But most important are the people. You can still leave your keys in the ignition in Roma.

It was the end of the best two weeks I had experienced in Queensland. We'd done all the work as a family and it was terrific to see the boys get so much out of it. Two weeks in the outback and the colour was back in their faces and they laughed a lot.

CHAPTER 17

The Dilemma

I arrived home to problems more complex than those I'd left in Queensland. The estate had lapsed into a position of impasse for the moment. The bank gave notice of closure on the company trading account, agreeing only to honour any cheques outstanding in Queensland. It was suggested I open a second trading account, secured by my meagre assets. Less obstinate individuals may have agreed.

During these worrying days we had a phone call from Scalp. He had never contacted me before. It was a breath of fresh air. He had mustered his weaners and sold them in Roma. Before heading north into the big scrub, as he called it, he planned a few days scalp hunting. He would telephone again when leaving.

I asked him about the cattle and he said another four had jumped the cattle grid and walked the sixteen kilometres down to the south bore. The others were watering and feeding out onto the open country. He had refilled the tank.

The situation with my mother did not appear to have changed, but her doctor told me the end was near. Sal and I went into Coonabarabran as often as we could and sometimes I went in alone and spent most of the day with her. Talking to her wasn't easy at this stage and when the nurses arrived to assist her I took the opportunity to exercise my leg. It was inclined to stiffen and the muscles above the knee had shrunk badly.

The days grew into nearly two weeks and still there was no word from Scalp. To begin with no news was good news, and then no news was ominous. There was no one we could call. Mum was slipping. Every two or three days I could identify some sign of deterioration. I hovered in indecision for two or three days and then a phone call from Injune wiped all that. The woman said she managed a service station in the town.

'I've had to trace you through directory assistance,' she said. 'And I've been very reluctant to become involved, but a stockman bought fuel here this morning and he said there was a mob of cattle out of water on Mt Kennedy. He thought they were yours.'

She said she didn't know who the stockman was. I am sure she did, but he understandably wished to remain anonymous.

I thanked her and I must have sat for some minutes before I told Sal, who was in the kitchen. We would have to pack immediately.

Sal packed up the clothes we were likely to need, a box of non-perishable food and utensils for outdoor cooking. By torch I loaded the truck with ten bales of hay, containers of fresh water, saddles, farrier gear and horseshoes, tents and mattresses. We set off at six the next morning.

It was about seven o'clock when we arrived at the nursing home in Coonabarabran. Sal and I walked into Mum's little room expecting to find her cheerful, as she usually was, and received another shock. Mum was in a coma. The nurse on duty had been trying to telephone me for the past hour. The doctor had been and advised Mum could go at anytime. The trip was off. For two days Mum drifted in and out of consciousness and on the third day she seemed to lapse into a deeper coma. It was a dreadful dilemma. The senior sister told us Mum could hang by a thread for days.

We decided to make a quick trip in the four-wheel drive. There were lots of bush tracks and with a bit of care I could negotiate most of them. If I found the cattle on water I could return immediately, stay with Mum in her last days and then mount a muster. If the situation proved to be grim I had no plan to fall back on.

It was a decision made with a lot of sadness. In my heart I felt I would never see Mum again. She was propped up on pillows and her face was deathly white. I looked at her for a while, a long last look, kissed her lightly and left.

We drove straight to Kooyong, Bill and Sandra's property, about ten hours away. Bill had two bikes and he suggested we load them onto his truck and he and I would head out to Mt Kennedy. It was the commonsense thing to do and I agreed, although reluctantly, as I knew Bill's annual bull sale was only days away and he could ill afford the time.

There was an eeriness about the rangelands that morning. It was probably all in my mind, but I know Bill felt it too. In the old south bore paddock where the steep slopes of the blue-grass tablelands formed a barrier to the east, we saw little mobs of cows chewing on tussocks of forest grass. Their stomachs had dropped since I last saw them and those that looked back at us through the trees may have been watching for the sign of a hay bale. The first to calve would be any day. With a calf to protect the cows in this paddock would be under double stress. They had to walk to water, forage deep into the forest and keep a wary lookout for dingoes. In normal conditions a maternal group will plant all the calves together and one cow will become the minder. But when nutrition is very low every cow is ravenous and these little arrangements seem to fall apart.

I directed Bill to the trough and we examined the cattle tracks. It was almost impossible to assess with any accuracy, but the pads suggested about fifty head were coming in for water.

The fact that the tank still had about twenty thousand litres of water confirmed only a small mob was drinking there.

At the trough watering the brigalow paddock there had been one or two days of chaos. The trough itself sat in black mud. When we got out of the vehicle the stench was strong, like a backyard pig sty. The smell indicated cattle had been hanging around the mud, trying to seek moisture from it and at the same time letting their faeces fall into it.

To get to the float valve I had to throw an old post into the mud and step on it. The float lifted freely in my hand and the valve closed. Sometimes when a float has been out of use for some time, corrosion will form on the hinges. There was no clue to its failure and when Bill stepped over the mud to check he too was at a loss to explain how the water had all let go. The trough was bone dry. The fibreglass surface showed the stains of frantic mud-covered noses.

We examined the most recent droppings and concluded the last beast had left maybe four days before. It was a good indication they had all found water. If cattle can't get out of a paddock they usually hang around where they last got a drink.

Bill drove back to the road and turned towards the cattle grid. From the grid a track ran east, following the fence. The track had almost disappeared under regrowth, but the cattle pad along the fence was fresh and the old grass had been trampled into the dust. Bill backed into a ditch on the side of the road and we unloaded the bikes.

I hadn't been on a two-wheel motorbike for years and the one Bill set up for me was a big trail bike. He showed me the gears and I suggested he lead the way.

It was only about half a kilometre to the first corner of the paddock and there we found the fence cut. The cattle had gone through and the tracks indicated they had walked in an easterly direction, tightly packed. The puzzling tracks were from those cattle that hadn't gone through the fence. They had followed the fence running north. They may have been the first to the corner, before the fence was cut. Close examination of the tracks showed they hadn't returned.

My immediate fear was for the cattle that had not gone through the fence. In the past I have found cattle bunched up in a corner because they could smell water in another paddock.

We spent the next four hours on the bikes looking for the cattle, though to be strictly accurate, Bill spent a considerable portion of the time waiting for me. He said it was like watching Mr Bean live and after an hour swapped bikes with me, but I don't think it made much difference as I still got the throttle confused with other levers.

It appeared all the cattle had found water, but they had spread over thousands of hectares. On the big open plains country of north-western Queensland the spread of cattle is normal and presents only minor mustering problems. In the rangelands of the Blank Space the mustering can be formidable. To compound the situation the cows were all about to calve.

The cattle which had walked the fence had been blocked by the escarpment on the western side. At that point they had left the fence, followed a game trail below the escarpment cliffs and found the gorge. About five kilometres beyond the gorge they found a spring near the charred remains of a homestead. Like the forlorn sight of a cross in a private graveyard, the darkened chimney stood alone.

There was no sign of a fence and we concluded the escarpment was the boundary for about three kilometres. If stock had to be kept separate in the past, a temporary fence must have been erected across the floor of the gorge.

The mob let through the fence, which may have accounted for three-quarters of our herd, had walked into a mob of station cattle and followed them to water. It was a huge dam about half full. The water marks on the bank indicated a rapidly receding waterline. Without knowing cattle numbers, Bill and I could only wildly guess, but we thought in ten weeks the cattle would only have a mud hole.

East and north of the dam there were no vehicle tracks. I think Bill might have handled the scrub and fallen timber, but he was particularly emphatic about me not having a go.

In one respect the day brought a wave of relief. The cattle had found water and most were on reasonable dry feed. The ones that had walked back to the old paddock were probably rogues, and based upon decades of observation very few rogues ever starve. If it were not for the imminent calving no urgent action would have been necessary. Once they began to calve little mobs of cows would poke away into hidden pockets in the forest and only water every two days. The stockmen of this country have told me cows will go three days without water in the wintertime. They drink copious amounts to get themselves through. It allows them to conserve energy and remain with the new calf.

I understood from conversations I'd had over the months I'd been in Queensland that seven hundred station cows ranged freely over this largely undefined area. These cows too were on the point of calving. A thousand head, dispersed through ranges, across great plateaus, tucked up in deep ravines and jungle-like belts of scrub locked me into a highly vulnerable situation. The riders of the rangelands could easily poke a hundred cows away into the more inaccessible ranges of the Great Divide. Once the calves were big enough they could drive the mob to one of the outstation yards scattered around the forested hills, or, if the stockmen were young, to just an open piece of ground for roping and bulldogging. When the calves were old enough to wean they would be trucked away and the cows bushed.

It was rumoured these herd-drafting operations had been

going on for some years and may have accounted for the long-horns and sundry brands I saw in the yards the day the drunk tried to pull me from the truck.

'You'll have to get them together as soon as possible,' Bill said, as we turned the bikes around to head back to his truck. 'Once they calve, mustering your cows from the others will be a nightmare.'

'I'll have to go home.'

'You've got a week or two. I think you'll get them all.'

Bill knew I was caught up in a very unpalatable situation and tried to soften the reality. The one thing that might give me time, I thought, was to make sure anyone hanging around the ranges or the camps with duffing in mind knew I was around. They didn't know I had to go south again. Bill thought it was a good idea too and we drove down to the old stockmen's hut, across to the yards, along a track through the horse paddock and back to the road. Unless the duffers saw me they would have no way of knowing it was me for certain, but no one else had sufficient interest at stake to ride a bike all over the place.

Back at Bill and Sandra's I received the inevitable news. Mum had died that morning. It was no shock of course, just that final realisation that I would never again see or speak to someone I had known from the first dawn of memory. That's what is difficult to come to terms with. I know it is the same for everyone, for no matter how long a loved one has been terminally ill, we have to grapple with that sudden void.

Next day Sal and I drove south again. For a lady in her eighties, Mum had kept in touch with the younger generations and they turned out in force at her funeral. Known to her grand-children as Nan, she'd had open house for my friends and my sister's friends over a long period of time. They hadn't forgotten her.

With the talking over and the usual references to memories—sometimes happy, sometimes sad—of times long ago still ringing in our ears, Sal and I were soon thinking of making our way back to Queensland.

CHAPTER
18 Gorge Camp Attack

When we packed again for Queensland it was about mid-August. The weaners had been at Jerilderie for a fortnight, the cows and calves on hand were battling along well on the basalt ridges and the struggling wheat crop badly needed rain. Greg was on repair work at Myall Plains, mainly fences, and he helped me load the truck.

This time Sal and I knew we could be away for months. The mustering alone might take a month, then we would have to live with the cattle on the stock route. Following our previous visit when we found the cattle bushed we knew we had to do something. The decision to go on the stock route was tough, but with cows roaming everywhere through cut fences, boxed up with other herds and water rapidly drying up, we had no choice. The whole thing was very daunting. Cows would be dropping off and having their calves, and the penalty for loitering on Queensland stock routes can be severe. I've heard of mobs being ordered off, despite having nowhere to go. And when cows and young calves are left behind they are exposed to theft.

Among the usual essentials I took on board two hundred litres of fresh water, enough oats and chaff for two months and twenty bales of lucerne hay. There were things I was undecided about, but threw on anyway. One was an old hammercock shotgun. I expanded my toolkit to include equipment for any breakdown short of stripping the engines.

The difference with this trip, apart from embarking upon a journey of incalculable problems, was the taking of two vehicles. The truck would be used to carry equipment, transport the horses, collect stragglers and, in general terms, become the base camp. The four-wheel drive we needed for trips to town to replenish supplies and have that occasional hot shower. Also, we'd need that little escape to 'Double Bay'.

Travelling in convoy we planned a three-stage trip. Money was tight now. I looked upon this trip as an expedition and sold the last of my sheep to finance it. We had to save everywhere possible and that meant no staying in hotels.

On the first stage we camped at St George by the river. With the seats folded down, the four-wheel drive provided a reasonable bed. We had company too on this trip—Ellie and Millie. The two little bitches would help flush cattle from thick clumps of scrub. They travelled in the stock float with all the equipment and felt very insecure about the whole operation.

It rained overnight in St George. We hadn't seen rain for weeks and when Sal and I got up and walked around to ease the stiffness there was that wonderful smell the wet soil gives after the long absence of rain. Galahs shrieked overhead and scores of birds chattered along the banks of the Balonne. Normally I may not have remembered such things, but it was the first moment following the funeral I felt alive again.

Puddles of water lay alongside the road all the way to Echo Hills. The farmers we passed on their way to town waved and one bloke fixing a fence waved both arms. People on the land rarely have anything to cheer about, but that day carried a rare light-heartedness.

At Echo Hills we were greeted with smiles by Ken and Rosie and coffee had already been made. The rain had come in time to spur the wheat crop into head. With cattle prices the worst for twenty years and wool down again, no one had to utter a word—the rain was like gold dropping from the sky.

Our coffee break at Echo Hills was lunch as well. We caught Circus and Yarramin with a bucket of oats. Yarramin looked well, despite his great age, but Circus hadn't put on much condition. At least he wasn't lame. The buckjumper had his nose in our faces and armpits. He was a big useless pet. We left him behind—he'd mated up with an old horse and I didn't want to split them. Something had gone horribly wrong with the initial handling of this horse and I felt a bit sad when I moved the truck away from the loading ramp for the last time. The cattle were gone. I knew we would never be back.

About mid-afternoon we topped a rise and the Roma hills broke the flat line of the horizon. No one ever wrote of scenery out here or ever would. It is the character of the land that envelops the people here. For me it's impossible to put a finger on it. Whatever it is I felt a sense of coming home when those hills hung on the horizon before us. There was so much worry and sadness down south that I think the prospect of being simply among the cattle and in the bush was a psychological relief.

Still, it was tempting to stop in Roma and have one last night in civilisation before going bush. But there was nowhere suitable for the horses and the dogs, so we pushed on to Amby. It was nearly a year since Circus had arrived in Queensland, spending that first night in the Amby railyards with the horses on the stock route smelling him through the rails. Sarah-Jane had been one of those horses and I wondered where she might be on that thousand-mile stock route that threads through the heart of Queensland.

Nothing had changed at Amby and I expect twenty years would have to pass before a new fence would be noticeable. I backed into the loading ramp and when I got out I saw the ashes of my old fire. Circus too remembered the yards and gave a bit of a snort. I fed them both hay and then Sal and I gathered some firewood. Sal had done a little bit of shopping in Roma, before catching me up. There was no ice or meat this time. We decided to get used to dry food and tins from the first day.

The most excited about our camp beside the rail track were Ellie and Millie. They were out like two little rockets when I pushed open the truck's sliding door and for the next ten minutes they sniffed nearly every square metre within a stone's throw of the yard. The smells were all new and their tails were upright.

After dinner, we walked across the railway line to the pub to telephone the boys, confirming that we had arrived and checking they were on track to leave. Richard was coming the day after tomorrow from Lismore in his little Brumby ute and Nick and Tommy were coming from Sydney by bus in about three days' time. The girls had been offended at being put back in the float, but not having been educated to behave in little towns they would have trotted into the bar.

We had two drinks. There were one or two familiar faces, but no one I knew to talk to. Back at the camp I tossed the mattress on the ground. 'It's so good you get to hate sleeping in a room,' I said to Sal.

James Blundell, the singer, wrote a song called 'Camp Fever'. In it he sings about the sunrise in the mountains. If I could sing, it would be about falling asleep while peering at the stars. With me it only takes one pot of beer.

The air was cold and still and when we woke after dawn the frost had settled over the top blanket. The girls were at our feet, curled up into little balls. There would be no smelling and sniffing for an hour at least, and with my nose back under the blanket there would be no breakfast fire for another hour either.

We had breakfast, loaded up and two hours later we were at

the gorge. It was an ideal camping spot for the job. I was going to make the brigalow paddock the holding one. Each little lot of cattle would be brought to it. By camping in the gorge we blocked the only way out and we were so far off the road I didn't expect camp visitors. And also, I had to admit to myself, it was wild with a rugged beauty. The last cattle to be mustered would be those that had already gone through the gorge.

To find a suitable camp site the vehicles had to be driven through the narrow gorge. At one time the blade of a bulldozer had pushed some large boulders to the side. Once through the gorge we found a protected spot with level ground and some lovely big gumtrees. It was among the trees I erected the tents, but after my experience with the ironbark crashing down in the storm several months before, I took note of the branches overhead. Before the boys arrived I wanted to have a fully established camp, so I put their tents up as well.

The floor of the gorge was a creek bed. It was principally sand with grey silt and covered in heavily grazed green grass. In fact the marsupials kept the green down to ground level. It was perfect for a camp fire, as elsewhere the rapidly warming days and brittle dry grass posed a fire hazard.

After unloading the horses and tethering them to a tree with some hay, I helped Sal set up her kitchen in the creek bed. Heavy rain never falls in central Queensland in August, so the chance of a flash flood was indeed remote. A cliff rose vertically from the bank of the creek and above the first fifteen metres the slope angled away to form a steep mountainside covered in rock-clinging shrubs and protruding boulders. With care, a man could scramble to the top, which I estimated to be about one hundred and fifty metres above us. The cliff itself was of fragile sandstone, more like a giant wash-out than a normal sandstone gorge. A metre or so above the cliff you could see the colour of the rock change from a grey to a heavy black basalt flow, indicating where periodic volcanic activity had burst through the earth's crust during the past forty million years.

While Sal and I were working the girls were having a ball. Ellie had put up several stinkers, but one shrill whistle from me and she stopped. She was always very obedient. Millie did whatever Ellie decided upon. A family of emus came poking around about lunchtime and Ellie retreated to me with furious barking. I was hoping the emus might stay around as they fascinate me, but the presence of the dogs was not to their liking and they stayed only a few minutes.

In the shadow of the gums in a slight northerly breeze it was hard not to fall asleep following lunch. There was still too much to do. The next job was to unload the hay, the water and fencing materials. I intended to load the horses again, before dark, and they needed more room.

About mid-afternoon we took the four-wheel drive back out to the road and went down to the old bore with some diesel. It started with no problems and on the way back I walked down to the corner of the paddock and strained up the fence. All we needed now were horses for Richard, Nick and Tommy. I felt too embarrassed to telephone Gil and ask him to lend us horses again. I decided to just turn up at Claravale in the truck, which didn't make it any better, but when I feel self-conscious about becoming a bloody nuisance around the place I prefer to talk directly.

Back at the camp we boiled the billy and went for a short walk. It was a lovely sunny afternoon and to be all set up, ready to start was a good feeling. Once the mustering was over Sal and I would have to just drift along on our own with Yarramin and Circus. The herd had become quite small now. There would be bad days, but I felt we would cope. Malameen, who was still being cared for by Brooke in Mitchell, was a handy horse on the stock route and I planned to pick him up after the mustering.

When we got back the emu family had made itself at home in the kitchen. They didn't eat much, but they'd knocked the card table over with all the plates and pots. It only took a few minutes to straighten up and I rather liked the feeling that we weren't alone.

I fed the horses again and watered them. Being tied up by a tree all day was a bit miserable for them, but I intended to build a night yard. There wasn't enough daylight left to get it up before dark, so I put it aside for tomorrow.

Yarramin had never been shod and never been sore. The Warrumbungle horses have extraordinarily tough feet. Yarramin was the third horse I had purchased from a farm up in the high crags and not one had worn a shoe. Circus, however, had to have two front shoes tacked on. I had lost the art of shoeing years ago and with a gammy leg thrown in, I didn't have to look for another job before camp fire time.

Our routine that evening was no different to any other. I loved to have a fire blazing before sunset and the red wine on the table. The horses I had reloaded onto the truck. The float was in two partitions and each partition became a stable. They usually sleep standing, but they had enough room to drop onto their bellies if they wanted to. Leaving them out was too risky. If something frightened them they would pull away and bolt. Tomorrow I would have to think about a makeshift yard, but for the moment I was going to relax. Sal had bought a couple of fold-up camp chairs in Roma. We were both sick of looking for suitable stumps, all of which offered dubious comfort.

'What were your happiest memories?' Sal asked as she sat beside me.

I looked at her, not catching on for a moment. I must have seemed far away. I was worrying again about asking Gil for the horses. It wasn't fair to expect other people to provide assistance. I should have been offering to buy the horses.

'There aren't many,' I replied frankly when I realised Sal was referring to Mum. 'It was a typical marriage of the orange and the green, with me in the middle in the early days. We belonged with the green, but Mum mostly had her way.'

'Did you ever take her to the mountains?'

'We drove right to the foot of the Tonduron once,' I said, feeling brighter with the memory of it. 'She loved it. She was excited and she said she understood my love of the mountains. It was music to my ears, I remember.'

'Your father ever go?'

'Once in a picnic party. He hated it. He loved sport and it was sad he never had a son who shared that love. I can't sit down long enough. It's not that I dislike cricket, tennis and football.'

We chatted into the dark and the wine bottle was half gone before we gave any thought to dinner. It was going to be very easy. Boiled rice and lamb stew from a tin. I'd had it often enough and with some spices it was very tasty. We had got to the coffee stage when our peace was interrupted. South of the gorge, in the direction of the burnt homestead we heard a vehicle. The direction of the sound bothered me, for no one lived out there anymore. As the sound grew I realised it was a small engine for these parts, the petrol engine of a car. Whoever it was they were coming through and I was pleased I had parked the four-wheel drive under a shady bottle tree, some thirty metres from the track. The truck I had in a ditch on the edge of the track. The tailboard rested on a mound of silt, washed up by the last flood.

My first reaction was one of irritation. I didn't feel like camp visitors, who invariably stayed, drank bottles of beer and had a meal. I knew Sal felt the same. Then the vehicle stopped and there was silence. We waited by the fire, expecting to see someone coming with a torch. No one came and I thought of the rifle back in the four-wheel drive. The sight of it would alarm Sal. The last thing I wanted was for her to be frightened.

'Why has no one come?' she asked anxiously.

I couldn't answer that.

'Whoever they are they mean no harm,' I said as casually as possible. 'If they did they wouldn't come here in a car and alert us.'

Minutes later the engine fired up again. We saw the head-lights catch the trees high up on the mountain. The driver was turning around. The foot went down again and the vehicle left under heavy throttle.

The presence of someone else out in the rangelands altered the whole camp atmosphere. I put the billy back on. I didn't need more coffee, but I had no intention of going to bed just yet. Sal had begun to wash the plates and pots when the vehicle came back. This time it didn't stop. With the engine roaring, the driver turned in the same spot. The lights flashed high again and I caught a glimpse of the dust. If you were camped on the edge of Mitchell you wouldn't take much notice, but here it was plain spooky.

'Someone camped out there on the piss. Take no notice.'

'I'm going to bed,' Sal said nervously. 'I want you to come too.'

'I've made more coffee. I won't be long.' I wanted to get the rifle without Sal knowing.

I waited a few minutes and then got the rifle and a packet of stinger bullets. The magazine and breech were dry. I hadn't fired or serviced it for some months. Sal had some sesame oil on the table and with my handkerchief I lubricated the whole mechanism. It was a small magazine, holding only six bullets. I pushed the magazine back and leaned the rifle against a small log I'd collected for firewood. The packet of bullets I put in my trouser pocket.

I soon forgot about the rifle and pondered over the days ahead. The boys could only come for a few days. Richard was in his final year of law and shouldn't have had his study time disturbed. It was tough on them too when they hadn't ridden for weeks. Then it looked like Sal and I might be away for weeks, perhaps months, and most of the time beyond contact. I was chewing these matters over when the vehicle returned. This time it kept coming. The headlights came over a low ridge and lit up the cliff, just above the camp. The tyres squealed on a bend and in the lights I could see the dust rising. For a dreadful moment I thought the driver couldn't possibly take the final bend before the crossing and that the vehicle would broadside towards the tents. But in a cloud of dust, which swirled across the camp, the driver was through. So bad was the dust I only caught a vague glimpse of the vehicle. It appeared to be an old model sedan. It was low and I heard the thump of hard dirt and the tearing sound of sucker growth as the car roared out of the gorge.

'Could you see who it was?' Sal called anxiously from the tent.

'Too much dust. Have no idea.'

'He's stopped,' Sal called again, alarmed.

'The track takes a swing to the east. The sound's not carrying through the gorge.'

'No, it's stopped.'

Sal had better hearing than me. With only a very slight breeze we should have heard that engine for two or three minutes. One night west of Camooweal I heard a vehicle heading into the Territory for fully twenty minutes. I threw the last bit of coffee out and headed for the tent with the rifle.

'It's definitely stopped,' Sal repeated.

'I don't think so.' Quietly I thought she was right. I had been through this sort of thing before and lying in the tent, rifle tucked beside me, was the best way to handle it.

I left my clothes on and my glasses as well. The night seemed unusually quiet. A dingo howled and was answered by another, and when I strained to listen I could hear the leaves stir in a slight breeze. Sal felt warm beside me, but her breathing was a little quick and I think she lay there listening too. I drifted into a light sleep and woke feeling cold. There was another blanket to pull up and this time I knew Sal was asleep. The moon was up and shadows of tree branches cast patterns over the ground. A persistent owl had moved on and the leaves too were still. I lay back again, relaxed now and gently put my arm around her.

I woke to vigorous shaking and I heard the last of the rocks fall.

'Someone's up there,' Sal gasped. Her hand was over my wrist and it was so tight I knew she was truly scared. The float rattled and banged as the horses jumped from their sleep into the wooden panels.

'Wallabies,' I said. 'A game trail cuts across just above the cliff. I noticed it yesterday.'

'I don't think so,' she said in a strained whisper. 'The noises I heard weren't wallabies.'

'The nights out here are often full of strange sounds. You get used to it.'

Sal remained sitting, her hand still locked over my wrist.

'Relax,' I whispered. 'If I had investigated every strange night noise I've heard in the past nine months . . . '

I didn't finish. It began high and I heard the boulders snap the trunks of small trees and as they gathered momentum the crash against lower boulders filled the gorge with a rumbling sound, not unlike thunder. In a matter of seconds the whole side of the mountain seemed to be falling apart, but it was an illusion of sound caused by the confined space of the gorge. Loose stone joined the tumble and a rock avalanche plummeted to the floor of the creek where the track crossed.

Sal's half scream rose from a depth of fear that most live their entire life without ever experiencing. I felt the adrenaline surge through my body and with it the instinct for survival. Sal was peering through the gap in the tent flaps and I pulled her back.

'Get your boots on.'

I had as much trouble as Sal finding my boots in the tent. You can't run barefoot in country under scattered galvanised burr. I had a terrible feeling we were meant to leave the tent, that it was all part of some terrible plan.

The rifle in one hand, I grasped Sal's wrist with my free hand and we ran to the trunk of the nearest tree, which was a gum. I pushed her to the ground behind me and cocked the rifle. The moon was brighter than before. The night was still again and the skyline trees were like a painting on the canvas of the moon. It was romantic and beautiful and I wondered how such a thought could flash through my mind.

'Let's go to the truck,' a little voice said.

'No. Wait.' I probably hissed at Sal, poor thing. When we ran from the tent I'd half expected a shot. The ground to the truck was too open.

I worked my eyes along the upper slope on an imagined grid basis. I was halfway down when I saw the dark form move. I heard the tiny snap of a twig. When I aimed I eased the barrel slightly to the left and fired. The bullet whined off the rocks like an angry insect. Strangely there was no echo. I let two more go in quick succession and shrank to the base of the trunk. Sal pressed hard against me. If he or they intended to shoot, now was their opportunity. In the dark, even under moonlight, the tiny flame discharged from a gun barrel is easy to spot.

There was no return fire. It seemed like a ploy to frighten us, force us to leave.

'I can see you,' I shouted. 'Move and I'll shoot your balls off.'

The only reaction was the horses snorting and blowing.

I swung the rifle up again and fired another three shots,

careful to place the bullets away from the last sign of movement. Much of the slope was quite dark where the moonlight couldn't penetrate through the clinging shrubs and stunted trees. Whoever it was could easily have left without me spotting them.

I loaded up again, thankful I had kept the box of bullets in my pocket. Nothing moved. We waited.

'We can go to the truck now,' I whispered. 'I can't work it out. If Frankie and Ike were up there drunk, having their idea of fun, I'm sure they would have yelled out abuse or threats.'

'No animal could start that,' Sal murmured, still gripping my arm.

'Falling boulders make a dreadful noise. It mightn't be as bad as it sounded.'

The lower gorge was in shadow where the track crossed the creek. In the gloom I couldn't see any sign of the boulders that had fallen.

'What do you mean?'

'Maybe it was a big buck wallaroo. Perhaps our camp had blocked his usual route to the sweeter country and he went over the top.'

Sal was angry. 'I know you mean well, but don't patronise me. You know bloody well that wasn't a wallaroo.'

Towards dawn we both slept a little. The fear of another attack was overshadowed by the cold. Most of our clothes were in the tent. We spread a couple of oilskins over us and I found an old dogs' blanket half under the seat which I folded and put against the window for a headrest. Sal dozed with her head on my knees.

I didn't leave the truck until it was fully light. The horses were strangely still. They do that when they have had a fright. It's something passed through the genes over thousands of years. When they were the prey of large carnivores, which at

one time roamed Eurasia, they learnt that sudden flight followed by total stillness was the key to survival.

The first thing that struck me was the boulders. Three of
them, the size of large garbage bins, lay on the track. There
was no way past them. The ground either side, right up to the
cliff face, was covered in boulders and logs. With a crowbar
and Richard's strength, maybe a passage could be cleared. But
for now we were trapped.

Before emerging from the cover of the truck I carefully
examined the cliffs where the dark mass met the blue of
the sky. I couldn't see anyone, but didn't expect to. In fact
no comfort could be gained by looking around. Our best
eyes and ears were the dogs and I knew where they'd be.
I walked over towards the four-wheel drive and Ellie's black
head appeared from underneath. She let go a volley of deep
barks and if I hadn't known her I might have stopped. She
was very disturbed and when she saw it was me she raced
over and put her head in my lap. Millie remained silent and
only left the cover of the four-wheel drive when I got closer.
I gave both of them a long pat and their little world changed
instantly. Soon they were on the smell-and-sniffing run, tails
cocked and wagging.

'It's okay,' I said to Sal, when I walked back to the truck. 'I'll
light a fire.'

Sal left the truck and walked over to her bush kitchen.
Nothing had been disturbed. Some of the smaller rocks lay
close to the table. She had an oilskin, not on but pulled tightly
around her. Her hair hung across her face. She looked frozen
and miserable and it was not all from the cold.

I made the fire as cheerful as possible with a few bits of dry
box, put the billies on and then unloaded the horses. I took
them to the same trees they'd been tied at yesterday on a halter
and fed them hay. They were nervous and looking everywhere
and ate the hay with great mouthfuls. It reminded me of young

foals sucking feverishly when slightly upset about the appearance of an intruder.

'We can't stop Richie coming here,' Sal said in a tone close to tears. She was sitting on the ground with her arms wrapped around her knees. 'We must stop Nick and Tommy.'

'We'll ride to Claravale. There'll be a gap in the range somewhere.'

'Shouldn't we wait until Richie arrives?'

'Tomorrow won't be any safer. The boulders were levered to fall on the road and trap the vehicles.'

'Be awful for Richie to arrive, see this, and we're not here.'

'We can stop Richard if we make the station by three o'clock. If there's a vehicle to spare we can meet him on the road. None of us should have another night here. We'll set up camp on the main road.'

'We can ring the police too.'

'They'll tell us to leave. They told me to get the hell out of the place months ago.'

One billy boiled and Sal made the tea. 'Like some toast?' she asked, as I turned to go over to the four-wheel drive. 'I wish you'd stay near me.'

'I want to get the shotgun.'

'You have the rifle.'

'They can see it on the front of a saddle. We need something they can't see.' I didn't wait. I got the gun and searched through my tools for the hacksaw. When I found it I brought both over to the fire and Sal passed me a mug of tea.

'You're going to shorten the barrel!' she exclaimed. I could see that she was still very frightened.

'I'm going to roll up one of the oilskins and fasten it to the back of your saddle. It will be in that. Out of sight.'

'I couldn't use it. Never, and cutting it down is a jailable offence.'

I moved across and looked at her directly. She was staring

into the fire, which threw out warmth we both needed so badly. I wished I could have picked her up and whisked her away from this place. It was alien to everything she had ever known.

'We're on our own,' I said as gently as possible. 'There's no police. No law. Through his telescope Frankie can see a fly crawling on my face. He can just about put a bullet through the fly.' The next part was the hardest: 'Older women in good shape are the sexiest women on earth. The ugly thing in the oilskin would be the only friend you have.'

When I had taken the barrel off the shotgun the weapon looked like a medieval pistol. I loaded it with no 6 shot. It was for ducks, but close enough would blow a hole in an elephant. Rolled up in the oilskin it was a perfect length. I put the oilskin by the saddles and went back to the fire. Sal was still sitting there. She wiped her eyes on her sleeve when I put my arm around her. There was a plate of toast and jam, all cold.

'You used to use it on the starlings,' I said. 'Just push the hammer down.'

I took a piece of toast from the plate and poured another mug from the billy. The girls were smelling around the boulders. I saw Ellie look up.

'You must eat. There's twelve to fifteen miles to ride.'

Sal turned her head. There was a faint smile; a trace of that old humour.

'You're one of them. You love it. The freedom, the wilderness, the knowledge you're beyond reproach from authority and society in general.'

'Sympathetic maybe. An unbridled culture of horses, gunsmoke and innuendo, born of the Civil War, died in the US and rekindled in Queensland.' I paused and squeezed her shoulders. 'How's that for a load of nonsense?'

Sal smiled fully this time. 'Most men are conformists. The more conformist, the more successful and women everywhere fall in head first.'

'I'm not sure what you mean,' I replied thoughtfully. 'But I'll take it as a compliment to a wild man. Although given my time again I would conform a little more.'

'Why do you say that?' Sal asked gently.

'I love music. When I was a little boy, a nun—Sister Sebastian—wanted me to learn to play the piano. She was in charge of a little group, including me, and she taught most of them. Not me though, I wouldn't conform and now I'd give anything to be able to play. But she taught so much more than the piano. It's moments like this I sometimes think of her, which is not difficult because she had such a pretty unblemished face. Come to think of it, her face and hands were all I ever saw. I loved her. She was the only woman who cared at the time. But if she were here now and we talked about Frankie she would probably say no one is all good and no one is all bad.'

I scanned the summit skyline once again. A pair of eagles had arrived to survey the scene. Silhouetted against the sky, they were perched in a dead tree. Ellie had come to sit beside me, but Millie carried on with the sniffing. Possums had been around overnight and she was very excited by their smell.

I threw the tea-leaves into the fire and got up. 'I'll saddle the horses. You better wear the thickest jeans you've got.'

Attaching the sawn-off shotgun to the saddle dees at the back took more than a few minutes. I had a box of spare leather and cut an old stirrup leather to size. On the barrel end of the oilskin I used a thin leather strap, simply by applying a tight knot. The butt end I pulled tight with the stirrup piece, careful to leave the buckle on top for quick undoing. The problem was the thick leather didn't fit through the dee, so I had to secure it with a cord.

I filled a couple of water bottles and placed them and the hastily made sandwiches in my backpack. On the rear of my saddle I fastened the other oilskin, taking care to make the shape of it look the same as the other. I think it was about eight-thirty when we rode through the gorge. The horses shied and veered away from the boulders. They were very nervous until we got through.

'What about the track out?' Sal said. 'If we run out of time at least we can meet Richie on the road. Send him back to Roma.'

'And we ride back in here in the dark,' I replied, unimpressed. It was a typical mother's outlook in the face of danger. 'Anyway, if there's any mischief afoot the track's the last thing we follow.'

Once clear of the gorge, I swung south, keeping the range to our right. Until we left the track I kept my eyes on the wheel tracks, but even if I thought the vehicle had stopped last night it was guesswork. My tracking was too rusty to be reliable, so I wasted no time on it.

Sal rode beside me, kicking Yarramin up whenever he lagged. She didn't look any better, with her hair still across her face. I hadn't washed either.

'Do you really think we're in danger of a psycho taking a sniper shot?' she asked timidly.

'God, no. We're not dealing with a psycho. We're dealing with professional cattle duffers. They want us out. But they don't want us dead and the place swarming with cops.'

Sal looked at me enquiringly. 'The sawn-off?'

'Frankie's an alcoholic and Ike's just no good. If they're drunk it's a little different and a pea rifle that they can see is useless.'

We rode on in silence for a while. The horses walked along well and I had already taken my jumper off and tied it around my waist. The girls trotted ahead to begin with, but there were so many stinkers to chase they knocked themselves out and settled back behind the horses, tongues lolling.

The strip of red country bordering the ranges was mainly

under stunted box with no regrowth. Away to our left the brigalow began, thick and impenetrable in parts. Ahead I could see a low range coming in from the east. It was the one we had to cross to enter the Claravale watershed.

'Knowing your man's a big start,' I said, as we rode on. 'Childhood abuse and violence. Hatred of his father. Some religious exposure. It all falls into the pot and creates a man destined for eternal conflict. People shun them. There's no compassion whatever.'

'What are you trying to say?'

'That they're not so bad, but lost—outcasts.'

I kept thinking about the rock fall. It was out of character. It wasn't Frankie's way and he would be too damn lazy to climb a mountainside in the dark. It kept bothering me and slowly another prospect emerged, one that sapped the moisture from my mouth immediately. The bloke released from jail six months ago. No one had ever mentioned him again. Surely he had gone?

We arrived at a point where two ranges met, joined by a rugged gap. The basalt-capped range we had been following terminated. The range ahead, to the south, was rimmed with a low sandstone cliff, perhaps only two and a half metres high in places. There was no way through.

'We'll ride east for an hour,' I said. 'If there's no gap a horse can manage we'll have to go back.'

'I'll be terrified if we have to stay another night.'

'We'll sleep in the four-wheel drive. The three of us. It'll be okay.'

Yarramin began to sweat and it became obvious we would have to ride as far as the fence and undo it. The fence ran east from the final spur of this range and crossed the road at the cattle grid. Distance was going to beat us. I reined in.

'Another night I am afraid.'

Sal looked down at Yarramin's sweaty neck.

'If you and Richie can lever the boulders we can leave anyway.'

'One I can pull with the chain. The big one's the problem. It's going to be inch by inch with the crowbar. I really think we've reacted out of shock. Richie's in no danger.'

All parents are the same. We tend to see our own lives as more than half spent and our greatest fear is one of our own being cut down early. That morning I think we did over-react in regard to trying to stop Richard. I had panicked and that's the reaction whoever had loosened the boulders may have sought. I should have quietly set about making the horse yard.

'We'll stay,' I said, after we had been riding for a bit. 'I've been slow to think through it. They're not going to hurt anyone. Maybe they'll try something else, but it will only be to scare us. Try and get us to leave for good.'

Sal didn't reply. She didn't like the prospect much, but she was adjusting to the Blank Space just as I had a year ago. My mind drifted back to that ex-prisoner I had never seen, but his presence defied logic. Frankie and Ike had climbed up the gorge, I decided, because if their scare tactics worked they stood to profit from them.

The only camp intruders had been the emus again. The dogs growled and the hair on their backs rose. The emus had decided to camp near our tents, among the gums. The big daddy must have stood more than two metres tall and he was used to confronting dingoes. The girls turned tail and we reined in. He wasn't going to stand for any nonsense. It was all bluff though. Once the dogs ran he stopped and the family retreated into the bush. They had been better fed this time. In our haste we had left the bread out.

I watered and fed the horses and after a late lunch I unloaded two used coils of ringlock and some steel posts. Sal had recovered and I saw her opening a little shower kit she had purchased in a Roma camping shop. It had to be hung in a tree. I must have put my head down for ten minutes, for when I looked across to the tents again she was standing naked under this thing, having a shower.

'Another week of this and you'll be ready for the Sierra Madre.'

Sal laughed. 'I've come through it. I feel great. They can go to hell.'

It was great to see. I went on with building the yard, feeling better myself. We had coffee about four o'clock and laughed and joked for the first time in weeks.

'I don't think you'll readjust,' Sal said.

'To what?'

'The farm life.'

'You mightn't fancy planting petunias either.'

19 The Dingo and the Omen

The last of the twilight had gone. Not even the skyline trees above the camp were visible and I was becoming quietly concerned that Richard hadn't arrived. With the coming of the night Sal had become subdued and a little of the old fear took hold again. I told her several times it would take eleven hours from Lismore. I was about to come up with something else, like engine trouble, when we heard the vehicle.

I snatched the camp torch from the table and strode over to the pile of boulders. The rock was so black. Anyone unaware of it would brake too late.

Richard drove into the gorge very cautiously and wouldn't have hit the boulders.

'You've been rockclimbing!' That's how he greeted me. He had his Uncle Henry's spontaneous sense of humour. It always had a bit of bite to it. I had been poised to relate some scarcely feasible explanation about the rock, but instead burst out laughing myself. Sal laughed too, but I think it was nervous relief. She had her arms around Richie, hugging him so hard that I hoped she would soon let go, or he would know something was wrong.

'Been a rock fall,' I said. 'Unstable bloody stuff it is.'

Richard looked a bit bewildered and focused his attention on the rock pile. 'You haven't been able to get out.'

'It's my leg. Not strong enough.'

Richard was too intelligent to accept the coincidence of a rock fall crashing squarely on the track, but he seemed to restrain himself from asking direct questions. I think it was because he knew there was a timid and very feminine side to his mother's make-up. Instead he asked indirectly searching questions and I began to think the pact Sal and I had made was a bit ridiculous. We had decided to say nothing about the attack on the camp. It was so bizarre that any thinking person would question it, even our own son, we'd thought. I believe everyone at some time in their life witnesses an incident or sees something that goes beyond the outer limits of credibility. In the monsoons of 1963 I stood out in heavy rain one day to observe little fish falling out of the cloud. It was near Winton in north-west Queensland. I spoke of it just once and received looks that shut me up for good. In February 1997, it rained fish from a monsoon that had swung as far south as Olary in South Australia. An ABC cameraman captured the scene for the national news. Thirty-four years later I felt free to talk about my experience. I hoped on this occasion it would only be a matter of days before I could relate the real source of the rockfall and not find myself looking into a highly sceptical face.

I helped Richard carry his things to one of the extra tents I had put up and then we all sat down for a drink. Richard was very disappointed when we told him the boys had to be stopped. They had all worked well together in June and more importantly, had loved it. Having driven seven hundred kilometres on his own he was tired and looked it, but as Sal and I talked and he did the listening, I saw him stare into the darkness several times, towards the rockfall. He knew: he knew the excuses were covering something ugly.

Dinner finished, the three of us retired to the tents quite early. Richard looked very tired. The suntan from the June muster had faded and I suspect he had crammed his study to give me this week. We had decided to face the boulder problem in the morning.

The temperature dropped sharply that night. Before midnight I pulled up an extra blanket. With only a little sleep the night before I should have slept like a log, but I lay on my back listening. Sal breathed easily, a slow and relaxed rise and fall of her bosom. Richie was safe and that combined with no more instances of malevolence had resulted in a heavy sleep. I envied her.

The girls nestled in around our feet. Ellie was a very alert dog and as good as any posted sentry. Sometimes she growled. Never loudly, just enough to signal a mischievous possum or the passing of kangaroos and wallabies. I only had to whisper and her tail slapped against my leg.

Slipping in and out of fragile sleep I had no idea of the hour, but I woke to low growls from Ellie. When I whispered there was no response from her and I sat up, moving slowly so as not to disturb Sal. Ellie was shivering. I patted her gently, but it made no difference and the little growls were more like whimpers. I felt for the rifle and lay back again.

Three long howls filled the gorge and sent shivers down my neck and back. It was the dingo. That same dingo from the high plateau and later the stampede. I had an image of a large pale yellow dog, long legged and graceful, standing boldly at the cliff's edge and staring down at the camp. Although a figment of my imagination, this creature of the Dreamtime seemed to be a spirit dog, left by people who had survived for thousands of years in these ranges, and I pulled up another blanket as pondering on the unknown always invites the cold, more so than the in-coming frost.

I fell into a troubled sleep with nightmares of absurd images. I was a priest standing on a high mountain spur and a young nun stood before me, her eyes askance as they always were when she looked at me. I told her weakness invited trouble and turning the other cheek and walking away ruined all the good intentions of men and women in the world. I told her I would walk with the gun in one hand and the rosary beads she had given me in the other. She said there was no conflict in her world and she would pray for me. Her face was soft and ageless and I wanted her to touch me again on the head, as she used to, but she was gone in the mist and I overstepped, almost falling. I woke with a start and Ellie pounced into my lap. I got up and lit the fire. The dogs went on their sniff-and-smell run. Before the billy boiled I put the sawn-off shotgun in the truck, under the seat. Then I made the tea and woke Sal and Richard.

After breakfast Richard and I got to work on the boulders. We had to roll some of the smaller ones away to get at the three big ones. In the daylight the suggestion of a natural rock fall was absurd. Rock falls occur when part of a cliff or steep rocky slope breaks away. There are several causes, but prolonged and heavy rain would cause ninety percent of them. The boulders and debris from this rock fall had come from a band of rock high up, where grass, bushes and dwarfed trees pointed to a stable composition of soil and rock.

'Two separate falls,' Richard commented. 'The smaller one was aimed at the camp.'

'I'm glad you said it,' I responded. 'Your mother and I felt you and everyone might begin to think we were not just visitors to the Blank Space, but victims of it.'

'You don't think we should shift camp?'

'That might give them encouragement.'

Richard glanced towards the camp kitchen, where his mum was cleaning up. With her floppy outdoor hat on, she looked set for a day among the roses.

'Mum must have been terrified,' he said at last.

'She had a few bad hours. We both did. Fear's like all other emotions. Its intensity doesn't last.'

and cartage. It was Wesfarmers Dalgety that saw me through my cash-flow crisis and I will never forget them. The bank's response had been to bounce a hire-purchase payment, the only cheque ever bounced on me.

Rowan was optimistic the job could be done in a week. He knew the country. In any event he could only give me about a week. He had commitments in the Northern Territory. I felt with his help there would only be stragglers to collect after a week. What further impressed me was his total lack of concern about the rangeland mob. Provided they didn't shoot at him, he wasn't interested.

While we were talking Sal made a reverse-charge call to Sydney to stop the boys coming up. She wasn't long and we all walked over to the yards. The Claravale yards were not just another set of stockyards. They were built in the 1890s and only rails had ever been replaced. In the early days the station covered a bigger area and ran more cattle. Two of the yards had been let go, but the rest had been kept in impeccable order. The same hardwood timber had been used to build the harness shed, the milking bales and the calf lock-up pens. For me it was a bush gallery of the Australian stockman.

Rowan told us to pick the two horses we wanted from the mob. He already had one saddled. I hadn't noticed it before. It was a leggy pale-skinned gelding with dark, striped patches down one side. He was in a yard on his own and a bit fractious. His neck was wet from sweat. Rowan said he had saddled him not long before we arrived and had then gone over to have a cup of tea.

We all watched while Rowan mounted. The horse ran sideways and lifted its head high, but didn't show any inclination to buck. Richard opened one of the gates and Rowan took his mount out into the paddock to trot and canter.

I gave Richard one of the bridles and we focused our attention on the mob. They had all been ridden at different times, but just run in from the ranges none looked too quiet. Richard saw Black Cotton and we both agreed on him. The black gelding had been taught to cut. We edged him into a corner and Richard managed to get the reins around the gelding's neck and slip the bridle on.

I looked carefully through the rest. The big snorty bay was among them. I didn't think he would be any good for cutting. In fact most of the horses were big, showing a marked infusion of thoroughbred. My eyes eventually fell on the dark bay Tommy had ridden. He still looked sour, but at fourteen and a half hands I thought he had potential for campdrafting. I caught him and led him over to the harness yard.

Richard had already collected the saddles from the truck. He saddled his mount and got on. There were no problems and we didn't expect any.

Sal had been watching Rowan hack his mount through the timber at the front of the yards. When she made her way back she had to walk through the mob and they all ran to one end of the yard. Horses are very much aware of the different sexes and I suspect none of them had been touched by a woman.

'We should be getting a contract team to go in and get them,' she said, watching me saddle up. 'It's ridiculous.'

'No money,' I said. 'They cut it off.'

'Well Rowan's coming with us on a zebra and I've been watching you on that leg. You couldn't ride a loosely bolted rocking horse on a merry-go-round in kids' corner.'

'It's weak,' I agreed. 'Not that bad.'

'Get Richard to lunge him for a few minutes off Black Cotton.'

I glanced to where I had last seen Richard. He had taken Black Cotton outside for a canter. I waved my hand, in a manner of dismissal. 'Look at him,' I said of the horse I'd chosen. 'He's nearly asleep. Don't take any notice of the ears. They're always back.'

I took the dark bay into the next yard, a big yard about forty metres by twenty. Before mounting, I led him around the yard once and checked the girth. He was very much aware of me, but there was not a sign of playing up. Quiet horse this fella, I thought.

I reached the saddle a bit like an old man would and sat loose, not wanting the horse to feel any tension. We walked down one side of the yard and when I turned him every muscle in that animal's body went rigid, as though he'd been poked with an electric prodder. I spoke to him quietly and urged him to walk on. The hump in his back grew. A horse thinking about a pigroot or two doesn't necessarily hump up, but one bent on the real thing transmits a sensation to the rider of being astride a forty-four gallon drum on the crest of a wave.

The bugger caught me in the first move. Ninety-nine times from a hundred a bucking horse's head will go down accompanied simultaneously by a skyward thrust of the rump. Instead this fella reared high, close to the point of overbalancing, and I was loose in the saddle before he recoiled into the first buck. Coming out of it I still had my feet in the stirrup irons but my bottom was on the edge of the saddle and I knew the best I could hope for was a safe landing. However, this fella intended to pelt me as high as the top rail before gravity took over. I left cleanly. The yard was spinning and I looked for the ground, arms wrapped in. Manure dust filled my mouth and through the fine powder of the same dust floating above, I saw the wild thrashing of hind legs.

There had been a thump on my back before I hit the ground. No pain, just a thump. The horse, still bucking, had moved on. I thought I had escaped injury.

It hit me with such force my mind reeled in confusion. I gasped for air and none would go in and I found myself clawing the ground with one arm. Down my right side there was a feeling of water, as though someone had doused me with a bucket of it. Sal was staring into my face, her lips moving and her hands clutching my shoulders. Slowly her voice came. I had heard her before, but the shock of pain was so consuming, my brain seemed to be locked in trauma.

Gradually I could breathe, then speak. The sudden onslaught of pain gave way to an overwhelming sensation of weakness. Sal and Richard helped me stand and I remember asking them to let me stand alone. Through the confusion I struggled against the consequences, the dark inevitability of shattered plans. Like the day at Echo Hills when I took the scalpel blade through my hand. Deep down in my subconscious there was a voice telling me the injury was bad and I might as well accept it.

There was no blood. The bleeding was all internal. Old Mrs Campbell—Stuart's wife—was trying to spoon hot sweet tea into me and a towelful of ice cubes appeared from nowhere. They lay me down in the shade and there was a brief conference about an ambulance. Mrs Campbell had been a nurse in her young days and said first aid could do little for haemorrhaging and it might be two hours or more before an ambulance arrived. Also, she was worried that if an ambulance was called they could get lost. The roads were little more than tracks and the few sign posts only indicated towns. There were no facilities for an air ambulance and even if there were, regulations were in force for safety purposes. A patient had to be transferred to a recognised aerodrome.

Mrs Campbell suggested Sal take me to Roma and go straight to a private doctor's surgery for immediate attention. She volunteered to telephone the surgery. Hands seem to gather around me and I was put into Richie's ute. Other vehicles were offered, but the Suburu had four-wheel drive and Sal knew the vehicle. She felt she could gain time by taking the Mount Bindango road. The normal route to Roma was a hundred and fifty kilometres as opposed to one hundred and twenty kilometres.

I recall almost nothing at this point, except old Stuart. He stood there ashen faced and I wondered vaguely about the trip myself. But I knew Roma was the only destination. I was bleeding inside, my breathing was fast and the light seemed sharper than it should have been, which was probably the onset of shock. All I remember of the trip was trying to cushion the pain, for the road was so rough. At Roma a doctor examined me and I was transferred to hospital. For Sal and Richard there must have been an awful moment of uncertainty. At the time we didn't know where most of the cattle were. The cut fences and the tracks gave clues, but for all we knew they could have been feeding along the tops of the Mt Hutton range or at that very moment held up in a rustler's break.

CHAPTER
20 Rescue

On the fourth day after being admitted to the Roma Base Hospital I became a patient of the western Queensland flying surgeon, Dr Tony Paul. I had haemorrhaged quite badly. Heavy internal bleeding in the peritoneum can be fatal, as the source may be the liver, or—slightly less serious—the spleen. He told me he had two options: drain the fluid and risk infection or wait and see if the body absorbed it, which is the option he took. Nothing was said about surgery, but if the haemorrhaging hadn't stopped he would have had no choice. Doctor Paul spared me the ominous implications at the time and I am very grateful.

The pain was the enemy. At times it put me into shock but at six o'clock each morning it had a humorous side. Before taking to the air and heading west Dr Paul came to see me and as quickly as possible I jammed my leather glasses case into my mouth. He had to examine my back and if I had something to bite on I could take the pain. It was an unusual spectacle, I should imagine, and it made him roar laughing on the first occasion. He said it reminded him of his Flying Doctor days way out in the Channel Country, where the west was raw all the time. Dr Paul was a most energetic man. Sometimes, fourteen hours after he had examined me at the crack of dawn, I would hear his voice somewhere along the hospital corridor. He had cruised through retirement age a decade earlier.

One morning, after the herd had been rescued and Sal spent much of her time reading by my bed, I asked her what had happened. From memory I had simply been thrown and apart from racetrack injuries I have survived about fifty peltings in the past.

'You got both barrels,' she replied soberly. 'The horse's kick was perfectly timed while you were still airborne.'

'Someone said I'd get both barrels.'

She smiled faintly and continued with her reading.

Sal's fate had taken an enormous twist since that day in February when she arrived in Roma. At that moment at the airport, bewildered by the circumstances and fearful of the country, the thought of returning and actually running the whole operation would have been beyond her darkest nightmare. But that's exactly what happened. Sal had to organise the rescue of the herd.

At Amby she found Smokie sitting on his backdoor step. Judging by the little pile of cigarette butts at his feet, he was bored. Sal had barely introduced herself before he was rolling his swag. Before they left Amby he got her to stop at the corner shop where he collected a dozen packets of tobacco. Sal drove him out to the camp, where Rowan had left a spare horse. Most men would have waited to start next morning, but not Smokie. He saddled up and tracked his way to where Richard and Rowan had made a start.

It was a gruelling time for Sal and Richard, made miserable by saddle soreness. Some horsemen ride so regularly they never experience it. For those thrown suddenly into days of twelve hours in the saddle, a day's ride is slow torture. The muscles from shoulders to toes are strained, especially the thighs, and the knees stiffen so much the rider struggles to walk after dismounting. Sal was to confide later there were moments when she wept, quietly and out of sight. In the evenings she was the cook.

The Campbell family were fantastic. Gil provided fresh horses and upon realising the hopelessness of our situation mustered his own cattle out of a ten thousand hectare paddock for our herd. When the last of the stragglers had been chased out of the scrub he instructed Rowan to walk the herd to Claravale and turn them into the paddock.

The final count was only three short. Some exasperating hours were spent catching baby calves, transporting them in the truck and then re-mothering them. It was a great feat of stockmanship to find three hundred cows in wild country and systematically horse draft them from a thousand head of mixed cattle. Richard told me later he learnt more in that nine days about handling cattle that he had in the previous ten years.

The first day out of hospital I insisted we go to 'Double Bay' for coffee.

'You'll have to write a book,' the proprietor said, quickly serving the coffee and ducking back into his world of pot plants.

After two tranquil days in Bill and Sandra's garden I felt well enough to fly. Richard had already returned to Lismore, once again looking lean, dark and fit. Sal had become a veteran of the Blank Space. When she drove out to see the cattle alone, sometimes along the back tracks to save fuel, she always had a shotgun on the passenger seat.

'I couldn't use it,' she confided one night. 'It just makes me feel safer.'

'Love to see Frankie's face if you pulled the sawn-off from a picnic basket.'

'I threw it into the Maranoa,' Sal said triumphantly. 'It was a flavour of Mexico we can do without.' Ironically the gun had been made in Latin America.

Two years later we were driving on a high treeless desert, west of Taos in New Mexico. The land seemed lifeless and parched and the sage studded the ridges and covered the low valleys from one horizon to the next. To the north the mountains loomed before us, thrusting another two thousand metres into the sharp blue of the sky, as though blocking any escape from the desert. Among the cluster of mud adobe architecture that has made Taos famous, we found a hotel and that evening we watched a Mexican duo sing and click their cuban heels.

'If only we could import the music as well,' I remember saying wistfully, well into my second tequila.

'You don't need them,' Sal said. 'You'd dance on a claypan to a didgeridoo.'

New Mexico is a harsh land, with a history of bloody uprisings against the Spanish and a crushing defeat by the US cavalry. We saw the crumbled ruins of a Spanish church where Pueblo Indians had fled for protection. We could almost hear the blast of cannonfire as we stood by the church fence, looking in on the hundreds of pathetic stick crosses. It was a time when indigenous people suffered atrocities across four continents, and none worse than in New Mexico. Yet this state has stormed ahead with tourism. The invaders and the native American have reconciled their differences. Old ghosts only fade away when the living let go, and many in Australia would do well to think about it.

But back in September 1995, Sal and I were far away from the romantic notions of Taos and D. H. Lawrence. I flew to Sydney with Sal and we rested at her mum's place for ten days before returning to Myall Plains. It really was good to go to a genuine Double Bay coffee lounge, sit out on the pavement in French style and watch people who didn't carry guns and had probably never touched one.

With the cattle held safely in one of Gil's big forest paddocks I had a feeling the characters of the stock route, the scrub riders of the Blank Space, the Mick Bourkes and the dreamtime dingo would become something of a memory, and despite the ordeals there was a sentimental feeling, as Irish as it may seem, that we were leaving an old friend.

There was a time when New South Wales breathed life under great forests and the fences were few. I never saw it and my father caught only a fading glimpse. But inland Queensland still survives as it once was, with its clean rivers, sweeping plains of native grasses and forests of fading blue on distant horizons. In a world where nature's resources are diminishing at a frightening rate, Queensland still has a splendid opportunity to combine organically grown beef with tourism. The international tourists of the twenty-first century will not simply be environmentally aware— they will be obsessed with it. Space under smogless skies, great plains rolling off the curve of the earth like the lost American prairies, men mounted on horses to work and Big Reds, the plains kangaroo, feeding out on balmy evenings, will become the symbols of paradise on a dirty and polluted planet.

If any lesson is to be gained from the Queensland campaign, for me or anyone else, it is the folly of overstocking on a dry, drought-prone continent. Since returning home I have pulled half the fences down and now run the breeding herd in one mob, which allows about eighty percent of the property to be unstocked. It does require specific management practices.

This has been a story of anything but success. Ironically, had the Queensland campaign been a brilliant success with no drama the only thing I would have written was my signature on a cheque. After a suicide in our district an old farmer said to me, 'Always count your blessings'. We couldn't count them all.

To pass through this world and never take a bold step for fear of rebuke and derision is to deprive yourself of the true vitality of life.

And as for the Wild Bunch without whom this story would not have been worth writing, I have a special quote: 'A man who dies without an enemy is neither a man of passion nor a warrior, nor will they remember him.'

Epilogue

Five months after my horse spill at Claravale we went back to brand the spring calves. Smokie and I mustered them up in the 'twenty-thousand-acre' paddock and Sal did the cooking. The paddock had kept the cattle in magnificent order, it was well watered and we hated the prospect of having to leave, but the paddock needed a long spell before the winter. Wesfarmers at Roma found me a thousand-hectare paddock at Yuleba on a station called Bendemere, about two hundred and twenty kilometres to the south-east from Claravale, and the whole herd was roadtrained there. Soon after they arrived buffalo fly descended from the north. The flies swarm in thousands, maybe millions, and if nothing is done the cattle rub themselves raw around the hindquarters and neck. We had to spray them all with a protective chemical.

The station was very well managed and for nearly four months Sal and I were able to forget about the herd and focus our attention on the home base. Farmers all over New South Wales were gearing up for a record wheat planting— the crop to get everyone out of trouble, or at least those who had arable land. The Coonabarabran district has large areas of grazing country not suitable for cropping and with only thirty millimetres of rain in four months the cattle and sheep producers entered the third year of drought with no reserves of stockfeed or cash. Some old pastoral families liquidated their farms and that included one holding selected in the 1850s. That awful dead-end, talked about in pubs for decades, had finally become a reality.

At Myall Plains the feed was so sparse we had to sacrifice most of our remaining breeders. That is, those cows that had been kept at home. To add to the sting the cattle market had crashed in April. Our only hope of avoiding a terrible sale result was in Victoria. Southern Victoria was enjoying a good season.

For Sal and me it was an opportunity for our first holiday in three years. I examined a map and saw that Wodonga was a little more than an hour's drive from the alps.

Geoff White provided a little paddock near the yards and we trucked the cows and calves down a week before the sale. Each morning Sal and I fed them hay out of our truck and then we took off for the day. The truck was a bit cumbersome, but in low gear it could go anywhere a car could. We tried our hand at trout fishing on the upper Murray, walked the imposing Mt Buffalo ramparts and on easy days found some delightful places: Beechworth with its yummy bakeries being the most memorable. At night we found Albury-Wodonga had live bands and on one occasion an impressive jazz performance in a smart-looking pub in Wodonga. In addition the city of Albury has probably the best cinema complex in inland Australia and wonderful restaurants. Needless to say we needed a good sale—and got one. The cows and calves were so close to the saleyards every agent in the city had an opportunity to see them and advise clients.

Towards the end of June 1996 the herd in Queensland had eaten out the paddock at Yuleba. I was faced with an immediate sale, which would have been disastrous. Cows and calves were fetching less than $200 per unit, or one third of pre-drought prices. Once again I had to study where the rain had fallen and I contacted stock and property agent Barry McGregor at Goondiwindi. I told him the whole story and two days later he drove three hundred kilometres up to Yuleba to inspect the herd. After several phonecalls he secured three paddocks, each on different stations. None of the paddocks was large enough to carry the herd for any length of time. The herd was split into three mobs and loaded onto trucks for the fourth time. My family and I will be forever grateful to Barry McGregor, who voluntarily rescued us from a sad ending with the cattle.

The cattle remained in the Goondiwindi district for six months. The cows had a fresh lot of calves and on the 20th January 1997 they were loaded for the final trip home.

Of the 1472 head roadtrained to Queensland only two hundred and ninety made it home with their calves. The cows had travelled three thousand kilometres. We'd sold 1160 head of cattle through the Roma saleyards.

Scalp I didn't see again. He sold his station and the last I heard he had purchased a lease in the Expedition Ranges north of Rolleston.

The Old Boy sold out and lives in the village of Amby, only a block from Smokie. I wouldn't mind a dollar for every minute these two spend over a billy of tea in the morning and a XXXX stubbie in the evening.

Mick Bourke I haven't seen since the stampede at South Bore. Someone thought he had gone back out to Quilpie.

Of the families nothing has changed, except their kids are all taller. Annette's boy Scottie had a week at Myall Plains in December 1997. After having ridden a racehorse for the first time and climbing two hundred metres to the summit of Balagurie Split rock in the Warrumbungles I am sure he returned to Mitchell with some tales.

In January 1996 the Campbell family from Claravale had a few days here with us as well and I remember Gil being fascinated with the fresh green lucerne in the horse paddock; something my family and I have taken for granted over the years.

Geoff White, manager for Wesfarmers Dalgety in Albury, still telephones me occasionally. It was Geoff who saw me through the financial crisis in 1995. He knows Sal and I are busting to take another draft of cattle to Albury for sale, so that we can walk the alps again and indulge in Albury's restaurants. But it won't rain down there and no one wants cattle when the paddocks are bare.

The other characters that came and went in this story I have not seen since. A lot can happen in three and a half years and I know that almost all of them have left the Maranoa.

I have four boys: James, Richard, Nicholas and Tom. It was James who uttered in disappointment one day 'and the horses too are gone'. It just slipped out of his lips and I said to myself, 'He's just named the manuscript I've started to write.' James and Kari live in Sydney. James is a full-time auctioneer and knows the history of every champion racehorse since the first Melbourne Cup in 1861.

Richard is no longer available for stockwork and his saddle is gathering cobwebs. He found his girl, Katie, who has an Irish born grandmother, in Queensland. Katie and Richard were married in March 1997 and the reception was at Myall Plains. Richard practices law in Sydney now and I get very embarrassed when he telephones me from the office at 7.00 a.m. and I answer the phone from the bed.

Nicholas left for Canada soon after the rescue of the herd and worked as a 'Lifty' at Whistler. He came back with such a glowing account of the Rockies it was too much for me and I began planning a trip to Colorado. Like Richard and James, Nick cannot get home much now. However, he did make it possible for Sal and me to make a brief trip to Arizona, Colorado and New Mexico by looking after Myall Plains while we were away. Nick has a degree in Business/Tourism and works in Sydney.

Tom has a Bachelor of Business degree and is headed, he tells me, for those cold little green islands some sixteen thousand kilometres away. For him it conjures up excitement and travelling on a shoestring. I am sure it will be. I will lose my chief tractor driver and when I am clocking up the hours in that mobile jail, maybe even I'll think about those green islands.

Of the horses, Circus grazes away in semi-retirement. There is a dam in the horse paddock and in the summer he rolls in the mud every day and has a tummy like a beer barrel. Malameen has been promoted to the number one stockhorse and is boss of the mob. Poor old Yarramin didn't make it back. He died at Claravale, but he was twenty-seven years old. Only a foal though compared with another old gentleman I have here, named Cloudy, who will have a fortieth birthday party in August 1998.

The old dingo died but Millie and Ellie are as full of life as ever. Millie will be given a pup soon, to look after and train before she gets too old.

The Bow-Legged Cow, veteran of the big lift, is fit and well. In 1995 she had twins; the only cow to have twins on Myall Plains in half a century. I see her regularly. She waters at the trough near the fowlhouse. She and Starlight's bull should have got together, because they both saw more of Australia than most people. I wonder what the calf would have been like!

Glossary

banker	*creek on verge of flooding*
beast	*head of cattle*
bore	*artesian well*
boree	*native tree, acacia species; grows on the western downs and around Longreach, Qld*
boss drover	*person in charge of a droving unit*
box	*native tree, eucalyptus species, widespread*
box-up	*when two separate herds of cattle get mixed up*
brigalow	*native tree, acacia species, widespread in Qld*
campdraft, draft	*separate particular cattle from the herd on horseback*
cast for age cows	*old cows, to be sold*
(marking) cradle	*frame that holds calf during marking, also known as a crush*
(calf) crush	*see cradle*

Flinders grass	*native grass, grows throughout northern Australia*
gidgee	*small native tree of the arid zone, acacia species*
hands (horse)	*method of measuring a horse's height*
herdsman	*stock route manager for each shire*
horse-tailer, tailer	*member of droving unit who tends the horses*
lunge (verb)	*to get a horse on the move before rider mounts. Method of avoiding buckjumping. Usually used with a horse not ridden for a month or more.*
(to) mark (cattle)	*to castrate, ear mark and brand*
mickey	*an unwanted bull; not required for stud*
Mitchell grass	*native, principal downs grass, Qld. Only grows on better soils*
mothering (cattle)	*cows and their calves that have been separated pairing off successfully when reunited*
myall	*native tree, flourishes on black inland soils*
night break	*cattle fenced off or cordoned off with tape for the night*
pad (cattle)	*cattle trail, eg to water*
pound (Qld)	*drafting yard; Qld cattle yards*
purse (cattle)	*testicle pouch*
ringer	*Qld stockman*
roadtrain	*line of linked trailers pulled by a truck, used for transporting cattle, etc*

scrubber	*beast that has gone wild in the bush*
stinker	*swamp wallaby*
strain (verb), strainers	*to taughten fencing wire, fencing tool*
(to) tail	*follow, watch, look after*
tonguing	*sign of overheated beast, such as frothing, tongue lolling from mouth, eg after running*
turkey's nest	*circular mound of soil with central depression to store water that has been pumped in from bore or large dam*
weaner	*a marked calf taken off mother at 6 to 8 months*
wilga	*small, drought-resistant native tree of the inland red soil plains*

IN THE MIDDLE OF NOWHER
Terry Underwood

"His smile was big enough to light the universe. He lay in an extended plaster bed which engulfed his body but obviously not his spirit.
'I'm big bad John,' he chuckled."

A city girl with dreams of the country, eighteen-year-old Terry Augustus was a trainee nurse working at St Vincent's hospital when she met John Underwood, a young, born-and-bred cattleman. Flat on his back in Ward 3, nursing a serious spinal injury sustained while mustering cattle, John was itching to get home. And home he finally went, to his family's cattle station, Inverway, up in the Northern Territory. He promised Terry he'd write. A postcard arrived a week later.

After five long years of writing letters, John and Terry married and moved to their new home — a tent and a newly drilled bore in the middle of nowhere. Modern-day pioneers, John and Terry built their station from scratch and raised and educated a new generation of Underwoods there. Times were tough and there was heartbreak, danger and struggle, but the power of love and the strength of family ties helped them overcome every obstacle.

In the Middle of Nowhere is their story. It's a story of beating the odds, told with warmth and a genuine knowledge of the Outback and its people, and the issues they face today. It's a *real* story of the Territory, and is as vast, dramatic and inspiring as the land that lies at the heart of this unforgettable book.

Bantam Hardcover
ISBN 0 73380 130 7

KINGS IN GRASS CASTLES
Mary Durack

When Patrick Durack left Western Ireland for Australia in 1853, he was to found a pioneering dynasty and build a cattle empire across the great stretches of Australia.

With a profound sense of family history, his granddaughter, Mary Durack, has reconstructed the Durack saga — a story of intrepid men and ground-breaking adventure.

... far better than any novel; an incomparable record of a great family and of a series of great actions.
BULLETIN

The best saga of pastoral Australia ever published ... hard to describe without superlatives ... in a hundred years the book will still be a classic.
MEANJIN

Bantam Paperback
ISBN 0 73380 156 0

SONS IN THE SADDLE
Mary Durack

The second generation of Duracks were not only hardy pioneers, droving cattle through untamed territory, they were also educated, travelled men at home in the worlds of commerce and politics. Through diaries, letters and legal documents, Mary Durack tells the story of her father, Michael, and Patsy Durack's vigorous family.

Mary Durack's Kings in Grass Castles *is an Australian classic. Since it was published in 1959 it has gone on selling as new generations of readers discover the pastoralist saga of the Durack family and their cattle spreads across the continent. Now ... the sequel we have been waiting for ...*
BULLETIN

Bantam Paperback
ISBN 073380 157 9

Also by Mary Durack

KEEP HIM MY COUNTRY

In the 1880s old Stanley Rolt had pioneered the country with cattle and made a fortune. To the outside world he had become a knighted tycoon, running a vast empire that stretched across the territories. But the land, a savage one of crocodiles, buffalo, wild cattle, flood, fire and drought, had killed his son and looked as though it was about to crush his grandson, young Stan ...

Corgi Paperback
ISBN 0 73380 024 6

TO BE HEIRS FOREVER
A true story recorded through the eyes of a remarkable woman

With her husband Will, six children, two servants, some livestock and tools, Eliza Shaw exchanged her world of drawing-rooms and embroidery in Leicestershire for the brushwood huts and back-breaking labour of a pioneer settlement in Western Australia. They were never to see England again ...

Corgi Paperback
ISBN 0 73380 000 9

THE ROCK AND THE SAND

Mary Durack's *The Rock and the Sand* is a fascinating account of early Catholic missionary work in north-western Australia — and of the dedicated men and women whose work was sometimes inspired, sometimes blind, but whose sole aim was to convert the Aborigines to Christianity.

Corgi Paperback
ISBN 0 73380 025 4